D0849985

The Devil's Device

Revised and Updated Edition

EDWYN GRAY

. The Devil's Device

Robert Whitehead

and the History

of the Torpedo

NAVAL INSTITUTE PRESS   ANNAPOLIS, MARYLAND

Originally published in 1975 as *The Devil's Device:*
The Story of the Invention of the Torpedo by Seeley,
Service and Co. Ltd., London
© 1975, 1991 by Edwyn Gray

Library of Congress Cataloging in Publication Data

Gray, Edwyn.
   The devil's device : Robert Whitehead and the history of the
torpedo / Edwyn Gray. — Rev. and updated ed.
      p.   cm.
   Includes bibliographical references and index.
   ISBN 0-87021-245-1
   1. Whitehead torpedoes—History. 2. Whitehead, Robert,
1823–1905.   I. Title.
V855.W5G7   1991
623.4'517—dc20   90-48675

Printed in the United States of America on acid-free paper ∞

9 8 7 6 5 4 3 2

First printing

For Vivienne with love

CONTENTS

ILLUSTRATIONS

PREFACE TO THE REVISED AND
UPDATED EDITION

Although *The Devil's Device* was completed in 1973 and published in 1975, research into the history of torpedo development has continued over the ensuing years, and this revised and updated edition for the Naval Institute Press has enabled me to include much new information as well as provided an opportunity to correct and improve the original text.

The section on underwater explosive devices from 1585 to 1865 has been expanded to provide a more detailed historical background to Whitehead's invention of the automobile torpedo while the critical analysis of the part played by Admiral Jacky Fisher in the Royal Navy's acquisition of the Whitehead weapon has been amended in scope and detail in light of recently located public documents, correspondence, and other material. The account of the Brennan torpedo and its inventor has been improved thanks to the research carried on by Norman Tomlinson, while some recently discovered family letters, which have been made available to me by Lady John Bowman, reveal further previously unknown sidelights on Whitehead's remarkable genius.

In addition to the numerous and detailed textual changes, a new system of source notes has been adopted and the layout of the bibliography improved. The appendixes have also been expanded and now contain details of some three hundred various torpedo models while, at the suggestion of the Naval Institute Press, much of the Whitehead family history prior to the inventor's birth has been either discarded or removed to the source notes. Last but not least the original final chapter has been completely rewritten to embrace the torpedo problems encountered by both the United States and Germany in the Second World War and to consider in more detail postwar weapon development. The inclusion of this new material has made it necessary to increase the number of chapters from fifteen to sixteen—an addition to the text which I am sure readers will appreciate.

I must again thank Lady John Bowman and Norman Tomlinson for their continued assistance and I am much indebted to Ruddock F. Mackay, whose book *Fisher of Kilverstone* led me to the various files of torpedo documents held by the Public Records Office in London which I had been unable to trace while preparing the original book. These have helped to shed much valuable and additional light on the 1866–1870 period. Other new material employed in the production of this new and revised edition has been incorporated into the source notes and bibliography.

My personal thanks, too, to all those who have provided me with information since the publication of the original edition especially: Dr. Marina Cattaruzza of Trieste; Ernest Hoyos; Dr. and Mrs. Rupert von Trapp; Maria von Trapp; Denis Cahill of the Maritime Archeology Association of Victoria (Australia); Michael Kitson, also of Australia; and finally, Mrs. Jennifer Holland, the Group Librarian, Attleborough, and her ever-helpful staff for assistance in tracing and obtaining scarce references and publications.

Acknowledgment is also made to the following publishers for the use of additional copyrighted material in this edition: Bantam Books Inc.; the Oxford University Press; Jonathan Cape; Athenäum Verlag; Edward Arnold; Conway Maritime Press Ltd; and the Indiana University Press. And finally to Dominic Thomas for his artwork.

Attleborough, Norfolk, England
1990

PREFACE TO THE FIRST EDITION

Ask almost anyone to write down the names of Britain's six greatest inventors of the nineteenth century and you can be quite sure that Robert Whitehead will be conspicuous by his absence. Yet this relatively unknown English engineer exerted more influence over the tactics of naval warfare and the design and development of warships than all the world's top admirals and naval architects put together. And the weapon he created twice brought Britain to the verge of defeat.

Until the advent of the atomic bomb in August 1945, Whitehead's invention, the torpedo, was the dominant weapon of destruction in warfare at sea for well over half a century. And although after 1905 gunnery and mines continued to destroy many warships and merchant vessels, the vast majority of ships fell victim to the relentless menace of the torpedo launched from any of three dimensions—from below the surface by lurking submarines, fired from the decks of fast-moving cruisers and destroyers, or dropped from the skies by aircraft. Only in the latter part of World War Two did the bomb seriously challenge the torpedo as the primary means of sending ships to the bottom. And even today in the face of nuclear bombs and guided missiles, the threat of torpedo attack by Russia's massive fleet of submarines remains an ever-present menace to the merchant shipping and naval forces of the Western world.

Whitehead's critics referred to his invention as "the terrible torpedo" while many gunnery specialists of the Royal Navy, bitterly opposed to any rival method of destruction, dismissed it as "the device of the Devil." To its admirers, though, Whitehead's torpedo was "the wonderful weapon" and, indeed, wonderful it *was* in the scope of its conception and in the light of contemporary engineering knowledge. No other invention has retained its original appearance so closely over the course of a hundred years of development and certainly no other has proved so comprehensive in its basic concept that major modifications have been unnecessary. The reader has only to compare a Benz automobile, a Wright biplane or a Holland submarine with its modern, sophisticated equivalent to understand and appreciate the depth of Robert Whitehead's genius.

Most works of reference give only the barest outline of the inventor's life and none give any insight into his character or personality. Although there are still several gaps this book reveals for the first time the story of Whitehead's eventful career and traces, in non-technical language, the development of the torpedo that bears his name and which is the progenitor of the modern weapon. It is not a peaceful story, for violence is the essence of torpedo warfare, but it is full of interest as well as excitement. It is an attempt to tell the story of the torpedo in terms of personalities and events rather than in dry technical detail. It is, moreover, a story that *had* to be written if only to bring due if belated honour to that virtually unknown "English engineer from Fiume"—Robert Whitehead.

I am most grateful to the many people who have helped me so willingly at various stages of my research and without whose help this book could not have been written. Firstly I must thank the members of the Whitehead family who have supplied me with documents, letters, and other information, especially Thomas Whitehead, the inventor's grandson, and Lady Frances Bowman, his granddaughter, both of whom gave me much of their valuable time. Also Count Balthazar Hoyos, whose grandfather was Whitehead's son-in-law and business partner, who assisted me with details of the years after 1870 and who regaled me with many fascinating anecdotes of the family.

I am also especially indebted to Denis O'Connor of the Bolton Industrial History Society for his painstaking research into the early years of the Whitehead family and their business ventures, and also Geoff Kirby, of the Admiralty Underwater Weapons Establishment, for so willingly making available to me the fruits of his technical research for his own book on the subject of torpedo development.

A full listing of sources is given in the notes and bibliography, but many other people contributed to my search for facts on Robert Whitehead and his torpedo and I am anxious to acknowledge their assistance: David Bowman, who spent many hours checking the private letters of Countess Alice Hoyos; E. M. Knight; Alex Anderson; Mrs. P. V. Windsor; Mrs. E. A. Whitehead; J. B. Whitehead; Commander Roy Corlett, RN; Mrs. Mary Fletcher; Christopher Short; J. H. Gray; Miss G. Thorn; A. N. Whitehead; P. H. Judd and P. Oxenham of Messrs. Vickers Ltd; R. G. Guinness; Lt-Com G. H. F. Frere-Cook, RN (Rtd.) the Curator of the Submarine Museum HMS *Dolphin;* Captain R. Garson, RN; Brian Clowes; J. Rowland-Hosbons; A. H. Appleton; A. R. Patterson of Messrs. Greenwood & Batley Ltd; Robert Chapman; Conrad Plessing; Mrs. Mary Deft; T. Ashworth, Borough Librarian, Bolton; Baron John Jordis; the Librarian and Staff of the Royal United Services Institute; the Librarian and Staff of the National Reference Library of Science and Invention; A. J. Brown of the Naval Records Club; Geoffrey M. Smart; Major J. B. S. Cottam, RA; Graeme G. Maclennan of the *Marine Engineer & Naval Architect Magazine;* E. R. Whitehead; the late Arthur Manns, Curator of the RNAD (Royal Naval Armaments Depot) Museum, Gosport; the Librarian and Staff of Westminster City Library; Mr. G. Serjeant of Messrs. Vickers Ltd; the Staff of the Public Records Office; Norman Tomlinson, Borough Librarian, Gillingham; Alastair Service; Barone Geoffredo de Banfield; Mrs. Vivienne Clarke; Lt-Cdr Callan, Weapons Officer, HMS *Vernon;* the Editor of the *Daily Telegraph;* the Librarian and Staff of the Naval Historical Branch, Ministry of Defence; H. F. Bowers, and C. D. A. Baggley, Headmaster of Bolton School.

I must also thank the authors and publishers who have kindly allowed me to quote from their copyrighted works.

In writing its obituary of Robert Whitehead *The Engineer* observed: ''There is reason to believe that he felt acutely that, although

honoured by other countries, the country of his birth did not recognise him in the same manner."

I hope that this book will go some way to rectify the omission.

High Wycombe
1974

The Devil's Device

"No one man has ever cost the world so much by an invention as did the late Mr. Whitehead of Fiume."

> *(Commander E. Hamilton Currey, 1910)*

"A First Sea Lord told me on one occasion that there were no torpedoes when he came to sea, and he didn't see why the devil there should be any of the beastly things now!"

> *(Admiral of the Fleet Lord Fisher, ca. 1870)*

"In the old days many of the torpedoes were distinguished and known by pet names. Those that were inclined to get out of hand were not allowed to run often, and then only when the omens were good. They still have their lucky and unlucky days."

> *(Rear-Admiral D. Arnold-Forster, 1931)*

CHAPTER 1

As Secret as Possible

W ith her black enameled hull, white upperworks, and buff funnel, the little paddle steamer looked as if she were setting out on a carefree excursion along the coast as she moved slowly across the sun-dappled waters of the Medway estuary on the last day of August 1870.[1] Picking up the 6-fathom channel, she turned northeast and her ungainly paddle wheels churned the water to foam as Sheerness dissolved into the morning haze astern. Only the White Ensign streaming from her staff and the Armstrong guns on her poop proclaimed that she was a man-of-war even though, by modern standards, a somewhat ludicrous one.

Yet below decks, in her bows and roped off from inquisitive eyes, lay the prototype of the world's most potent weapon, a weapon that could transform the puny sloop into a lethal David capable of slaying and sinking the Goliath ironclads that made up the backbone of the Victorian Royal Navy. It was, in the strictest sense of this now overworked phrase, a secret weapon. So secret, in fact, that its inventor had not dared to patent his design for fear that someone might steal it. And that "someone" could as easily be a government as a private

3

individual. One day it would be the dominant weapon of naval warfare. And when that day came it would be worth a fortune. In the
meanwhile Robert Whitehead had no intention of revealing any part
of it to anyone unless he was paid hard cash in return.

Cramped uncomfortably in the bows and working in the light of a
swinging oil-lamp Whitehead carefully checked the mechanisms and
valves for the hundredth time. Then, moving further forward, he
examined the strange tube-like contraption the installation of which
he had designed in a small drawing-office at Chatham Dockyard just
over two months earlier. Satisfied that everything was in working
order he climbed back over the rope barrier, nodded to the Marine
sentry standing guard, and made his way up on deck.

Three naval officers and a tall, handsome "Austrian gentleman"
were grouped together by the starboard paddle box.[2] They were
talking quietly amongst themselves, and as Captain Arthur saw the
bearded inventor appear in the hatchway, he gestured for him to join
them. At first the conversation was stilted and awkward, for it was
plainly apparent that the three officers were sceptical. Secret weapons
were not uncommon in the Victorian era, and few inventions lived up
to the aspirations of their creators.

Yet there was something about Robert Whitehead that warned
them he was no ordinary harebrained inventor. His reputation had
gone before him, and they were fully aware that, after a series of
exhaustive trials the previous year, the Imperial Austrian Navy had
taken up Whitehead's "fish" torpedo—although they took care to
remind themselves that the Austrians had cautiously refused to buy
the exclusive rights and had been content to place a small order for
the new-fangled weapon. And, of course, he was already famous for
designing the engines for the flagship of the victorious Austrian fleet at
the Battle of Lissa.

HMS *Oberon* pounded out of the Medway, steering for the Kant
Sands where the trials were to take place, and somewhat naturally—
for Whitehead's son-in-law and business partner Georg Hoyos had
actually fought at Lissa—the conversation turned to the revolution in
naval tactics, which Wilhelm von Tegethoff, the Austrian admiral,
had created by his victory in that battle. Despite their avowedly open
minds the three officers, Captain William Arthur, Captain Morgan
Singer and Lieutenant Arthur Wilson, were convinced that the ram
was the ultimate weapon of future warfare at sea, and they made no

attempts to hide their belief. From now onwards, they explained, both tactics and warship design must be directed towards one goal—that of sinking the enemy by attacks with rams.

With its tradition of close-range fighting it was only natural for the Royal Navy to accept Tegethoff's tactics as the fundamental tenet of future warfare. A trained and disciplined crew could stand up to the murderous carnage of gunfire as rival ships closed for the fatal impact; what else, they asked, could stop the inexorable onslaught of the heavy iron ram. What indeed? And, of equal importance, what other weapon could inflict damage below the waterline in battle for, with the increasing use of armor, it was becoming virtually impossible to sink an opponent unless he could be damaged underwater where there was no protection.

Robert Whitehead kept his own council as Hoyos and the British officers argued their cases. He knew that he had produced the very weapon that could make rams as obsolete as the ancient triremes of Rome that had first used them in battle. And he knew, even more assuredly, that only a successful demonstration of his weapon would convince the professional sceptics of the Royal Navy.

The Nore lightship was fine on the starboard bow as the *Oberon* turned east, and excusing himself politely, Arthur went up to the bridge for a quick check of the chart as the two anchored lighters heaved into view two miles ahead.

Whitehead was under no illusion that the committee set up to test his weapon had anything but grave doubts about its viability. He would have been even more apprehensive had he seen the letter of 3 August 1870, which the Admiralty had sent to Captain Arthur in his capacity as chairman of the committee: "As Mr Whitehead had not patented his invention, he was desirous that everything connected therewith should be kept as secret as possible, and, consequently, they [the committee] could not be permitted to examine working parts of the machine."[3]

It was a far from encouraging letter, for although Whitehead only had himself to blame for the excessive secrecy, it created an unfortunate impression of charlatanism in the minds of the three officers appointed to examine what he had to offer. Nor did Whitehead's background make them any more optimistic. He had forsaken England some twenty-four years previously and had, since then, worked continuously abroad. In addition he had no social background and, even worse, he was a common engineer—and everyone knew that engineers were not exactly *persona grata* in polite circles. In fact, very sensibly, the Navy's own commissioned engineers had to mess separately and were not admitted to the wardrooms lest, so it was whispered, their oil- and coal-grimed hands should besmirch the spotless table linen. It was an attitude exemplified in its extreme by the remark of a young midshipman to an engineer lieutenant who had reminded him of the seniorities of rank: "You may be senior to me, Brown—but *my* mother wouldn't invite *your* mother to tea!"

Robert Whitehead was accustomed to the social snubs that went with his profession. But outwardly he seemed little concerned about it. He *knew* he had produced the world's most sensational naval weapon, and the proof of the pudding was in the performance thereof.

Lieutenant Wilson, the junior member of the committee, destined to become Admiral of the Fleet Sir Arthur Wilson, VC (Victoria Cross), professional head of the Royal Navy, felt a certain kinship with the inventor who, with his dark waistcoat and large gold watch chain, looked such an incongruous figure on a man-of-war. Wilson, too, was an inventor of no mean ability and several of his devices were to play an important, if small, part in the development of Whitehead's strange new weapon.

Robert Whitehead had arrived in England in June 1870 to make arrangements for the trials and, accompanied by Captain Arthur and a Mr. Crossland from the Admiralty, had gone to Sheerness to select a suitable vessel for his experiments. Having picked the iron paddle-wheel sloop *Oberon* he proceeded to prepare drawings for the dockyard constructors so that they could fit a torpedo discharge tube, also built to his own design, into the bows of the ship.[4] Then, while the work was carried out, Whitehead returned to his factory in Fiume to collect the torpedoes which he intended to use in the trials.

Returning through France by train, with the weapons carefully boxed and crated, he had the misfortune to time his arrival in Paris with the start of the Franco-Prussian War. The French capital was full of rumors and a fever of spy mania had gripped both the police and the military authorities. The sudden appearance of a strange foreigner, complete with an entourage of mysterious crates the contents of which he firmly refused to disclose to anyone, produced predictable results. A senior police officer was called and Whitehead, in halting French, explained politely that what was in the boxes was his own private affair and need not concern the gendarme. The fact that he was traveling from Austria, an ally of Prussia, to England, still regarded by the French as a potential enemy, only made matters worse.

"Perhaps Monsieur would avoid the possibility of an unfortunate misunderstanding by opening the boxes."

Monsieur demurred. The police officer tried again.

"I am quite sure it is only your personal baggage and if Monsieur would open the boxes he will be quite free to continue his journey."

Whitehead was, perhaps, being pigheaded. On the other hand he was only too well aware of the scene that would follow if he opened the crates and revealed a number of obviously lethal weapons in the center of Paris. So he stuck to his guns—or more accurately his torpedoes—until his repeated refusal led to his inevitable arrest and, of course, the added danger that the mysterious crates might be confiscated and opened.

Fortunately news of the incident reached the British embassy where the ambassador, aware of Whitehead's identity and the nature of his luggage, quickly intervened. Exactly how he explained the affair to the French authorities is not recorded, but a few hours later, Whitehead and his secret weapons were safely on board the Calais train. It was a doubly fortunate escape for, only a few days later, he might well have been cut off by the advancing Prussian armies.[5]

By the time Whitehead reached England the preparations for the vital trials had been completed. The *Oberon*'s torpedo tube had been fitted at Chatham Dockyard, and the sloop had moved up to Sheerness ready to embark the committee. A sturdy net, 100 feet long and 15 feet deep, had also been constructed to trap the torpedo at the end of its run and two lighters were adapted to support its ends. On 31 August 1870 the lighters took up position on the Kant Sands, two miles east of the Nore lightship, while the Admiralty Committee, Whitehead's party, and the torpedo itself went on board the waiting sloop.

It was a clear day and the morning mists that had shrouded the Kent coast as they left Sheerness had dispersed in the heat of the sun. The *Oberon* took up her prescribed position, dropped anchor, and the committee gathered on the fo'c'sle to watch proceedings. There was a strong tide running and the bows of the sloop swung with the ebb, but a few revolutions of the port paddle-wheel lined her up on the target net and, at last, all was ready. For Robert Whitehead the moment of truth had arrived.

The first torpedo hissed from its tube and the committee made no attempt to hide its smugness as the cigar-shaped weapon curved away to the right and then rose to the surface forlornly 95 yards off the starboard beam. For a moment Whitehead looked disconcerted. Then, suddenly, he remembered the way the bows of the sloop had swung with the tide while the final preparations were being made. The Austrian trials—in fact *all* the previous experimental runs—had been made in the Adriatic arm of the Mediterranean. And the inland sea was, of course, tideless. Judging by the wording of their report the committee, however, did not seem unduly impressed by the inventor's explanation: "Mr Whitehead stated he had not allowed sufficient motive power to counteract the action of the tide against the range."[6]

And the fact that the committee "was never permitted to inspect any part of the machinery in the body of the torpedo" led them to the inevitable conclusion that Whitehead's weapon was more probably propelled by proverbial "hot air" than its official motive power of compressed air.[7] Leaving the committee scribbling their comments in their notebooks Whitehead and his son-in-law hurried below to rectify the error. He had got off to a bad start and the next run could well make or break the experiments.

The *Oberon*'s whaler recaptured the torpedo and towed it back to the sloop where it was hoisted on board and sent below. After a brief discussion with Hoyos, who, as a former naval officer, was familiar with tidal problems, Whitehead lifted the cover of the compressed air engine and turned the regulator valve to admit an increased pressure of air into the two-cylinder power-unit. Then, having supervised the refilling of the air reservoir, the two men went back on deck to watch the second run.

This time the torpedo behaved almost perfectly. It left the tube in a dead-straight line, maintained depth with reasonable accuracy, and ended its short but impressive trip against the net strung between the anchored lighters. The committee's scepticism began to melt as the strong arms of the whaler's crew brought their boat alongside the torpedo, now gently bobbing up and down on the surface, hitched a line to its pointed snout and started to tow it back to the sloop.

Whitehead remained impassive as the weapon was hauled aboard, but he undoubtedly breathed a silent prayer of relief at the success of the second run. Even if things went wrong next time, he had at least demonstrated the *potential* accuracy and behavior of the fish torpedo. And, as a quick glance at the committee showed, he had certainly whetted their appetites for more.

The third run was also satisfactory and, having concluded the first day's trials, the *Oberon* weighed anchor, swung her bows in the direction of the Nore lightship, and started back on her homeward course for Sheerness. Up to a point Whitehead was satisfied, but he had noticed a tendency for the torpedo to veer to the left on discharge with the result that the point of impact on the target was to the left of the line of projection. It was not a serious fault but it fell short of the high standard of perfection at which its inventor aimed.

The *Oberon* left for the experimental area early next morning, 1 September, and this time the 14-inch-diameter torpedo made six satisfactory runs before a broken piston brought the day's work to a premature end. The cause of the breakage was not revealed to the committee who were forced to observe vaguely that the pneumatic engine broke down from the fracture of a piston due to its "weak form." This was presumably Whitehead's own explanation for he still steadfastly refused to allow anyone to examine any working parts of the device. Irritated by the inventor's excessive secrecy the committee retaliated by seizing on the weapon's continued tendency to run slightly to the left of its line of axis.

Whitehead was asked the cause of the directional aberration and, at a loss to explain it even to himself, he tried to evade the question with vague generalities. The committee were not impressed and noted, rather testily: "[We] do not consider that Mr Whitehead produced any sufficient explanation to account for this.[8] "It was clear, however, that they were more than a little impressed by the way the torpedo measured up to its inventor's claims and were anxious for the trials to continue.

Working into the small hours of the night with the aid of Georg Hoyos and one of his Fiume mechanics, Whitehead lifted the pneumatic engine, drew out the offending piston, and replaced it with another in good time for the next day's experiments.

Five more satisfactory runs were made the following morning and afternoon, but the engineer was uncomfortably conscious that Captain Arthur and his companions were still casting a critical eye at the weapon's inability to hold a true course. Satisfied that there was nothing wrong with the torpedo itself Whitehead went down into the bows to carry out a careful scrutiny of the discharge tube. It proved a worthwhile investigation for he quickly located the source of the trouble—the dockyard fitters had omitted to fix the guide rods in the fore part of the tube in accordance with his design drawings. Whitehead was angry with himself for not noticing the mistake earlier, for as a practical engineer he was only too aware of the need to leave nothing to chance. But it was too late for recriminations and he called Captain Arthur to a hasty conference at which it was jointly decided that the *Oberon* would have to return to Chatham for refitting before any further tests could take place. At the same time, on the committee's suggestion, a new target net was to be made up from seining twine so that it would drift with the tide for easier handling.

The trials were resumed eleven days later and continued, at intervals, until 20 September. In all a further forty-one runs were made and, thanks to the guide rods, there was a considerable improvement in accuracy. There were also, rather naturally, a few setbacks. On one occasion a piece of wood jammed the torpedo in the discharge tube and the resulting damage caused the weapon to behave somewhat wildly on its next run. It was clearly not due to any inherent design fault and the committee agreed to allow the substitution of a second 14-inch torpedo which was being held in reserve.

Whitehead was by now getting restive at the exhaustive duration of the tests. And, judging by the committee's note of his complaint, he was also worried whether the torpedo engines would stand up to further prolonged testing. "Mr Whitehead stated that he considered the trials of his small-sized torpedo had been very severe as it had made upwards of 30 runs in comparatively muddy water without having been thoroughly examined or its pistons replaced."[9] His plea was apparently noted with sympathy for, two days later, on 22 September, the larger 16-inch torpedo was taken to sea for the next set of tests and the small 14-inch was given a well-deserved rest.

The committee, however, were still irritated by Whitehead's exceptional secretiveness. On one occasion when the experiments were held up while the inventor worked on an unspecified fault Captain Arthur reported impatiently that one hour fifteen minutes "was occupied in repairing defects the nature of which were not disclosed."[10]

The first run with the 16-inch weapon proved a sharp disappointment after the predictable accuracy of the small torpedo. It lurched through the water like an inebriated porpoise for 300 yards, then stopped abruptly and finally floated to the surface as if it had passed out under the strain of its exertions. The whaler's crew brought it back to the *Oberon*, where Whitehead hastily explained "that this torpedo, never having been in the water before, was not properly adjusted."[11] He then proceeded to spend two hours adjusting it only to be rewarded with an even more calamitous anticlimax when it was finally launched from the bow tube. This time it managed to stagger 50 yards. And then sank.

The *Oberon* was anchored in 6 fathoms but the bottom, as Whitehead had already complained, was muddy. Although "all efforts [were] employed for recovery" they proved fruitless and the torpedo had to be written off as lost. As there was no spare on board, the trials had to be abandoned for the day and the sloop headed forlornly back to Sheerness while Whitehead and Hoyos discussed the probable reasons for the failure.

Fortunately the replacement torpedo proved as reliable as its smaller brother and the trials continued for a further two weeks, the last taking place on 7 October 1870. The weapon was on its best behavior and, completely fascinated by its accuracy and stability, the committee became more ambitious in their demands. Whitehead raised no objections for it was becoming increasingly clear from the friendly attitudes of Arthur, Singer, and Wilson that they were completely sold on the idea. And Whitehead was only interested in hard cash sales.

Several runs were made with the target moving and one shot was tried, successfully, with the paddle-steamer going full astern. Experiments were also carried out in launching the torpedo from a small steam launch with the aid of "boat frames," a method of attack still in use during the Second World War. There were smiles all round. "The property which this torpedo has of making its run at any given depth forms the principal part of the secret . . . and is undoubtedly a most valuable one," the committee observed enthusiastically. "[We] therefore consider that the inventor has completely established the property of the torpedo."[12]

But their enthusiasm was tempered by critical observation and it was apparent that very little escaped the notice of the three hawk-eyed officers. "As Mr Whitehead appeared unwilling, except on a very few occasions, to admit the full pressure of air to the engines, it is probable that there was no great margin of strength in the machinery." Their wholehearted support for the weapon, however, led them to qualify the acid bite of their criticism, "but it is only fair to him to state that, as the torpedo is only intended to be used once on active service, there would be no object gained by giving it sufficient strength to stand continued running."[13]

So far so good. But one question still remained to be answered. Could this revolutionary new underwater weapon sink a ship? With typical simplicity the Royal Navy decided to find out by means of a practical demonstration.

An old coal hulk, the former wooden corvette *Aigle*, was selected as the victim.[14] A special net, 80 feet in length and 12 feet in depth, was suspended from spars to protect the hulk from the torpedo's explosive warhead. It also served the purpose of a subsidiary experiment designed to test the potential of nets as a means of defence. The bottom of the net was weighted so that the lower edge was some 14 feet below the surface and, as an added precaution, large chains were passed under the target ship to facilitate raising her from the bottom should she be sunk.

Explosives were obviously regarded as too dangerous for a mere civilian engineer to handle, and although Whitehead was already producing torpedoes for the Austrian government fitted with warheads containing either guncotton or dynamite, a War Department chemist, Professor (later Sir) Frederick Abel, was called in to prime and charge the weapons. With unexpected foresight, the Admiralty also deputed a young officer from the Royal Engineers, Lieutenant Abney, to take photographs of the historic event—the results are still available for inspection at the library of the Naval Historical Branch of the Ministry of Defense in London.

The *Aigle* was moored in the Medway in 20 feet of water, with her stern to both wind and tide but broadside on to the sloop. The *Oberon* took up position at a range of 136 yards. A Force 7 breeze chopped the estuary into short sharp waves and there was a 1-knot tide running in the same direction.

In the excitement, however, no allowance was made for the tide and, as on the very earliest runs, the torpedo "left the tube slightly to the left of the keel line." At such point-blank range it was impossible to miss and, despite the slight inaccuracy of its course, the 16-inch weapon "passed just clear of the left-hand edge of the net, struck the ship direct {*sic*} under the starboard quarter, and exploded."[15]

Judging by the photograph taken by Lieutenant Abney there was a very satisfying bang, for the old coal hulk is almost completely obscured by a cloud of dense smoke and erupting water. The torpedo's point of impact was 18 feet from the target's sternpost and some 10 feet below the waterline. The 67-pound guncotton warhead tore a hole 20 feet by 10 feet in the hull—or as Admiral Fisher put it more picturesquely: "a hole as big as the First Lord's carriage"[16]—and the *Aigle* settled on the river bottom without further ado.

The smaller 14-inch torpedo was then fired but this exploded—against the net without causing further damage. In Whitehead's opinion it had struck a rope and exploded prematurely. But no one cared what the reason was. The only thing that mattered was the fact that a torpedo, a Whitehead torpedo, had sunk a ship. And that was really what it was all about.

Despite the committee's recommendation "that it was unanimously of the opinion that any maritime nation failing to provide itself with submarine locomotive torpedoes would be neglecting a great source of power both for offence and defence"[17] there was still a strong streak of conservatism in some of its conclusions. They felt, for example, that torpedo tubes could not be fitted to large ships and that broadside tubes would interfere with the internal workings of ironclads and lacked accuracy. And, still clearly obsessed by the tactics adopted at the Battle of Lissa, they added that bow tubes would weaken the strength of the ram. It was, however, the only error in their analysis and considering the revolutionary nature of Whithead's new weapon it was understandable in the light of their otherwise unanimous approval.

Thus did the Royal Navy accept Robert Whitehead and his invention. The Establishment, however, ignored him. And, although foreign governments showered him with titles, decorations, and orders, he remained, like the proverbial prophet, without honor in his own land.

Genesis of a Genius

R obert Whitehead was a Lancashire man both by birth and temperament. His family had made its money in cotton and his ancestors had all shown a marked disposition for independence allied, in many instances, with considerable mechanical and business skill. Indeed, the history of the Whitehead family goes some way to explaining the source of Robert's undoubted genius as well as revealing the origin of his firmly independent character.

Although his great grandfather, Thomas Whitehead, was a clergyman, his grandfather, also named Robert, proved to be more interested in the excitements of commerce than the call of the Church.[1] Moving to Bury some time before 1771, he opened a bleachworks at Elton—reputed in local records to be the first in England. Serving a booming industry, the business prospered and Robert (Senior) prospered with it. In fact, he soon accumulated enough money to buy his own country mansion, Haslam Hey at Elton—a fine old house ideally suited to the ambitions of a man who intended to make a fortune and found an industrial dynasty.

His eldest child, James, was born there in 1788 and two years later his wife, Alice, presented him with another son, John.[2] The two children grew up happily amongst the woods and meadows of rural Lancashire secure in the family's new-found wealth and mercifully free from the misery and squalor of the millworkers and artisans crowded into the hideous towns that were growing up around the mills and factories of England's industrial north.

Conscious, however, that although he had two fine young sons he unfortunately had only one business, Robert (Senior) began casting his eyes around for fresh fields of expansion and in May 1794 bought a plot of land in Bury Street, Little Bolton, where he erected a three-story warehouse to which, a few years later, he added a modest dwelling house. Then, although he continued to run the Lowercroft Bleachworks at Elton, he began to build up a new and independent business calendering—a process used to finish cloth.

At some time during the Napoleonic Wars, however, there appears to have been a cataclysmic upheaval in the family, for contemporary Bolton trade directories suddenly show the younger son, John, as sole proprietor of the Lowercroft Bleachworks and, even more strangely, also in occupation of the family home of Haslam Hey. His father, by contrast, was noted as living in the much smaller and less salubrious house adjacent to the calendering business in Bury Street.

The possibility of an internecine power struggle cannot be ruled out for it is otherwise difficult to understand why Robert Whitehead (Senior) should have yielded control of the prosperous bleachworks to his younger son. It is apparent, too, that from this period onwards John's branch of the family was seemingly more wealthy and socially secure—due, no doubt, to his marriage to Elizabeth Oram, a descendant of John Kay, whose invention of the flying-shuttle in 1753 first sowed the seeds of the Lancashire cotton boom.

John's elder brother, James, remained very much the practical industrialist.[3] And, like his father, he too lived in the Bury Street premises—an area bounded by mills and foundries and a far cry, indeed, from the rural delights of the old family home of Haslam Hey. James had married Ellen Swift in 1814 and it was undoubtedly this intermixing of blood that produced Robert Whitehead's inventive genius, for Ellen also came from engineering stock and the family firm of Thompson, Swift & Cole demonstrated a considerable versatility in the scope of their products. A contemporary directory described them as "iron and brass founders, steam engine makers, hydraulic presses, weighing machines, gas light apparatus, mill machinery, sugar mills, and the construction of fireproof buildings." Their premises at Hope Foundry in St. George's Street, Bolton, must indeed have been something of an engineering emporium, and coming from such a background it is not surprising that Robert showed a similar versatility in his inventions before finally concentrating all his genius on the torpedo.

William, the eldest son, was born in 1821 and Robert, the subject of this book, on 3 January 1823. Another son, James, was born in 1825 and a fourth, John, two years later. There were also four daughters—Elizabeth, Alice, Ellen, and Mary.[4] They were a happy close-knit family, and although Bolton was rapidly becoming industrialized—in the year of Robert's birth there were 28 cotton mills in the town employing 4,139 workers as well as other factories and foundries—they were still close to the fields and woods of the surrounding countryside.

For a young and eager boy there was much to see and, equally, much to do. The new steam locomotives were a constant source of wonderment as they hauled their loaded wagons along rails of polished steel. Steam, too, was encroaching on the canals, and strange craft with long spindly funnels and lathering paddle wheels towed strings of laden barges up and down the inland waterways of Lancashire to the delight of the children watching on the canal and river banks. The cotton mills had also surrendered to the new god of steam, and by 1823, when Robert was born, Bolton boasted 39 steam engines totalling 913 horsepower at work in its factories and mills. Thirty years later Whitehead's own marine steam engines were producing as much power from a single unit.

In 1829 Robert began his formal education at Bolton Grammar School where he joined his elder brother William who was already into his second year of studies. Nothing is known of his progress at the school for no records exist prior to 1837 but it can be assumed, judging by his later achievements, that he was a brighter than average pupil. He left the Grammar School in 1837, the year in which Queen Victoria ascended the throne, and spent the next two years being privately educated at the establishment of the Reverend Franklin Baker at Fairfield House, two minutes' walk from the Whitehead family home in Bury Street.

At some time between 1834 and 1841 Robert's father suddenly

gave up his cloth finishing interests and set up business as a wholesale brewer with premises in All Saint's Street. It was certainly a family affair for the ubiquitous firm of Thompson, Swift & Cole built and supplied the brewing machinery—adding this new accomplishment to their already versatile range of engineering skills. And although only a schoolboy, Robert took more than a casual interest in the installation. The pumps used in the brewing processes exercised a special fascination for him and memories of their functional design probably influenced his work in Italy when, some eleven years later, he built the pumping machinery used for draining parts of the vast Lombardy Marshes.

In 1839, after his two-year stint at Parson Baker's educational establishment, Robert found himself abruptly transferred from the peaceful calm of academic life to the noise and bustle of an engineering workshop when his father apprenticed him to Richard Ormerod & Son of Aytoun Street in Manchester.[5] It was a tough transition for a sixteen-year-old boy but it had, in Robert's eyes, two saving graces. Firstly, he was at last in close contact with his beloved engines, and secondly, his favorite uncle, William Swift, was the manager—a fact that had undoubtedly influenced James Whitehead's choice when he selected Ormerods for his son's training. The practical experience Robert gained from working on engines and machinery remained a valuable asset through the rest of his long working life, and guided by his uncle, he was also quick to appreciate the importance of acquiring a sound theoretical knowledge to back up his manual skill.

One of his first jobs as an apprentice was the great span of the iron roof of Manchester's London Road railway station where, perched on narrow girders high above the ground, he helped fitters bolt the various sections together.[6] Next he moved to the workshops to gain practical experience in handling machinery before proceeding to the drawing office where he quickly gained a reputation for his "exquisite draughtsmanship," a skill that was to remain with him until he was nearly eighty years old.

Not content with the knowledge he was acquiring as an apprentice he began attending classes at the Mechanics' Institution in Cooper Street from 7:30 to 9:30 every evening.[7] And here, for the sum of five shillings per quarter, he studied mechanical drawing and pattern designing as well as the more theoretical aspects of engineering and mechanics. A contemporary advertisement by the institution proclaimed: "The object of the Institution is to instruct the working classes in the principles of the arts they practise."[8] Clearly Robert Whitehead had no illusions of grandeur when it came to a quest for knowledge.

No precise date can be fixed for the end of his apprenticeship with Ormerods although two Austrian sources indicate that it lasted for six years. It is unlikely, however, that it extended beyond 1844 by which time he would have reached his twenty-first birthday. Nor is there any evidence to show where he worked between then and 1846. One thing, though, is fairly certain. The 1844 date usually quoted in reference books for his emigration to Marseille is, in the light of known facts, incorrect.

Be that as it may, his father's brewery business had certain recompenses not the least being a wide acquaintance with the local tavern and innkeepers who, by repute, are usually blessed with pretty daughters. Even in his old age Robert's portraits show a merry twinkle in his eyes. But, when romance finally blossomed, the old family connections with cotton proved stronger than suspected for he fell in love with the daughter of James Johnson, a "dry-salter" from Doncaster, and Anne Boville of Swainby, Northallerton.

Frances Maria was an attractive and charming girl who proved more than capable of dealing firmly with the occasional eccentricities of Robert's inventive genius yet retaining sufficient wit to keep up with his intellect. No details of their courtship have survived but there can be little doubt that Robert approached his task with the same single-minded determination that had characterized the Whitehead family over past generations and which, in later life, he was to demonstrate again in the struggle to perfect the greatest of his inventions. It need hardly be added that he won her heart.

The marriage took place at All Saints' Church, Old Byland, on 30 March 1846 in the presence of the entire family. Robert's father, James Whitehead, had by then apparently retired from active business for he was described in the marriage documents merely as "gentleman" while Robert himself was shown as an "engineer" residing in Manchester. Having embarked on matrimony, he immediately began preparing for the second momentous step in his life—to leave England and seek his fortune abroad.

France, still recovering politically from her defeat in the Napoleonic Wars and endeavoring to reestablish herself under the restored monarchy of the Citizen King, Louis Phillippe, was also struggling to become an industrial power. Old enmities forgotten in the rush to make money, the French turned their eyes to Britain for guidance and technological know-how in the new world of steam and steel. English engineers were at a premium and there were many anxious and willing to take up the challenge in a foreign land.

One of the industrialists to take advantage of these new opportunities was an English mercantile adventurer, Philip Taylor, who had started life as the fourth son of an obscure hymnwriter—a somewhat odd beginning for a brilliant if eccentric engineer. After a varied career that took him all over Europe and in which he made and lost fortunes in quick succession, Taylor opened an engineering business in Marseille, where he was joined in partnership by his sons Philip and Robert. In 1845 he purchased the La Seyne shipbuilding yard— no doubt inspired in his endeavors by the success of his friend Brunel's *Great Western*, which had set a new Atlantic record with a sixteen-day east-west crossing on its maiden voyage in April 1838.

But steamship building was a complicated business requiring the skills of men already well-versed and experienced in the new technology and there were few such men available in France. Taylor therefore turned to Britain for his engineers and, with the bait of high wages and good living conditions, he inaugurated a form of Victorian ''brain-drain'' to obtain the skilled labour he needed for his expanding shipyard. One of his targets was Richard Ormerod & Son in Manchester, where Robert Whitehead had served his apprenticeship and where his uncle, William Swift, was still manager. A deal was done and William quickly packed his bags to take up an appointment as works manager at Taylor's yard in Marseilles.

Robert was impressed by the letters he received from his uncle and it was soon apparent that without working capital, there were much better opportunities for young British engineers on the Continent than there were in England. William Swift, for his part, was equally anxious to secure the services of his nephew, who was already gaining a reputation as a brilliant draughtsman. It did not take Whitehead long to make up his mind and within a few months of his marriage the young engineer and his bride were facing the discomforts of the Channel passage en route to Marseille.

No details are known of Whitehead's work at La Seyne, but this early experience with ships and marine engineering was to prove a valuable asset to him in his later career. Once again he came under the protective wing of his Uncle William, who helped to develop his mechanical skills still further and, in addition, he undoubtedly took more than passing note of his flamboyant, if eccentric, employer. Known as "Papa" to his workmen, Taylor had the respect of his employees and was both popular and admired by the French craftsmen who worked for him in the La Seyne yards. Robert Whitehead's own benevolent paternalism towards his workers in later life owed much to the influence of Philip Taylor during those early days in Marseille, and his friendship with Taylor's son was maintained well into the 1890s.

But the young draughtsman was already yearning for independence and, within two years, he was on the move again, traveling this time across the tiny kingdom of Piedmont, eastward, over the great plains of Lombardy, to another area of Europe where industry was struggling to grow, and, more important, where fortunes could be made.

Much of Northern Italy was under the control of the Austrian Empire in 1847 following the division of spoils at the Congress of Vienna after Napoleon's defeat in 1815. Various minor states in Italy and down the Illyrian coast had been handed over to Austria for, as Tsar Alexander remarked when some of these petty provinces protested at being brought under the Hapsburg yoke, "Republics are no longer fashionable."

The damp climate of the Po valley, the abundance of cheap labor, and the traditional silk-spinning industry of northern Italy gave Milan, like Bolton, a natural advantage in the textile sector of the new machine age, and the old city quickly became the center of the cotton trade. It was therefore hardly surprising in the circumstances that Robert picked on Milan to set up business on his own account as a consulting engineer. And with the high reputation which British engineering skill enjoyed throughout the world at that time he had no shortage of customers.

Concentrating mainly on the new textile industry he soon invented a number of ingenious improvements for silkweaving machinery. And with memories of the unscrupulous opportunists and rogues he had encountered while working in England, Whitehead prudently protected himself by registering his designs and inventions with the Patent Office in Vienna for, although working in Italy, he was within the administrative borders of the Austrian Empire. The patents covered machines designed for use in the Milan weaving industry and included, among other things, a device for winding silk direct from a cocoon. His consultancy business was soon flourishing and with the security of his patented designs, which would, in time, yield a comfortable royalty income, the future looked decidedly encouraging. But, engrossed in his work, Robert failed to notice the dark clouds building up on the political horizon—clouds that would gather into a storm fierce enough to destroy his new venture completely.

By 1848 Europe was in a ferment of revolution brought about by the rising tide of nationalism, the excesses of various petty despots, and the grievances of the working classes, who were suffering, for the first time, from the miseries of the new industrial era. Once started the fever of revolution swept the Continent like an epidemic. By mid-March both Austria and Prussia had succumbed to the infection as rival national and political factions struggled for power and there were ominous rumbles throughout the Hapsburg Empire.

In the tiny kingdom of Piedmont, the state which was to later become the catalyst of Italian unification, King Charles Albert proclaimed a new constitution as a sop to the liberals, whom he needed as allies in his projected war against the Austrian giant and, within days, Pope Pius IX was also forced to agree to similar reforms after an uprising in the Papal States, which were at that time a completely independent community.

As rumors of the riots and rebellions trickled through into Northern Italy, Robert Whitehead must have many times regretted his choice of domicile. England may have lacked the opportunities he needed but at least she was politically stable and relatively free from civil violence and war. The worst, however, was yet to come.

On 17 March 1848 Metternich fled from Vienna in the face of a threatened revolution and, the following day, the people of Milan rose up against their foreign oppressors. Many of the wealthier merchants and mill-owners had already fled the city but Whitehead remained behind to be caught in the middle of the conflict. Austrian press censorship was total and complete and their propaganda machine operated with smooth efficiency. The newspapers gave no hint that the Austrian government was crumbling or that embryonic nationalist revolutions were anything more than minor civil disorders in outlying provinces. The empire was secure according to the calmly worded editorials and, not for the last time, Whitehead believed them implicitly.

The street fighting that followed was bitter and bloody—the poorly armed Italians exhibiting an unexpected ferocity that surprised even the Austrians. Within five days the citizens of Milan had expelled General Joseph Radetsky and his twenty thousand troops and the city, bullet scarred but unbowed, celebrated its liberation with gay abandon. Venice, too, threw out its Austrian garrison and it was apparent that all Italy was about to explode in revolution.

For Whitehead the popular surge of Italian nationalism meant disaster. Industry was at a standstill with most of the factory hands manning the barricades against their foreign oppressors and, to make matters worse, the newly formed Provisional Government promptly annulled all patents on the premise that they were issued under the authority of a foreign government and therefore invalid. Whitehead's patents were his only asset and without them all his hard work had been brought to nothing. And, aside from the business aspect of the situation, he now had to concern himself not only with his own personal safety but also with that of his young wife, Frances.

Yet despite these bitter experiences, and until his dying day, Robert Whitehead tenaciously clung to his belief that anything printed in a newspaper must be true.[9] It was this same stubborn streak in his character which, when disciplined into other more positive directions, was to lead to his most famous invention.

Der Küstenbrander

The five days of street fighting Whitehead had been forced to witness at close-hand in Milan left him with a repugnance of war which, at first glance, seems strange for a man who, twenty years later, was to create the deadliest weapon of naval warfare the world had ever seen. But, like so many other well-meaning inventors, Robert was convinced that the terrible nature of his weapon would be a means of preserving peace rather than a cause of national conflict. As *The Times* commented: "He was no lover of war . . . [and] believed that the torpedo would rather tend to prevent war than provoke it."[1] History, unfortunately, was to show the fallacy of his belief.

The liberation of Milan was not, however, the end of the struggle in central Europe. The "March and April Laws," sponsored by Louis Kossuth, were voted through the Hungarian Diet and these new statutes raised the former vassal state of Hungary to political equality with her former master, Austria. And further riots in the imperial capital of Vienna forced the Austrian government, now deprived of the strength and leadership of Chancellor Metternich, to appoint a special minister for Hungary. Even worse, a general war involving the whole of central Europe was threatened when the Piedmont king, Charles Victor, took the opportunity of Austria's internal troubles to launch his troops against the tottering empire as the first step to creating a united Italy.

These political upheavals may seem to have little relevance to the life of an obscure English engineer struggling for existence in the north of Italy. But Whitehead was already directly affected by the loss of his Austrian patents and was to discover, in the aftermath of revolution, a fertile breeding ground for the development of armaments and new weapons. New figures were to emerge, a new political climate was to be created, and the inevitability of a major war was to grow. And, not least, a sense of national grievance and a hunger for revenge brought about by the events of 1848 was to exercise a baleful influence over the areas bordered by the Adriatic for the next seventy years. They were also to have a considerable effect on Robert Whitehead's life and work in the years to come.

General Radetsky, ousted from Milan, skillfully regrouped his army in a strong defensive position known as the Quadrilateral and, at the Battle of Custozza, defeated Charles Victor's Italian troops. The Piedmontese army fled in disorder leaving the roads to the north open and Radetsky's soldiers returned in triumph to Milan.

The victorious return of the Austrians was a welcome occasion for Robert Whitehead. It cannot be doubted that his true sympathies lay with the expropriated Italians but, as a man of business, he was more concerned that the restoration of stable government and the prospects of civil peace would start the wheels of industry and commerce turning again. And *that*, so far as he was concerned, was all that really mattered.

Even so the events of 1848 made a profound impression on the young engineer leaving him, as already noted, with a loathing for war and violence. His dislike of killing, in fact, grew so intense in later years that he became almost vegetarian in his habits and avoided eating meat except when social etiquette made refusal impossible. He also showed a similar distaste for shooting and, throughout his life, he avoided any form of contact with the more popular blood sports.[2]

Revolution and civil disorder had left him disillusioned and unsettled, and by the time the Austrians returned to Milan he was already planning to leave the city. Apart from business considerations a more personal event influenced his decision to move on. His first child, James, born during this period, had died in infancy and Frances was pregnant again. It was therefore essential for them to find a more secure area in which to settle for it was patently apparent that Northern Italy would soon become a battlefield again as the struggle for unification continued.

First thoughts led, rather naturally, to the idea of returning to England, but his elder brother, William, who had been engaged on a series of civil engineering projects along the Adriatic coast, encouraged Robert to make tentative enquiries about employment in the various shipyards and engineering concerns that were growing up in that region. The prospects looked good but before finally leaving northern Italy Robert was given an unexpected opportunity to demonstrate his skills as a civil engineer. The Austrian provincial government, in an attempt to win the support of the defeated Italians, had set in motion a vast project to drain sections of the Lombardy marshes, and Robert was invited to design and supervise the building of the necessary pumping machinery.[3] Calling back his memories of the pumps which Messrs. Thompson, Swift & Coles had installed in his father's brewery at Bolton and adding to their efficiency with the aid of his own technical knowledge and fast-growing experience, Whitehead's designs proved admirably suited to their task, and the success of his pumping engines added further lustre to his increasing reputation.

As soon as the drainage contract was completed, Robert and his wife left the unhappy memories of Milan behind them and set off across the north of Italy to Trieste, on the Adriatic coast, where Robert had obtained an appointment with the famous shipbuilding company of Austria Lloyd as a constructor.[4] Once again Whitehead chose to settle in an Italian region of the Hapsburg Empire even though he was careful to remain within the well-ordered sphere of Austrian administration. The economic stability of Austria offered the secure base he needed for his business ventures although, at that period, he seemed to fight shy of involving himself too deeply in the more Germanic regions of the empire. The easy-going way of life of the Italians appealed to him far more than that of Austrian society, and there is ample evidence to show that Italian was the common second language of the Whitehead household.

The child that Frances was expecting when they left Milan was born on 19 May 1849, but parenthood merely acted as a spur to Robert's ambitions. Already dissatisfied with his prospects at Austria Lloyd he was actively seeking another appointment that would give him the freedom he needed to develop his engineering talents. He did not have long to wait.

Stabilmento Strudthoff were the leading pioneers of marine engineering on the Adriatic coast. Based at Trieste, with their works almost opposite those of Austria Lloyd, they had already, in 1845, established their reputation by building the first marine steam engines in the region and, shortly afterwards, they were given a contract to supply power plants for the warships of the Austrian Navy. Whitehead's own reputation was also growing and before many months had passed Robert was able to tell his wife that Strudthoffs had offered him the post of technical director.[5] For a young man of twenty-six it was a tremendous step and he accepted the offer without hesitation. And so, once again, the Whitehead family packed its belongings and, with the recently arrived baby, Frances Eleanor, they moved to the other side of the city so that Robert could live closer to his new job.

He soon found that the shipbuilding experience he had acquired at Philip Taylor's yards at La Seyne was an invaluable asset and within a very short time his agile brain was evolving improved techniques and designs for use in the engineering shops of the company. Strudthoff's board of directors undoubtedly felt they had good reasons for congratulating themselves on finding this outstanding young English engineer.

Robert's early period with the firm, however, was marred by personal tragedy when he learned that his youngest brother, John, probably the most brilliant member of the talented Whitehead family, had died at the unexpectedly early age of twenty-three. But the tragedy was mitigated when on 31 March 1851 Frances presented Robert with his second daughter, Alice, and there were further celebrations two years later when his elder brother, William, married Christina Foster in Trieste. For a while it seemed likely that the entire Whitehead family would settle in the city but William, like Robert, was an ambitious and independently inclined man, and he was soon off on his travels again in an adventurous career that took him all over Europe, into Asia, and even to America—wherever, in fact, there was a bridge to be built or a viaduct to be constructed.

So far as Robert was concerned, however, the responsibilities of providing for his growing family curbed any thoughts of following in his brother's peripatetic footsteps, and it was fortunate that his new job at Stabilmento Strudthoff was able to provide, at least for the time being, a sufficient challenge to satisfy his restless genius. He concentrated his energies on the design of marine steam engines and built a number of power units for Austrian warships including, in 1851, the machinery for the 1,560-ton paddle-wheel sloop *Taurus*.[6] In 1854 his reputation received another boost when he produced a screw-propulsion unit—the first to be manufactured by Strudthoffs.[7] 1854 also proved a good year for more personal reasons. On 23 November his son John was born and Robert now had another incentive to set up his own independent business, especially because, even from early childhood, the boy showed a marked aptitude for things mechanical.

Two years later, in 1856, Whitehead designed and built a cylindrical marine boiler—possibly the first to be produced in the Austrian Empire.[8] Standing at the very edge of contemporary advanced technology, this latter achievement singled him out as being already in the top flight of his chosen profession. Marine boilers of this period were usually rectangular in shape with squared corners reinforced to withstand the pressures built up by the expanding steam. Indeed, although the Royal Navy installed a few experimental cylindrical boilers before 1860, old-type boilers were still being fitted as late as 1874, and the first British capital ship to be equipped with cylindrical boilers was the *Alexandra*, laid down on 5 March 1873.[9]

The cylindrical boiler, which allowed much higher steam pressures and thus more efficient engines in terms of power-weight ratio, posed two problems—one practical and the other theoretical. The former was no more than a lack of experience in the production of curved cast-iron plates while the later involved the calculation of the internal stresses. The long and arduous hours of study at Manchester's Mechanics Institute provided him with the necessary theoretical knowledge while his work at the La Seyne and Austria-Lloyd shipyards had given him sound, practical experience in the handling of cast iron. This continually enlarging reservoir of technical know-how was to stand him in good stead when he came to design and build the air chamber for his first torpedo some ten years later.

Robert's technological skill—he was now only a little over thirty years of age—was attracting considerable attention in Austrian marine circles and it was abundantly clear that if he was not soon offered a seat on Strudthoff's Board of Directors he would begin searching for more fruitful pastures. Indeed, with industry developing along the Adriatic coast, there were plenty of wealthy men eager and anxious to back anyone with the training and experience required to run the new factories, mills, workshops and shipyards that were springing up in the region. Anyone, that is, who could be relied upon to work honestly and, more important, who could return a good profit on their investment.

One such group of financiers, operating under the name of Stabilmento Tecnico Fiumano (STF), had established a new engineering works at Fiume a few miles along the coast from Trieste. All they needed was someone with the "know-how" to turn it into a thriving concern. Almost unanimously their eyes turned to the dedicated English engineer working at Strudthoffs.

By 1856 Whitehead was quite comfortably situated and, with Strudthoffs paying him a salary commensurate with his skill, he had no financial worries. In addition, he was held in the highest esteem as a brilliant engineering designer and enjoyed an enviable reputation as a man who was "scrupulously honest and straightforward."[10] His family, too, was happy in Trieste and Frances had proved a steadfast companion and an admirable wife in every way. Yet the driving urge for independence—the Whitehead family characteristic for generations past—continued to unsettle him and he refused to regard Trieste as their permanent home. And so, when Stabilmento Tecnico Fiumano offered him the post of manager at their new works with all the independence that such an appointment implied, the opportunities presented proved too attractive to turn down and, with very little hesitation, he accepted the job.

To begin with he traveled daily from Trieste to Fiume, but after a short while his wife and the children took up residence in a small red-brick house, the Casa Rossa (Red House), situated inside the grounds of the STF factory and overlooking the main gates, which opened on to the road from Fiume to Abbazia.

Under Whitehead's skillful guidance the new company flourished from the outset. The men financing the concern were influential and well connected and it was not long before they had obtained a number of highly remunerative contracts from the Imperial Navy Office in Vienna and, wisely, they concentrated on the financial side of the business, leaving Robert with a completely free hand in matters of design and production. At first the works were engaged on minor engineering projects such as power winches, donkey engines, and so on, but it was not long before contracts for marine engines were obtained and no doubt Whitehead's reputation played a large part in the sudden influx of important orders.

The marine engines he designed for STF functioned perfectly and proved utterly reliable in service—or, at least, as utterly reliable as any other marine engine of that period. Robert produced nothing startling or revolutionary and his designs were based on tried and tested principles with the emphasis on good solid workmanship. It was, indeed, not uncommon to see him in the yard with his coat off and his sleeves rolled up showing a machinist or fitter how a job *should* be done by practical demonstration.

Whitehead was in his element at last. The directors of STF had given him complete and unquestioned control of the engineering side of the company and he thrived on the responsibility that flowed from his autonomy, often working into the small hours of the morning revising drawings and preparing new designs. It was perhaps fortunate for the family peace that they were living at the *Casa Rossa* inside the factory.

His second son, James Beethom, was born on 21 July 1858—his unusual second name stemming from Robert's sister Alice, who had married John Beethom of Manchester some time earlier—and the elder son, John, by now almost four years old, was already showing signs of inheriting his father's engineering talents. The factory drew the boy like a magnet and whenever "Jack," as he was known by the family, went missing there was rarely any difficulty in finding him for he was usually in one of the machine shops "helping" a mechanic with his work.[11]

The future was already beckoning brightly and the inventor was astute enough to recognize the possibilities of great things just a short way ahead. It is unlikely, though, that Robert thought much further ahead than the probability of a directorship with STF or, at most, the realization of his dream to become his own master. And, absorbed in his work, he failed to notice the storm clouds gathering again over the political horizon as both Germany and Italy moved relentlessly forward towards national unification. Already, in 1859, Italy had realized part of her ambition when in alliance with the France of Napoleon III she recovered the lost province of Lombardy during a brief

war with her old enemy Austria. But Venetia with its valuable seaport
of Venice remained in the hands of the Hapsburg Empire and it was
apparent that a further conflict was approaching when Italy would
attempt to wrest the province from Austrian clutches.

The prospects of a naval war in the Adriatic emphasized the need
for a strong Austrian fleet to defend the empire's small but vulnerable
coastline and Italy's navy was, with the exception of the French, the
most powerful in the Mediterranean. A strong navy was Austria's only
hope of retaining her grip on the glittering prize of Venice, but the key
question was—could she catch up and match Italy's strength at sea
before war finally broke out?

The impending naval race brought Whitehead the most important project of his career so far when the Vienna government approved the construction of a new armor-plated screw frigate, the
Archduke Ferdinand Maximillian. She was to be flagship designate of
the new fleet and the contract for the design and construction of her
engines was awarded to Stabilmento Tecnico Fiumano. For all practical purposes the contract was awarded to Robert Whitehead for, so
far as design and construction were concerned, he *was* Stabilmento
Tecnico Fiumano.

Forerunner of the ironclad proper, the armor-plated steam frigate had originally been developed by the French when they laid down
the *Gloire* and her three sister ships in March 1858. Until then the
mainstay of the world's fighting fleets were updated versions of the old
three-deckers of the Trafalgar era and earlier. True, they had been
revamped by the addition of small steam engines and, in some cases,
also given minimal protection by screwing iron plates onto their vast
oak hulls, but basically they were still the stately wooden-walled
sailing ships of the late eighteenth century.

The *Gloire*, however, was an entirely new concept. A warship
designed and built from the keel up as an armored fighting ship, she
had a single deck of heavy guns firing on the broadside and was fitted
with engines powerful enough to give her a substantial margin of
speed over the old type "wooden-walls." In fact it was claimed, quite
accurately, that a single *Gloire* could have taken on and destroyed the
entire British Mediterranean Fleet in a single afternoon without assistance.

Britain naturally replied to this new threat from across the Channel and, the following year, laid down the *Warrior*, the first in what

was to be a long line of ironclad battleships that ended only under the threat of nuclear warfare in the early 1950s. Her power unit, a Penn horizontal single expansion trunk engine with a jet condenser, was regarded as the best and most advanced in the world. By dispensing with piston rods there was a considerable reduction in wear and tear on the bearings and the engine was fed by no fewer than ten rectangular boilers. It is interesting to recall that Whitehead had produced his first *cylindrical* boiler for Strudthoffs some three years earlier.

A comparison between these two ships, one British the other Austrian, gives some idea of Whitehead's skill as a marine engineer. To add balance to the comparison, details are also given of the Spanish ironclad *Numancia*, built by the La Seyne shipyard where Whitehead had worked in 1847 and which Philip Taylor had sold to the *Compagnie des Forges et Chantiers de la Méditerrannée* in 1855.

Taking into account the smaller size of the *Ferdinand Max* it is apparent that Whitehead's marine steam engines were only marginally inferior to those built by his more experienced rivals in Britain and France; for performance depends ultimately on the lines of the hull and Robert, as an engineer, had no say in the design of the ship itself.

Table 1
Comparative Details of Contemporary Ironclads

	Warrior	*Ferdinand Max*	*Numancia*
Launch date:	20 Dec 1860	24 May 1865	19 Nov 1863
Displacement (tons):	9,137	5,130	7,189
Engine:	Penn horizontal single expansion	2-cyl horizontal single shaft	French-designed compound
IHP	5,267	2,925	3,700
Speed*:	14.08	12.45	10 but reached 12.9 on acceptance trials
Armament:	10 × 110-pdr[†] 26 × 68-pdr SB[‡]	16 × 48-pdr SB [Krupps deliberately failed to deliver her main armament of rifled guns.]	40 × 68-pdr SB

Source: All details from *Conway's All the World's Fighting Ships 1860–1905.*
* Knots
[†] Gun with rifled barrel.
[‡] Smooth-bore gun.

But, most important, in battle Whitehead's engines were to perform fautlessly. And *that* was the acid test.

The 1860s and 1870s were revolutionary years in warship design. The period started with the old three-deckers and ended with the prototypes of the modern twentieth-century capital ship. Gone were the sails, although the Royal Navy showed a strange reluctance to part with them entirely for many years; gone too were the old smooth-bore guns ranged along each broadside. In their place were two, or perhaps four, heavy rifled guns of large caliber operating in armored turrets or barbettes, supported by light quick-firers.

At the beginning of the period the famous 68-pounder, almost identical to the guns used by Nelson, fired solid shot. The introduction of the shell, a hollow sphere filled with an explosive substance, made the use of armor imperative, and the ironclad developed as a direct consequence of this new artillery. Yet such was the conservative nature of the naval mind that the process of evolution took more than fifty years—for British ships had been using a form of shell gun, the carronade, as early as 1799. It was only after the Battle of Sinope in November 1853, when the Russian fleet completely destroyed Turkey's wooden-walls with their explosive shells, that the admirals of Britain and France were finally persuaded to adopt this revolution in naval armaments. And even then they had reservations.

A similar struggle took place between the supporters of wooden ships and the proponents of iron—a struggle also quickly settled by the Battle of Sinope—and between sailpower and steam engines, followed later by paddle wheels versus screw propulsion. Always the traditionalists fought hard to preserve anything that had been tried and tested. Always the newcomers struggled to gain adoption of the latest invention. And such is the frailty of human nature that the newcomers of one generation often become the conservative traditionalists of the next. Whitehead himself was to become one of the challenging newcomers when he first produced his torpedo, yet he, too, showed signs of becoming a traditionalist later in life when new minds sought to change and modify his designs.

At this stage, however, he kept clear of experiments and continued to produce his simple but well-tried power units for the Austrian Navy, and cut off from the rivalries of the French and British warship designers, he was little influenced by the wildcat schemes that marred development in Western Europe. In any case his orthodox upbringing would have led him to discard most of the wilder experiments as impractical even if he had known of them. For Robert, despite his ability and willingness to break new ground, was a strictly no-nonsense engineer of the "old school."

Even so there were certain other experiments in progress, which were to change completely the shape and construction of the ironclad and revolutionize the tactics of naval warfare over the next few years. And although he did not realize it at the time, Robert Whitehead was to find himself the leading figure in the coming upheaval.

Somewhere around 1860 an unknown officer in the Austrian Marine Artillery had devised plans for a small surface boat, only a few feet in length, which, when loaded with explosives, could be used to attack blockading warships operating close inshore.[12] His ideas never developed beyond the drawingboard stage but, when he died, his papers came into the hands of a retired officer of the Austrian Navy, Fregattenkapitän (Commander) Giovanni de Luppis.[13] De Luppis found the idea fascinating, and with plenty of leisure time on his hands, he began working on and improving the drawings. Finally, after many months of work, he built his own scale model of the design.

The prototype was constructed of wood and propelled by a clockwork motor which turned a screw at the stern. Also at the stern and situated behind the propeller was a large rudder the operation of which was controlled by an observer on the shore with the aid of tiller ropes while the gunpowder charge packed into the hull was detonated by means of a percussion pistol device in the bows. When the little vessel struck its victim on the waterline the pistol detonated the charge and, so its fond inventor hoped, inflicted fatal damage on its opponent.

De Luppis experimented and modified *Der Küstenbrander* (the coastal fireship), as he named his device, until he was satisfied and then, without further ado, presented himself and his model to the naval authorities in Vienna. Unfortunately the experts were singularly unimpressed. They considered it to be "unworkable" and criticized —not without just cause—both the steering mechanism and the primitive method of propulsion. They agreed, however, that it had possibilities of eventually becoming a serviceable weapon and de Luppis was advised to develop his idea further, possibly with the aid and cooperation of a consulting engineer.

The retired Fregattenkapitän was at that time living in a villa on the Adriatic coast, and with a lively interest in maritime affairs, he was already well acquainted with the reputation of the English engineer working at Stabilmento Tecnico Fiumano. Convinced that *Der Küstenbrander* was the prototype of an important weapon, he had little hesitation in visiting Whitehead to sound him out on the prospects of cooperation with a view to partnership in the invention.

Robert met de Luppis some time in 1864 and was immediately struck by the possibilities of the device although, equally, he could see the serious faults inherent in the design as it then stood. It was a challenge to his ingenuity—no more than that—and somehow he felt impelled to take up the invitation. With the Austrian officer's help he set about building a full-scale working model and, together, they tested it in the bay facing the STF factory. The engines proved unreliable and the complex web of tiller lines, which de Luppis usually operated with the enthusiasm of a small boy playing with his first electric train set, were ill-suited to accurate navigation. The speed, too, was ridiculously slow and the range, even when the tiller lines kept the weapon on a straight course, was woefully short. Yet, somewhere along the line, Whitehead felt that the primitive contraption contained the germ of a workable idea.

The engineer first restricted himself to improving the motive power and redesigning the steering gear. But every modification brought fresh frustrations and finally, after months of work, he was forced to admit that de Luppis's conception was doomed to failure from the outset. Running on the surface at slow speeds *Der Küstenbrander* was hopelessly vulnerable to her victim's defensive guns, and its pathetic lack of power meant that it could be pushed aside by a stout boathook when it came too near to its target. Having reached his conclusion on engineering principles, and after a considerable amount of mental argument, Robert reluctantly informed the Austrian that his device was unworkable and the short-lived partnership was dissolved.

Yet there was something about the idea that retained his interest, and almost unconsciously, he found himself turning the problem over and over in his brain until the whole thing took on the proportions of an obsession. Perhaps something stronger and more powerful was needed. Or maybe a form of self-steering mechanism. The question was--*what?*

Unable to concentrate on his main work Robert began sketching

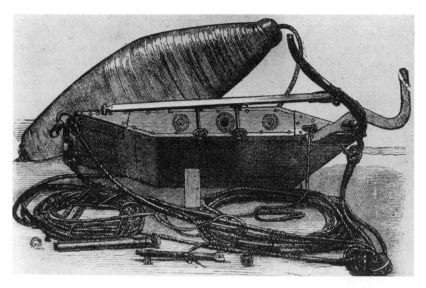

A contemporary picture (ca. 1870) of the notorious Harvey towed torpedo.

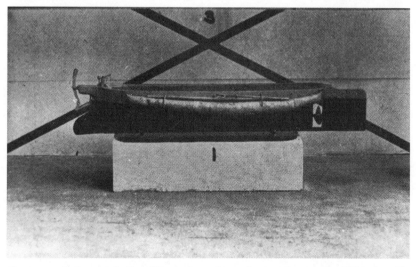

Giovanni de Luppis's *Der Küstenbrander*—the inspiration for Whitehead's automobile torpedo.

out fresh plans while he considered the problem in a new light. He recalled that most warships of the period, including the *Ferdinand Max*, were fitted with ram bows on the premise that damage below the waterline was more likely to prove fatal than damage to the upper side of the hull. Clearly, then, any new weapon would be most effective if its explosive charge could be detonated *below* the surface. And with his logical engineer's mind it did not take him long to extend the idea to its rational conclusion—that *the weapon must travel beneath the surface right through the attack.*

The more Whitehead considered his new theory the more convinced he became that this was the only sensible answer to the problem. By traveling beneath the surface of the water not only would the point of impact on the target be below the waterline but, of equal importance, the approach of the device would be invisible to the defenders on the target vessel. The combination would be irresistible, and by deciding to make his torpedo an underwater weapon, Robert ensured its success at a single stroke. On reflection, however, he soon appreciated that the attendant engineering problems would make the troubles experienced with *Der Küstenbrander* seem like child's play in comparison.

Once bitten by the torpedo bug Whitehead concentrated his entire energies on the project. Locking himself away in a small hut in an obscure corner of the factory and helped only by his son John, now rising twelve years of age, and a single trusted mechanic, he began turning his thoughts into reality.[14] The difficulties were manifold. First there was the detonator and trigger mechanism to consider, then the power unit itself, for the weapon must clearly be self-propelled if it was to be a viable proposition, and finally, most difficult of all, the guidance and depth-keeping gear. It would have been a formidable task for a complete team of men, for nearly every aspect of the new weapon ventured into uncharted and unexplored regions of engineering science. For one man to succeed in creating such a revolutionary device would require genius of a high order. And Robert Whitehead was such a man. The result was a strange new weapon that took the generic name of all underwater devices—the torpedo—and gave it a new and potent meaning.

Although Robert had visualized the torpedo he still needed to perfect the reality of his inspiration and for the next two years, hidden away in his lonely hut, he struggled to bring his creation to life. No midwife ever fought so hard over a birth as Whitehead did with his torpedo. And no midwife has ever been so well rewarded for her efforts. In the circumstances it is not surprising that, from the moment it first saw the light of day, the original torpedo was always affectionately referred to by the Whitehead family as the "baby."[15]

But while he struggled with his precocious infant the clouds of war were once again gathering over Austria. Italy, still questing after her lost province of Venetia, found an unexpected ally in Chancellor Otto von Bismarck, who needed to crush the Hapsburg Empire in order to place Prussia at the undisputed head of the new German Empire. It was a classic stab-in-the-back strategy, for only two years earlier, in 1864, Austria had allied herself to Prussia against the helpless kingdom of Denmark in a war to win the duchies of Schleswig and Holstein to the fast-growing German confederation. Austrian warships under Kommodore Tegethoff had entered the North Sea to support the infant Prussian Navy and Whitehead's engines had helped to power the ships that blockaded the Danish coast. The result of the war was a resounding victory for the unholy allies but the triumph was somewhat soured when the Prussian chancellor grabbed most of the conquered territory at Austria's expense. The Convention of Gastein, at which Bismarck admitted, "we have papered over the cracks," did little to restore Austro-Prussian amity and it was clear to all that the new confederation was too small to contain both first-class powers within its borders.

The war between Prussia and Austria finally erupted on 14 June 1866, and Italy, seizing her opportunity, joined the struggle a few days later. The climax of the Austro-Italian conflict came when the opposing fleets met off the island of Lissa on 20 July 1866. It was the first major sea battle in which ironclads fought ironclads. It was also the last naval action to be fought without the threat of the weapon that Whitehead was to unveil to the world later the same year.

Thus the Battle of Lissa proved not only a watershed in the history of naval warfare but also the crucial turning point of Robert Whitehead's own by no means uneventful career. And although he took no active part in the fighting, the events of this historic battle were to drag him from comparative obscurity into the dazzling glare of international fame.

Thanks to Your First-class Engines

On paper the Austrian fleet was completely outclassed. Her two biggest warships, the armored frigates *Ferdinand Max* and *Hapsburg*, mounted no rifled guns at all, thanks to Krupps conveniently defaulting on delivery shortly before war broke out, and the total broadside of her seven ironclads was a mere 1,776 pounds. They were opposed by no less than twelve Italian armored ships, the largest of which, the *Affondatore*, *Re d'Italia*, and *Re de Portogallo*, could let loose a broadside of 6,373 pounds between them without the assistance of their equally well-armed consorts. As one historian summed it up: "On paper these three ships [alone] ought to have blown the Austrian ironclads out of the sea."[1]

The situation was even more daunting in practice for, taking into account Italy's other nine ironclads, their ratio of superiority increased to 208 rifled guns against the Austrian's 74 and a total weight broadside of 20,392 pounds in reply to the enemy's puny 1,776 pounds. When the two fleets met in battle, the result was surely a foregone conclusion. As the Prussian army had routed the Austrians at Sadowa less than three weeks earlier so it seemed inevitable that the Italians must utterly destroy them at sea.

The Austrians, however, had one advantage. Their commander in chief, Konteradmiral (Rear Admiral) Wilhelm von Tegethoff, was a fighter in the grand tradition. He had already seen plenty of combat experience in a period when most naval officers had never heard a gun fired in anger. He had served in the blockading force off Venice during the 1848 revolution, fought in several battles in the Black Sea during the Crimean War, and had latterly commanded the steam frigate *Schwarzenberg* in a sharp action with the Danish fleet off Heligoland in the Schleswig-Holstein affair of 1864 as an erstwhile ally of Prussia. Now, at the age of thirty-nine, he was Austria's only hope against the overwhelming power of the Italian fleet.

When war broke out Tegethoff concentrated his seven ironclads at Pola and sent a terse signal to the Navy Office in Vienna demanding every available ship in the navy, no matter how old or how obsolete, to be sent to join him. "Give me every ship you have," he answered his superiors when they demurred. "You may depend on my finding some good use for them."[2] Events were to prove the justification of his boast.

In the end he succeeded in assembling a motley assortment of twenty-seven ships ranging from an old three-decker, some obsolete wooden frigates, and a group of ancient gunboats, to the modern but only partially armed *Ferdinand Max*, which, it will be recalled, was powered by one of Whitehead's 800-horsepower steam engines. As an aid to identification—Tegethoff's battle experience warned him that distinguishing friend from foe at sea was no easy task—he ordered all the Austrian ships to be painted black. "When we get into the fight," he told his captains, "you must ram away at anything you see painted grey."[3]

Ramming! That was the tactic on which Tegethoff intended to rely in the face of the overwhelming odds ranged against him. His puny smooth-bore guns stood no chance against the Italian armor and the sheer weight of the enemy's broadside threatened to annihilate his fleet if the battle stabilized into a toe-to-toe slugging match at close range. Ramming was a relatively untried and untested maneuver but there was no alternative in the life and death struggle that lay ahead. It was a matter of guts versus guns, and Tegethoff placed his reliance on Admiral Farragut's favourite maxim: "Give me iron in the men and I shall not much mind the iron in the ships."[4]

The Austrians were also fortunate in another respect. The Italian commander, Admiral Count Persano, was as irresolute as Tegethoff was determined, and his moral weakness was compounded by his incompetence. He showed a marked preference for remaining in harbor and often seemed more adroit with the pen, writing a series of plaintive excuses to the Italian government, than in taking his fleet to sea. It was only when faced with the threat of dismissal that he agreed to sail against the enemy and even then he balked at a direct attack on Venice, proposing instead to land troops on the island of Lissa off the Dalmatian coast while the fleet gave gun support to the assault. He fondly believed that his object could be achieved by a swift hit-and-run raid from which he could escape to the safety of his harbor at Ancona before the Austrian fleet discovered and engaged him.

Persano, however, counted without an opponent of Tegethoff's caliber. As soon as the Austrian commander learned of the attack on Lissa, he hurried his motley fleet to sea, and although the Italian admiral received an intelligence report that the enemy was sailing against him, Persano demonstrated his usual irresolution and remained in the vicinity of the island throughout the night with the intention of landing the waiting troops at dawn the following morning, 20 July. Suddenly, at 6.40 A.M., a startled look-out in the Italian fleet sighted the first of the Austrian ships approaching and Persano found himself caught on the wrong foot.

Tegethoff's fleet was drawn up in three "V"-shaped lines, one behind the other, and spearheaded by his flagship the *Ferdinand Max* with the armed liner *Stadion* scouting a short way ahead of the van. Persano, on receiving the sighting report, exhibited his characteristic aptitude for panic. The landings, which were in fact already taking place, were called off and the Italian fleet were hurriedly formed, first, into line abreast, and then, three divisions in line ahead with the ironclad ram *Affondatore* posted out on the starboard beam of the second division.

There was an early morning mist over the sea which at one time reduced visibility to a few hundred yards, but between nine and ten it lifted and both fleets could see each other—the Austrians driving firmly ahead SSE in a workmanlike wedge formation with their heaviest ships in the van while the Italians snaked untidily to starboard as course was changed to NNE in a vain counter to the enemy thrust.

At this precise moment, when action was imminent, Persano chose to create his own private confusion by transferring his flag from the *Re d'Italia* to the *Affondatore*, which was still detached from the main fleet and steaming on the *disengaged* side of the Italian line. He may have had solid tactical reasons for his choice of flagships, but inevitably it led to subsequent charges of "leading from behind" and similar well-loaded criticisms. The ill-timed transfer also threw the Italian line into confusion at a critical moment in the coming battle for the *Re d'Italia* had to slow down while the admiral's barge was lowered away, and as result, the First Division under Vacca moved some distance ahead of the two trailing divisions. To add to the confusion Persano did not see fit to inform the rest of the fleet that he was shifting his flag, with the result that when action was joined, all eyes remained fixed on the signal yards of the *Re d'Italia* for the admiral's commands.

Tegethoff saw the sudden widening of the gap between the Italian First and Second Divisions and made his decision. At 10:35 A.M. the executive signal streamed from the Austrian flagship's halyards:

"Panzerschiffe den Feind anrennen und zum Sinken bringen" (Ironclads will ram and sink the enemy).[5]

The Italian fleet was now passing directly across the bows of the oncoming Austrian formation—crossing the "T" of their enemy in the approved textbook maneuver. By all the rules it should have given them yet one more advantage in a battle that was already well weighted in their favour. But Tegethoff was unperturbed and the Austrian van division drove forward at full speed. Persano was still on his way to the *Affondatore* when Vacca, commanding the Italian First Division, opened fire on the advancing enemy and his tenuous control of the battle was lost in the first minutes.

Tegethoff, intent on ramming, held his fire and the Italian shells wreaked heavy damage and casualties on the Austrian ships as the range closed. The 3,065-ton *Drache* on the flagship's starboard beam took enormous punishment. Her captain, von Moll, had his head blown off and one of his lieutenants, Weiprecht, rushed to the bloodstained bridge to assume command. The mainmast went down and then a direct hit put the 500-horsepower engines temporarily out of service. Somehow the *Drache* remained in formation and, with the other ironclads of the Austrian First Division, smashed through the gap separating Vacca's squadron from the rest of the Italian fleet in a movement reminiscent of Nelson's tactics at Trafalgar.

The smoke from the blazing guns created a thick fog over the surface of the sea through which could be heard the rumbling roar of broadsides and the heavy thud of shells striking home. Tegethoff suddenly found himself on the disengaged side of the Italian line and, without hesitation, ordered his ships to reverse course and plunge back into the smoke again. This time they met the enemy at close quarters. The *Hapsburg*, *Salamander*, and *Kaiser Max* on the port wing of the formation engaged Vacca's ships while the *Don Juan*, *Drache*, and *Prinz Eugen* fell upon the Italian Second Division led by Persano's recently abandoned flagship the *Re d'Italia*. The admiral himself was by now busy dashing up and down the line in the *Affondatore* addressing urgent signals to all and sundry—none of which were even observed let alone obeyed.

The old wooden ships forming the center wedge of the Austrian formation were also now in the thick of the battle, having been engaged by the Italian Third Division, which was bringing up the rear of the line. Faced by modern ironclads firing explosive shells they stood no chance. Yet, battered and blasted, Kommodore von Petz somehow managed to hold them together. His flagship, the *Kaiser*, an ancient three-decker, stood out high and massive in the smoke, and Persano, espying what he thought was an easy target, ordered the *Affondatore* to ram. Despite the fact that she had been designed primarily as an armored ram, the Italian ship was an unwieldy beast to handle and it took her captain a full ten minutes to bring her round on to the desired course, by which time von Petz had neatly eluded his attacker by wheeling sharply like a toreador avoiding the charge of a wounded bull.

Tegethoff, however, had better luck. He rammed first the ex-flagship *Re d'Italia*, and then the *Palestro*. Both ships succeeded in swinging away as the Austrian ironclad closed and Tegethoff only managed a glancing blow at each ship. But, even so, he caused considerable damage. The *Palestro* was dismasted and the *Re d'Italia* circled out of control with her steering gear disabled. Climbing halfway up the mizzen rigging of the *Ferdinand Max*, Kapitän von Sterneck, her commanding officer, peered out over the smoke and shouted down to his admiral on the bridge that the Italian flagship was "not under full control." Tegethoff took command. The men battened down below decks tending Whitehead's engines were ordered to raise full power from the boilers. The engines responded magnificently and the *Ferdinand Max* seemed to leap forward as the

The Austrian ironclad *Ferdinand Max*, for which Whitehead designed the engines.

The Italian *Re d'Italia* sinking after being rammed by the *Ferdinand Max* during the battle of Lissa on 20 July 1866.

steam valves opened. There was a horrendous crash as her bows sank deep into the side of the *Re d'Italia* and the murderous ram pierced the vitals of its enemy like a dagger thrust into the heart. Torn metal screamed under the hammer blow, great beams of oak split and splintered with the impact, and the shrieking cries of the Italian sailors crushed in the collision mingled into a frightful symphony of death.

Whitehead's engines never faltered and full power was maintained as the Italian ironclad heeled over under the force of the ram. Then Tegethoff ordered the engines to be reversed and the victorious *Ferdinand Max* slid smoothly astern as the shattered *Re d'Italia* sank beneath her bows.

The utter demoralization of the Italians was quickly apparent. As the Austrians lowered a boat to pick up survivors of the *Re d'Italia* struggling in the water the ironclad *Ancona* seized its opportunity to try and ram the *Ferdinand Max*. Once again Whitehead's engines behaved impeccably as von Sterneck swung the helm and shouted for full speed ahead. The Italian missed by inches and, as she swept past, she fired a broadside into the Austrian flagship at point-blank range. Her crew, however, had overlooked one important point. Although their guns were loaded with powder bags they had, in their excited anxiety, forgotten to add the shot!

The battle was now nearly over. The two fleets gradually drew apart—Tegethoff quickly reforming his scattered ships into three divisions so that they lay between the enemy and the island of Lissa, while Persano brought his command back into its original line-ahead formation. But the Italian admiral made no effort to resume action with the weaker fleet and, after a few hours, his demoralized ships returned to harbor.

It was a tremendous victory for the Austrians. Three Italian ironclads had gone to the bottom and three more were so severely damaged they were out of service for several months. Persano was disgraced. Tried by court-martial he was deprived of his rank and dismissed from the navy.

Tegethoff, by contrast, received a hero's welcome. The emperor promoted him to Vizeadmiral and showered him with honors and decorations while his royal brother, the Archduke Maximilian, a former commander in chief of the Austrian Navy and by that time the ill-fated ruler of Mexico, rewarded the victorious admiral with the

Grand Cross of the Guadalupe Order and told him: "Your name is added to the list of naval heroes of all time."[6]

Yet despite the personal glory of the moment Tegethoff did not forget the man whose engines had contributed so greatly to the Austrian victory. A few days after the battle he sent a telegram to Robert Whitehead at Fiume: "Thanks to your first-class engines I was able to win the Battle of Lissa. Tegethoff."[7]

The newspapers soon got hold of the story and, suddenly, Whitehead found himself a public figure. And recognition of his engineering skill did not end there, for some weeks later, he was personally thanked by the Emperor Francis Josef and given an enamel and diamond ring to commemorate the occasion.[8] It was something of an anticlimax that Austria, having won such an overwhelming victory at sea, should lose the war itself. But her armies could not withstand the efficient onslaught of her main enemy, Prussia, and after a seven-week struggle she was forced to admit defeat. The Battle of Lissa came as a valediction to the bravery of her arms, for the formal peace negotiations were opened on 22 July 1866, only two days after Persano and the Italian navy had been so soundly beaten.

Having obtained all he needed Bismarck could afford to be magnanimous and the Treaty of Prague, signed on 23 August, was lenient in the extreme. Austria withdrew from the German confederation, thus acknowledging Prussia's leadership, and renounced her claim to the duchies of Schleswig and Holstein. She yielded up some minor territory to Prussia but, despite defeating the Italians on land at Custozza and on the sea at Lissa, had to cede the disputed region of Venetia to Prussia's beaten ally. No reparations were claimed, for drained dry by the war, the Austrian Treasury was empty, and Francis Josef and his government were left alone to pick up the pieces.

The Battle of Lissa, the first to be fought by ironclad fleets, attracted considerable attention among naval experts and it was generally held that the ram was now the supreme instrument of destruction. Admiral Touchard summed up the consensus of informed opinion by stating publicly: "The ram is now the principal weapon in naval combats—the *ultima ratio* of maritime war."[9] It was not, however, to remain *ultima* for long. Whitehead's long hours of work inside the locked hut at Stabilmento Tecnico Fiumano had not been wasted. The torpedo, the answer to the ram and the true *ultima ratio* of maritime war, was now almost ready.

The precise plans of this original prototype have never been revealed. The torpedo itself was lost at sea during tests in 1866 and Whitehead chose not to publish its design details for reasons best known to himself. When Lieutenant Sleeman wrote to the inventor in 1879 asking "for a more complete description and a drawing of the first fish torpedo" for use in his book on torpedo warfare the author noted rather acidly: "[Mr Whitehead] has not seen fit to comply with the request."[10] Neither were the designs registered at the Patent Office in Vienna for, as a result of his bitter experience in Milan, Whitehead had no faith in the protection afforded by patents and he refused to disclose details of the weapon to anyone who was not prepared to pay for them.

It is possible, however, to deduce the form and mechanical workings of the original torpedo from the details published of the early model tested by the Austrian Navy in December 1866. It was, indeed, a far cry from the surface *Küstenbrander* visualized by de Luppis, but although lacking many important refinements of the later models, it bore a strong family resemblance to the modern weapon.

From the tip of its sharp-pointed nose to the end of its tail it measured 11 feet 7 inches and its cylindrical body had a maximum diameter of 14 inches. It was built "in the shape of a dolphin" and fitted with a pair of vertical fins that ran the full length of its sleek body.[11] The purpose of the fins was to prevent the torpedo from rolling or spinning on its axis while running. The sharp, almost needle-pointed, nose contained a pistol impact detonator actuated by a firing pin of simple design. On hitting the target the pin thrust back to detonate an 18-pound charge of dynamite which was packed into the nose section. Some authorities maintain that the charge was made of guncotton, but it seems probable that, at this stage and working independently of the naval arsenals, Whitehead was more likely to have utilized a purely civilian form of explosive which he could obtain without undue difficulty.

The main body of the torpedo was made from wrought-iron boiler plates and weighed approximately 300 pounds. Immediately behind the dynamite-filled warhead was the air chamber holding the compressed air, which provided the motive power for the engine. The air chamber was, in itself, a brilliant piece of engineering, for although constructed only from boiler plate, it was capable of containing a pressure of 370 pounds per square inch—a capacity which American

The Devil's Device—one of the earliest known pictures of the Whitehead torpedo.

engineers were unable to emulate when they tried to copy the design four years later. At the after end of the chamber was an ingenious valve arrangement which regulated the air flow so that it was released at an even and constant pressure to feed the engine in the next compartment.

Whitehead's superb mechanical skill was also demonstrated in the engine itself. No power unit suitable for use in the restricted confines of a torpedo existed in the 1860s and the inventor had to get down to the drawing board and design a new engine from scratch. Steam with its attendant boilers was out of the question and clockwork was discarded as it lacked the required durability. In the end Whitehead evolved an unusual air engine capable of operating under water completely independently of the atmosphere. Unfortunately none of the original drawings have survived but it was described in a contemporary paper as consisting of "a cylinder placed eccentrically within another and in contact with its inner surface actuated and made to revolve round the axis of the outer one by compressed air admitted through a specially contrived valve opening in the circumference of the latter. A sliding plate next to the valve moved in and out at each revolution, always remaining in contact with the inner cylinder, and compelling the air to act always on one side and in the same direction. The propeller was on the central shaft of the outer cylinder to which the inner one was keyed eccentrically."[12] Thus the sliding vane between the two eccentric cylinders divided the volume into two parts and the pressure of the compressed air caused a directional rotation of the outer cylinder which was coupled to the propeller.[13] Although a pure pneumatic motor with no form of combustion involved, Whitehead's remarkable conception contained the germ of the idea on which the modern Wankel rotary engine works and his power unit, built for a specific purpose and subject to a host of physical restrictions, provides a good index to his genius.

A simple hydrostatic valve acting directly on the elevator controls was intended to hold the torpedo at a predetermined depth under the water while trim tabs on a primitive rudder gave a measure of azimuth control—both ideas foreshadowing, in many ways, the elevators and ailerons of the flying machine. The torpedo was fitted with a single, twin-bladed propeller running at 100 revolutions per minute, the blades themselves being protected by a circular iron guard. The rudder was fitted behind the propeller—a significant detail in view of later developments. All controls were preset by trial and error and the completed weapon had a range of about 200 yards at 6 knots, which would be extended a further 50 percent by a reduction in running speed.

It was, however, by no means perfect in either function or performance, and Sleeman noted that "in one important particular it continually failed and that was in the regularity with which it kept its proper depth in water. At times it would run skimming along the surface whilst at others it dived down to the depths and explored the bottom." With Whitehead's mania for perfection there can be little doubt that he was not, at that point in time, satisfied with his creation. He had solved the propulsion problem with his novel air engine and had more or less overcome de Luppis's reliance on tiller lines for directional control. Even more important, he had gone far beyond the Austrian's original conception by producing an *underwater* weapon with all the advantages that followed. *But,* and it was a big *but,* until he could devise some means of maintaining a regular and predictable running depth all these advantages were worthless.

Had it not been for the unexpected fame that followed in the wake of Tegethoff's telegram it is probable Whitehead would have continued to perfect his machine before offering it for sale. But the sudden publicity and important contacts that flowed from the success of his engines in the *Ferdinand Max* made it imperative to strike while the iron was hot. Robert had been in business long enough to realize that sheer skill was not enough if one lacked access to the right ears, and even though his torpedo was not yet completely satisfactory, he snatched the opportunity to ensure that news of his weapon reached the most influential people.

One such person was Fregattenkapitän Heinrich von Littrow. He visited Whitehead at Fiume soon after Lissa and was sufficiently impressed to bring the invention to the notice of Archduke Leopold, who at that time was engineer-general of the Austrian Navy. Quickly realizing the potential of such a revolutionary underwater weapon the archduke wasted no time, and in December 1866, Whitehead was invited to submit his torpedo for official trials.

The trials proved impressive although the erratic depth keeping of the weapon made it apparent that the torpedo was not, as yet, in a sufficiently advanced stage of development to merit its acquisition by the Imperial Navy. The Austrian government admitted that the device had considerable possibilities but it was abundantly clear from the demonstration that a great deal more work was required before it could be accepted by the navy.

Despite the relative failure of Whitehead's revolutionary new weapon and the associated problem of maintaining depth, details of these first Austrian trials were passed to the British ambassador in Vienna by a gentleman identified only as Mr. C. T. Hill. "The Machine is self-propelled with necessary force, and has speed under the water's surface, at some 6 feet depth, less or more, so as to be perfectly invisible to the Enemy. . . ." Hill reported to the ambassador, "I am able to learn that the Experiment, so far as it concerns Speed, Depth of Water, and Direction, was most satisfactory. I am not able to give . . . any particulars of the Form, Force, Speed, etc of the Torpedo, for Mr Whitehead. the able Mecanick [sic], keeps all to himself, it being his head work and personal labour; the public were kept off the Works at some distance."[14] This latter observation, plus the poor standard of English employed in the report, suggest that Hill was merely a patriotic bystander rather than an official representative of the British government.

Hill also appeared to have contacts close to Whitehead for he informed the ambassador: "I hear also that the parties interested are most sanguine of complete success and intend making an exorbitant demand on the Imperial Royal Government (of Austria-Hungary) for possession of the Secret; the amount however I fear is too high (£300,000) for the Imperial Government to meet, and so the parties will have to look elsewhere for a purchaser."[15]

Hill's mention of "the Secret" in December 1866 is strange. The key to the torpedo's ultimate success, the pendulum depth-keeping system or balance chamber, which was described officially and in documents as *The Secret*, was not devised by Whitehead until after the trials of October 1868—nearly two years *after* the report was made. The price, similarly, was more appropriate to the 1868 trials for there had been no question of the Austrian government buying the rights to the torpedo in the aftermath of either the December 1866 trials or those of 1867. The question of outright purchase, or a nonexclusive licence, only arose *after* the successful 1868 trials, by which time Whitehead had evolved the balance chamber or "Secret."

It seems possible—although this can only be conjectural—that Hill submitted another report following the October 1868 trials and that this has been inadvertantly included in the December 1866 report—or that the papers held by the Public Records Office are an amalgam of more than one report. This would explain both the £300,000 price for an exclusive contract *and* the reference to *The Secret* in a document that purports to have been written in 1866.

The ambassador passed this interesting item of intelligence back to the Foreign Office in London and it was forwarded, in turn, to the Admiralty on 11 January 1867. But their lordships were seemingly unimpressed. They had heard of similar inventions before and none had lived up to the claims made of them. No doubt they would hear of many more in the future. The report was therefore pigeon-holed in the best of Whitehall traditions and was not dusted down and considered again until the receipt of Vice-Admiral Lord Paget's reports in August and September 1868, by which time Britain had lost the initiative and the Fiume torpedo was creating a considerable stir in naval circles around the world.

Whitehead was neither surprised nor disappointed by the verdict of the Austrian Navy. He himself knew that the torpedo was unsatisfactory until some method of controlling its depth keeping could be devised and he returned to Fiume to continue his development work. Small detailed improvements were made and, day after day, the torpedo was taken out into the Adriatic for tests. Yet no matter how much he struggled with the problem the secret of maintaining a constant depth continued to elude him. Even so, a further series of tests was carried out by the Austrian Navy the following year and it was obvious that the admirals were more than usually interested in the new weapon. But, as always, the erratic depth-keeping behavior of the machine tempered their enthusiasm with reservations and Whitehead returned wearily to Fiume once again to wrestle with the problem.

Despite the setbacks with the torpedo Whitehead's personal career, however, continued to flourish. At the Paris Exhibition of 1867 he exhibited a fine working model of the steam engine that had powered the *Ferdinand Max* and was rewarded with a prominent place amongst the prizewinners.[16] Once again his name featured in the newspapers and, on 26 May of that year, he and other prizewinners were received by the Emperor Francis Josef at his Vienna palace.[17] This was his second meeting with the Austrian monarch, the first being shortly after the Battle of Lissa, and this royal acknowledgment of his growing reputation as one of the country's leading marine engineers extended the horizons of his social circle still further.

Another event that was to widen these horizons even more occurred when his daughter, Alice, fell in love with a handsome young officer of the Austrian Navy, Count Georg Hoyos.[18] The story of their first meeting has all the romanticism one would expect from this colorful period of central European history and has, indeed, a certain fairy-tale quality that will be seen again in the subsequent story of Whitehead's family.

One afternoon a young naval officer was leading a column of sailors down the road from Fiume to Abbazia. As befitted his rank the Kapitänleutnant was riding a spirited charger, and as the column passed the main gates of the Stabilmento Tecnico Fiumano factory, the horse suddenly reared and tried to throw its rider. During the ensuing tumult Whitehead's daughter, Alice, then only sixteen years old, rushed to the window of the *Casa Rossa* to investigate the commotion outside. Just as she appeared in the window the officer brought his steed under control and, glancing upwards, he saw the lovely young English girl framed in the sunlight. Bowing gravely from the saddle, he raised his cap in salute, and then rode on down the dusty road followed by his column of marching sailors.

That evening Kapitänleutnant Georg Hoyos asked his mother if she knew who the girl in the window was. Mama, it seemed, knew *everyone* in Fiume. It must have been the daughter of the English manager at the engineering works, she told her son. A very pretty girl, the countess admitted, but how *can* she live in such a dirty smelly place as the factory. Georg listened quietly as his mother chattered on. Then he dropped his bombshell. "Well, Mama, I don't care *who* she is or where she lives. She is going to be my wife."

The count proved as good as his word. A few days later, aided by an introduction from a naval friend, he visited the works, met the manager, and chanced to make the acquaintance of the girl he had seen in the window. From then on Georg was a frequent visitor both to the Whitehead's home and also to the factory, for not only had his good looks won Alice's heart, he had also made a considerable impression on Robert as well.

The two men had much in common for Hoyos, like Whitehead, was a keen inventor and competent mechanic. He had already designed and patented a pneumatic life-saving apparatus which, as with Robert's torpedo, worked on compressed air, and Alice frequently found herself languishing alone in the drawing room while Georg and her father spent hours discussing drawings and comparing calculations. But, in addition to his engineering interests, the count was also a man of action. He had served on board the *Drache* at the Battle of Lissa and seen her captain, von Moll, killed on the bridge almost at his feet. And his intimate knowledge and experience of naval matters was to prove of great value to Whitehead in the exciting years to come.

Robert was delighted with his prospective son-in-law and there was further happiness in the family circle when, on 12 May 1867, his wife presented him with a third son, who was christened Robert Boville a few weeks later.

1867 passed into 1868 but still the depth-keeping problem of the torpedo refused to yield a solution and Robert labored for long hours into the night as he struggled to find an answer. It was a problem that no one had ever faced before, for like all major inventors, Whitehead was now striking out into the unknown. No similar weapon existed and there was nowhere he could seek advice or assistance. And yet until the difficulty was overcome there was little hope of anybody taking up the invention despite its unique design and unquestioned potential.

But Whitehead, having slaved over his torpedo for more than four years and watched it grow from a primitive surface version of the spar torpedo into a sleek underwater weapon with its own self-contained power unit and directional control, was growing despondent over his continual failure to solve this final problem. By the early spring he was certain that the solution was as unattainable as the proverbial crock of gold at the end of the rainbow and seriously began to consider dropping further development so that he could concentrate all his energies on marine engines again.

Two events took place during the spring, however, which provided him with the incentive to continue. Firstly, on 4 May 1868, the emperor awarded him the Order of Francis Joseph, which carried with it the style of baron, in recognition of his services to Austrian engineering and in honor of his success at the Paris Exhibition the previous year.[19] And, secondly, the Austrian Navy began pressing for yet another series of trials of the torpedo.

Thwarted in his efforts to perfect the weapon itself Whitehead turned his attention to the methods necessary to launch the torpedo and, in a short space of time, produced a discharge tube that enabled the device to be fired underwater. It was both ingenious and simple. The tube consisted of an openended cylinder slightly larger in diameter than the torpedo itself. A watertight door was fixed at each end so that by closing the further door, water could be kept out of the tube while the torpedo was loaded into the breech end. Once inside the tube the breech door was closed and locked while the opposite door was opened to admit water into the tube. The torpedo was fired by compressed air and a guiding bar ran out to hold the weapon on a straight course as it was ejected from the tube. Finally a sluice valve enabled the tube to be emptied of water again ready for reloading after the outer door had been closed.

The submerged torpedo tube was, in itself, a remarkable piece of original engineering thought, and its creation marked Whitehead down as a man who had sufficient vision to see well beyond the weapon itself. It also had certain practical advantages. Placed well below the waterline it had an inherent measure of protection against enemy shellfire and the dangers of accidental explosion following a direct hit in battle. And, situated below the surface, the moment of firing was effectively masked from the target ship thus making the task of avoiding action that much more difficult. Its only real disadvantage was its lack of pivotal movement, for by its very nature, the submerged tube was normally fixed in one position with the result that the entire ship had to be maneuvered into a precise firing position, whereas with a gun, it was only necessary to hold the ship's course and traverse the weapon about its axis.

The Austrian trials, initially arranged for May, were a full-scale affair to be held on Whitehead's home ground of Fiume. A gunboat, the *Genese*, was made available and Robert fitted one of the new discharge tubes into its bows. The outer end of the tube was closed by a conical door which was opened and shut by means of a strap hinge and a lanyard. An internal watertight door was worked up and down through an arrangement of gears, and at the inner end of the tube, a third watertight door acted as the breech. Ejection was by means of compressed air and a small withdrawal pin on the side of the torpedo started the weapon's own engine at the moment of firing—a sophisticated touch that reflected Whitehead's determination that every action should be self-contained or automatic.[20]

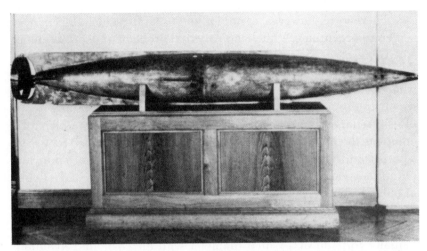

A very early Whitehead torpedo (ca. 1868–70). (Photograph courtesy of Count Hoyos.)

The trials of the Royal Laboratory torpedo at Woolwich Arsenal in May 1872, attended by the first lord, Mr. Goschen. (Courtesy of the Radio Times Hulton Picture Library.)

There were, however, certain inherent faults, which, by chance, served to accentuate Whitehead's eternal problem of depth keeping. The *Genese* was too small for her purpose and he was forced to fit the seaward end of the torpedo tube only 3 feet beneath the surface whereas the weapon itself was designed to run at a depth of 12 feet. It was therefore necessary for the torpedo to pick up a running depth after discharge and this, of course, was quite outside its ability. To complete the trials an old yacht, the *Fantasie*, was provided for use as a target and was given special protection in the form of spunyard netting suspended from booms along the beam. The nets had a depth of 6 feet below the surface and the total target length was 200 feet.[21]

For various reasons the trials were delayed until October and Whitehead produced two different models for demonstration—the "small" torpedo of 14-inch diameter with an 18-pound dynamite warhead and the "normal" 16-inch pattern carrying an explosive charge of 67 pounds of guncotton. Whitehead had also made some significant improvements in his invention since the last tests, the most important of which concerned the air chamber. This was now constructed from a solid piece of iron which increased the air pressure from 700 pounds to 1,200 pounds and boosted the speed to 11 knots over short distances.[22]

Whitehead's high hopes were, however, doomed to disappointment, for although the range was set at only 700 yards and both ships were anchored, only eight of the first fifty-four shots struck the *Fantasie*'s nets and the "small" torpedo showed a marked predilection for diving straight to the bottom. About 50 percent of the runs, twenty-four to be precise, held a sufficiently straight course to either hit the target or pass beneath it, but this was not good enough for Austria's stringent requirements.[23] It all seemed hopeless and Whitehead asked for a three-week adjournment of the experiments "to carry out further adjustments"—although what adjustments he had in mind is a matter for conjecture and it seems clear that he was merely playing for time hoping for some miracle.

But the miracle happened!

According to Princess Flugger's account Whitehead had a sudden flash of inspiration while he lay in bed. Meeting her at a ball sometime later he told her that "one night he had dreamed how the problem was to be solved. Quickly he jumped out of bed and put everything down on paper before the night was over."[24] Whitehead's great-grandson, Count Balthazar Hoyos, also told the author a similar story, although in his version, it was Robert's wife, Frances, who made him get up and write it down because the inventor was so restless he was keeping her awake.

Whichever account is correct there seems little doubt that the crucial answer to the depth-keeping problem came to him in a flash of inspiration as he lay awake in bed. But although it came seemingly by chance it was, in reality, a revelation born from sound engineering knowledge and many years of hard work and experience. In all probability the answer had gestated in his subconscious while he struggled to find the solution, and while he was relaxing and trying to sleep, the final pieces of the jigsaw clicked together in his mind.

Whitehead immediately dubbed his new depth-keeping device *The Secret* and it remained known as such for many years. It became the main bargaining counter in his various contracts with foreign navies and for more than a decade only a handful of sworn torpedo specialists were admitted to its mysteries. As with many of his other inventions and devices *The Secret* was not patented for a number of years, for Whitehead was afraid that unscrupulous pirates from foreign governments would steal the patent drawings and produce their own imitations. Events were to prove his fears justified for although there were no patents to steal there were still plenty of pirates around. And they proved to be not averse to stealing the entire torpedo when the time was ripe.

The Secret was as simple as its title was dramatic and it remained unchanged in its basic form until the end of the Second World War—in itself a remarkable tribute to Whitehead's genius. The "balance chamber," as it came to be called in later years, was situated in a compartment behind the warhead although this arrangement was changed in 1875 to the more familiar layout of the balance chamber behind the air chamber and in front of the engine, which is still with us today. It consisted of a movable disc fitted in the shell of the chamber and made watertight by a rubber joint. This hydrostatic disc, or valve, worked against a spiral spring and was either "in" or "out" according to the pressure of the water surrounding the weapon.

The pressure of water increases with depth and, with the aid of such a valve, it was a relatively simple matter to preset the disc for a certain depth of water so that it sought its equilibrium by operating a series of connected levers that raised or lowered elevator flaps on the rudders causing the torpedo to rise or dive until the point of equilibrium (i.e., the correct preset depth) was obtained.[25]

A pendulum device incorporated into the mechanism compensated for any inclination or tilt of the torpedo and the movement of the pendulum weight acted as a further correction to the horizontal rudders and assisted the action of the hydrostatic valve by acting as a "damper." By utilizing the pendulum principle the depth error of the torpedo was reduced in one dramatic swoop to plus or minus six inches.

When the tests were resumed Austrian enthusiasm knew no bounds, and it was only the parlous state of the empire's treasury, bled dry by the Seven Weeks War, that prevented the government from buying the exclusive rights to the torpedo from Whitehead. The committee appointed by the Austrian Navy reported that:

(a) The exploding power of 40 pounds of gun-cotton was quite sufficient to sink any ship.

(b) The certainty of hitting was as great as could be expected from such a weapon.

(c) The firing apparatus never failed.

Only their last finding contained any criticism when they noted: "The velocity is indeed not great enough to catch a fast-going ship in chase; but it is quite sufficient for the defence of harbour entrances and for attack on ships at anchor; and as ramming is now the principle mode of attack in naval battles, and they therefore become nothing short of a *mélée*, torpedoes can even then be employed with great advantage."[26]

It was obvious that the officers of the committee, still influenced by the Battle of Lissa, failed to realize that Whitehead's torpedo had not only made ramming an almost impossible tactic but that, over the years, it would also gradually widen the fighting range of battles as each side strove to keep out of torpedo range of the other.

But whether their tactical foresight was faulty or not the Austrians realized that the torpedo was an essential weapon in the armory of a modern navy and by the end of the year their government had signed a nonexclusive contract with Robert Whitehead for a supply of the new weapons which gave him unfettered freedom to sell his product to any other nation prepared to pay the asking price.

There seemed to be an element of sour grapes in Sleeman's final comment on the Austrian contract occasioned, no doubt, by the Royal Navy's initial reluctance to acquire the torpedo: "Looked at in the light of the present day [1880], it seems a most extraordinary piece of good fortune for Mr Whitehead to secure the adoption of his invention by the Austrian government in its then most imperfect and crude condition."[27]

CHAPTER 5

A Barbarous Method of Warfare

H aving secured his first contract—Vice-Admiral Lord Clarence Paget, the Royal Navy's C-in-C (Commander-in-Chief) Mediterranean, put the price paid by the Austrian government at no less than £20,000—Whitehead began casting a wide net for further potential customers.[1] "Employing no agents, giving and taking no commissions, but dealing direct with (all) Governments," Whitehead handled all matters himself and wrote personal letters to the leading European governments, the United States, and various other foreign nations, in a quest for new orders.[2]

Unfortunately, despite the new and revolutionary nature of the weapon that Whitehead had produced, his description of it as a "torpedo" was neither new nor revolutionary, for in the mid-nineteenth century, "torpedo" was the generic term used to cover *all* forms of underwater weapons and explosives. And as not a single government responded to Whitehead's letters, it is apparent that no one troubled to look at the details of his invention.[3] All, it seems, assumed that the Fiume "fish" torpedo was no different from what

Admiral Fisher's oft-repeated
claims that he was responsible for
the Royal Navy's acquisition of
the Whitehead torpedo have
proved to be totally unfounded.

had gone before. And the asking price of £20,000 made it utterly
ridiculous.

The torpedo's name was derived from the cramp or torpedo fish,
which stuns its intended victim with an electric shock. ''Torpedoes
deliver their opium at a distance and stupifie beyond themselves.'' So
said Sir Thomas Browne over four hundred years ago, and it remains
an apt description of the torpedo's function even today. Although the
American inventor David Bushnell first applied the term to underwater weapons in 1775, similar devices had enjoyed a long history: as
far back as 1585 the Italian engineer Frederico Gianibelli had produced an infernal machine that was used to blow up a barrier which
the duke of Parma had erected across the river Scheldt. The vessels
that Gianibelli built were constructed of wood, filled with gunpowder
and other combustibles, and roofed with 6-foot thick tombstones. On
top of these was placed a pyramid of marble slabs filled with cannon-
balls, shots, and pieces of iron—an early example of an antipersonnel
device—and when the flotilla was ready, the boats were launched

This picture, found in the archives of the Royal Naval Armaments Depot Museum, is thought to be the first photograph of Robert Whitehead. The much-battered weapon, however, bears no similarity to the 1868 model and lacks both fins and propeller guard. Might this be the lost 1866 prototype?

downstream to drift with the current towards Parma's barrier.[4]

Whether intentionally or by chance, Gianibelli's invention directed the force of the explosion horizontally. The ensuing blast killed eight hundred unfortunate Spanish soldiers and blew a 200-foot hole in the barricade. But, successful though it was, this particular infernal machine was certainly neither a torpedo nor even a drifting mine, and although the Italian is frequently hailed as the inventor of the explosive sea mine by over-enthusiastic historians their claims are misplaced. Gianibelli's device was a surface, or at best an "awash," weapon and as such was more in the nature of an explosive boat—an idea that had originated with the ancient Greeks and Romans, whose fire ships were the probable inspiration for *Der Küstenbrander*.

Credit for the concept of the spar torpedo rests with the Dutchman Cornelius van Drebbel, who is, perhaps, more famous for producing the world's first authenticated submarine, which he demonstrated on the river Thames in 1620 in front of King James 1 and thousands of excited Londoners. Modern historians are now doubtful about both the validity of van Drebbel's claims for his submarine and the veracity of contemporary chronicles. The vessel was, they allege, no more than a semi-submersible, which ran awash and was carried downstream from Whitehall to Greenwich by the current rather than by the exertions of the four rowers inside. Bearing in mind that the "submarine" was little more than an upturned boat constructed of wood, covered by greased leather, and propelled by two pairs of oars, the experts are probably right.[5]

Nevertheless, as he was the first man to devise and produce an *underwater* explosive device, van Drebbel, despite his somewhat dubious reputation, cannot be dismissed out of hand. Born at Alkmaar in the Low Countries in 1572, he trained initially as an artisan and, after learning the art of glass making, moved into engraving, and then to alchemy.[6] He arrived in England somewhere around 1603 and so impressed King James I with his *perpetuum mobile* that he was appointed as tutor to the sovereign's eldest son, Prince Henry. On the latter's premature death he returned to the king's service. Work on his famous submarine apparently began in 1618 although some unkind critics—and van Drebbel did not appear to be the most popular of men—claimed that he had merely copied a diving bell which his fellow countrymen in Alkmaar had built and patented some years earlier. It was also whispered that he had pirated ideas from the plans for a submarine drawn up by the mathematician John Napier.

From the standpoint of torpedo history the most interesting feature of van Drebbel's submarine was its weapon system, for the Dutchman had the wit to realize that an underwater vessel would only rise above the status of an eccentric toy if it had the ability to sink enemy ships. A contemporary account by the inventor's friend Constantyn Huygens, which was written three years before van Drebbel's death in 1633, described the boat in detail and continued: "From all this it is not hard to imagine what would be the usefulness of this bold invention in time of war, if in this manner (a thing which I have repeatedly heard Drebbel assert) enemy ships lying safely at anchor could be secretly attacked and sunk unexpectedly by means of a battering-ram—an instrument of which hideous use is made nowadays in the capturing of gates and bridges of towns."[7]

The phrase *battering ram*, however, is misleading. Huygens was referring to an explosive battering ram or petard, and it is clear that

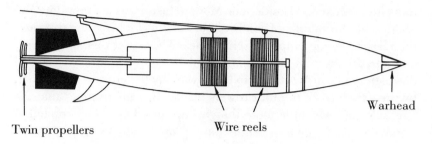

Warhead

Twin propellers

Wire reels

1885 BRENNAN WIRE-GUIDED TORPEDO

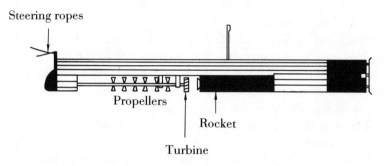

Steering ropes

Propellers

Rocket

Turbine

1885 BERDAN TORPEDO

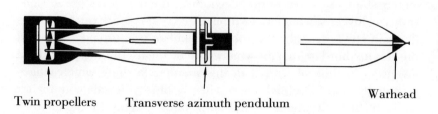

Twin propellers   Transverse azimuth pendulum   Warhead

1892 Model HOWELL TORPEDO

Diagrams of various torpedoes. (Diagrams by Dominic Thomas.)

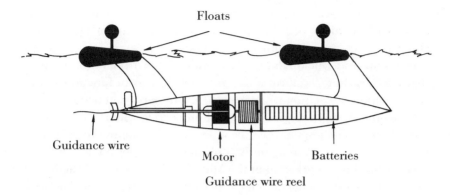

Floats

Guidance wire

Motor

Batteries

Guidance wire reel

1888 NORDENFELT 29-inch ELECTRIC TORPEDO

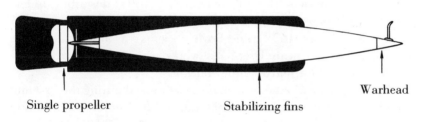

Warhead

Single propeller   Stabilizing fins

1868 WHITEHEAD 16-inch TORPEDO

what van Drebbel had in mind was a *water* petard—an early example
of the spar torpedo. Huygens indicates the intention of an underwater
operation by his phrase "secretly attacked and sunk unexpectedly"
and this is supported by contemporary documentation. In January
1626, for example, the master of ordnance received a Royal Warrant
"for making divers water mines, water petards, and boates to goe
underwater"[8] And on 29 June of the same year the duke of
Buckingham, preparing for his expedition against La Rochelle, submitted an order for "360 forged iron cases with fireworks, 50 water
mines, 290 water petards, and two boats to conduct them underwater
. . . to go with the fleet."[9]

Contemporary engravings of the water petard reveal it to be no more than a canister of explosives mounted on the end of a long pole. Other pictures show it being detonated against the underside of the target ship and Buckingham's reference to "two boats to conduct them underwater" confirm it to have been similar in function to the spar weapon subsequently pioneered by Robert Fulton during the Napoleonic Wars and which was still in service when Whitehead's torpedo made its appearance. Neither were they mere paper inventions as were so many imaginative products of this period, for Drebbel was installed in a workshop at the Minories, a district near the Royal Mint in London, under the auspices of the Admiralty and was paid the then princely sum of £100 for each "water engine" produced. It is just possible that van Drebbel's "water engines" and "water petards" were successfully exploded during trials (which would explain the government's willingness to provide him with premises and a salary). The physicist Robert Boyle (1627–1691) describes underwater explosions in his *New Experiments Physico-Mechanicall* (1660) and *Tracts* (1672), and Boyle it seems was also familiar with several aspects of van Drebbel's work, especially the inventor's "quintessence" for rejuvenating stale air.

It is not clear whether any petards were used during the first and second expeditions to La Rochelle but the inventor was enlisted to take a personal part in the third at a salary of £150 per month. His presence, however, did nothing to help his cause for the water engines failed and, not surprisingly, van Drebbel was blamed. All payments to him were halted, and abandoning his experiments in disgrace, he spent the last years of his life as an innkeeper and brewer—this latter occupation being, by coincidence, also that of Robert Whitehead's father some two hundred years later.

It is difficult at this distance in time to evaluate van Drebbel's contribution to the history of the torpedo. It is, indeed, probable that many of his claims, such as, for example, his chemical liquid for revitalizing stale air, were fraudulent. And he certainly enjoyed no great reputation with his comtemporaries, being variously described as "an alchemist and charlatan" and a "jackass, braggart, and windmaker" on different occasions.[10] But it seems clear that he was the first person to devise a spar torpedo—although, perhaps, it did not work—and certainly among the first to visualize underwater attacks by submarines even though, like his water petards, these failed to live up to his extravagant claims.

A hundred years or so were to pass before the appearance of the next definitive character in the torpedo story—this time an American, David Bushnell, who was born in Westbrook, Connecticut, in 1740, and educated at Yale. He is often described as the first man to demonstrate that gunpowder could be detonated beneath the surface of the sea, but this may not be wholly correct—although his was certainly the first authenticated experiment.

Like van Drebbel, David Bushnell also built a submarine, the *Turtle*—undoubtedly the world's first practical underwater vessel. Egg shaped and foot propelled it was designed to sail submerged beneath an enemy ship so that the operator could fasten a 150-pound explosive charge, actuated by a clockwork fuse, to the keel with the aid of a large wooden auger. Bushnell's device was more correctly an antecedant of the modern limpet mine, but as it happened, he called his weapon a "torpedo"—and the name stuck.

The *Turtle* itself made history on the night of 6 September 1776 when it set off from the Whitehall Stairs near the Battery on Manhattan Island to attack the British frigate *Eagle*, which was lying at anchor offshore. Contemporary accounts claimed that the pedal-powered submersible, piloted by Ezra Lee, reached the *Eagle* but that the gallant sergeant was unable to pierce the frigate's copper-sheathed bottom with his wood screw. The *Eagle*, however, was not coppersheathed until 1782 and surviving evidence suggests that, in truth, Lee failed to reach his target. Indeed, physically weakened and mentally befuddled by carbon dioxide poisoning, he was more than a mite lucky to have propelled his tiny one-man craft back to the safety of Manhattan.[11]

Bushnell's interest in underwater warfare did not end with the *Turtle*, and after two further failures with the submarine, he turned his attention to the design of mines—which he still misleadingly called "torpedoes." These crude weapons were little more than wooden kegs filled with gunpowder, which, having been floated downstream with the current like Gianibelli's infernal machines of 1585, were detonated by a spring-loaded flintlock mechanism, which triggered the explosive charge on contact with the target. Although unmoored and drifting, these devices were more correctly primitive ancestors of the modern contact-detonated sea mine than Robert Whitehead's automobile torpedo.

Next on the scene was the redoubtable Robert Fulton, another American pioneer in the science of underwater warfare, who not only

built a thoroughly seaworthy submarine but who also made considerable progress in the development of sea mines—both static and
towed. Earlier biographers claimed that Fulton and his friend Joel
Barlow built a self-propelled torpedo somewhere around 1797 and
that they were both nearly killed when it exploded during experiments
on the Seine.[12] But modern researchers have dismissed the story and
in his 1981 biography of Fulton, Wallace Hutcheon states: "There is
no solid primary evidence to support an allegation made by some that
Fulton and Barlow had conducted experiments on some crude type of
propelled torpedo on the Seine River."[13] Robert Whitehead's place in
history as the sole inventor of the automobile torpedo thus remains
secure and unchallenged.

Fulton was born at a farm in Little Britain, Pennsylvania, on 14
November 1765 and showed an early inclination for inventions while
still at school, although on moving to Philadelphia in 1782, he
emerged as a talented miniature portrait painter. Bad health led him
to England in 1787, where he met two major British inventors and
engineers, the earl of Stanhope and the duke of Bridgewater—the
latter inspiring Fulton to enter the field of canal development where
he produced a number of useful and technically valuable inventions.

During the middle of 1797 Fulton traveled to France to obtain
patents for some of his canal projects and on 12 December of that
year wrote to the French government offering to build and operate a
submarine for use against the British navy. Fulton's conditions regarding the ownership of prizes and legal safeguards for his crew
against charges of piracy led to a breakdown of negotiations and on 5
February 1798 his proposals were formally rejected. Fulton,
however, remained in France and continued to work on his submarine, the *Nautilus*, which was finally completed in 1800. Unlike
van Drebbel's vessel and Bushnell's *Turtle*, Fulton's submarine
proved to be a reliable and practical design within the constraints
imposed by contemporary technology.

In the context of torpedo history the most interesting aspect of the
Nautilus was its weapon, which, according to a detailed sketch made
by Fulton in 1798, consisted of a single towed torpedo—the first such
device to be built and a direct ancestor of the infamous Harvey
torpedo, which will be described later. The *Nautilus* itself was made
from copper and was first tested in the waters of the Seine in Paris on
13 June 1800—a date that suggests Fulton was not a superstitious

man. The American also had sufficient confidence in his boat to be on board the first time it submerged and, with his two companions, remained beneath the surface for forty-five minutes without ill effect. It was also tested on the surface, where it proceeded under sail—a somewhat anachronistic system of propulsion for a submarine! For progress beneath the surface it relied on a hand-cranked screw similar to that employed by the notoriously dangerous *Hunley* submarine—a terrifying contraption that sank on six separate occasions bringing death to a total of forty-two brave crewmen.

Following further tests at Rouen in July, during which the submarine successfully achieved depths of down to 25 feet, Fulton moved on to Le Havre, where the boat remained under water for over an hour. Various explosive devices were also tried out, and on 27 August, Fulton "tested a contact mine containing roughly 30-pounds of powder which he used to blow up a barrel serving as a target."[14] Although no further details of this device can be traced it seems safe to assume that Fulton was testing the business end of the towed torpedo that had appeared in the original sketch of the *Nautilus*.

The inventor had meanwhile developed "submarine bombs" made from copper, which contained from 10 to 200 pounds of gunpowder. These weapons were fitted with a gunlock to ignite the charge on contact and were apparently part of the towed torpedo envisaged in the *Nautilus* design, although, in the event, the trials were conducted not by the submarine but by a surface vessel. In fact, Fulton is on record as having "quit the experiments on the boat [*Nautilus*] to try those of the Bomb Submarine [sic]" because of the difficulties which he was encountering with his underwater vessel.[15]

During trials on 3 July 1801 he successfully sank a 40-foot sloop with a 20-pound bomb—the first occasion on which a ship had been sunk in European waters by means of a submerged weapon. The world's first recorded maritime casualty to result from an underwater explosion seems to have occurred in August 1777, when one of Bushnell's drifting mines, having missed its intended target—a British naval vessel off New London, Connecticut—struck and sank a small boat killing three enemy sailors. Five months later Bushnell's explosive kegs claimed more victims when two boys accidentally exploded a device on the banks of the Delaware River with fatal results.

Fulton, meanwhile, was concentrating on mines—which he called "torpedoes," "submarine bombs," or "carcasses" as the mood took him—and his interest in the submarine gradually waned although he was to design several more before his death. By 1801 he had already envisaged the use of floating and anchored mines with detonation either by contact or with a timing device. But by now the French were tiring of the American and his inventions—it seems that, rather shortsightedly, they were more interested in the submarine than in underwater weapons—and soon after the trials in September 1801 Fulton changed sides and offered his services to the British. There were the usual bureaucratic delays, which were compounded by a damning report from a commission of experts which unanimously wrote-off his submarine, but finally on 20 July 1804 Fulton was given a contract to develop and produce "submarine bombs," for which he was to be paid a salary of £200 per month with an appropriation of up to £7,000 in payment for the devices when completed.

As a result of this contract Fulton produced twenty mines of three different sizes which were ultimately used in an attack on the French fleet at Boulogne—an operation that began during the late evening of 2 October 1804. These weapons, however, were only a little more advanced than Bushnell's floating kegs and, like the latter devices, relied for motive power on the drift of the tide although Fulton devised a new attack technique in which the mines were released in pairs with one tied to each end of a line. They were triggered by a clockwork timing mechanism rather than by contact, and the linking line was intended to snag the target's anchor cable in similar fashion to the South American bolas entangling the limbs of animals. The raid, however, was not a great success and the French only admitted the loss of one vessel.

A second attack on 1 October 1805 was similarly unsuccessful, and to restore confidence in both his weapons and his reputation Fulton organized a demonstration of his "torpedoes" in Walmer Roads near Dover on 15 October, during which the old Danish brig *Dorothea* was blown up by a pair of linked mines, which were towed to the target by pulling boats or galleys. The clockwork timing device, which detonated the explosive, was set for eighteen minutes—a delay that would have probably rendered the device impractical in combat conditions, for the crew of the target ship would have had ample time to cut the line free from the cable, leaving the charge to drift harmlessly away with the tide before the fuse ignited. But both Fulton and the observers were exultant with the success—it was, after all, the first time a large ship had been destroyed by an underwater explosion—and the inventor was rewarded with a handsome Admiralty contract to produce bigger and better torpedoes together with an advance on account of £2,500. But only a week later Nelson's overwhelming victory at Trafalgar meant that the Royal Navy no longer had need of a weapon which, as the Earl St. Vincent had told Fulton, "They who commanded the sea did not want, and which, if successful, would deprive them of it."[16] Many historians have ascribed St. Vincent's strictures to the submarine, but in the context of Fulton's note, he was undoubtedly referring to the mine or towed torpedo as no submarine was involved in the demonstration.

Fulton returned to his native America, disillusioned, perhaps, by his failures, but £15,640 the richer and still full of enthusiasm for underwater warfare although he was by now deeply involved in the development of the steamboat, which seemed to offer better prospects of commercial success if only because it was not tied, like the torpedo, to the vagaries of politics.

He was soon back in business, and on 20 July 1807 he demonstrated his "torpedo" off Governor's Island in New York Harbor, where, at the third attempt, it sank a 200-ton brig. As in the Dover demonstration the torpedoes, each containing 170 pounds of gunpowder, were towed in pairs linked by a 100-foot-long chain and a 15-minute delay was incorporated into the clockwork firing mechanism. Fulton was now also using floats to keep the chain some eight to ten feet from the surface—a system similar to that employed sixty years later by the Harvey brothers, who used an otter-board to keep the explosive cannister under the surface during an attack run.

Fulton's towed torpedoes were, of course, suitable only for use against vessels at anchor. But his ever inventive mind soon overcame this inherent disadvantage, and he devised a flintlock harpoon gun for attacks on moving ships. Mounted on a swivel and fired from a small boat it could hurl "a single bolt of iron two feet long with an eye and a barbed point" into the wooden hull of the target.[17] A line reeved to the eye of the harpoon was linked to a time-fused explosive device, which, having been pulled out of the attacking boat, would be drawn against its victim by the "action of the [target ship] through the water." The cost, according the the inventor, was $150 for the torpedo and $30 for the gun—an attractive price for a weapon with such a potential for destruction.[18]

The inventor recognized, however, that the threat of his harpoon torpedo could be neutralized by skillful ship handling. An experienced captain would be able to keep the device away from the ship's side by intelligent use of the helm and also hold the ship off at a safe distance until the timing mechanism detonated the charge. But thanks to the low cost of the weapon, Fulton suggested that this tactical defect could be overcome by launching mass attacks with at least twenty small boats, each armed with a harpoon, which would overwhelm the target by sheer weight of numbers—a tactic subsequently adopted by torpedo aircraft in the Second World War that swamped the gunnery defenses of the target ship by coordinated attacks from a variety of different bearings.

In a dissertation on the morality of torpedo warfare at the end of his monograph Fulton admits that "it is barbarous to blow up a ship with all her crew" but then proceeds to the premise that "all wars are barbarous" and lists various examples of such barbarity ranging from the sinking of a merchant vessel by gunfire to the bombardment of Copenhagen. He concludes somewhat piously: "If Torpedoes should prevent such acts of violence, the invention must be humane."[19]—a view shared by Robert Whitehead, who sincerely believed that the torpedo was a deterrent to war.[20]

The nearest Robert Fulton came to producing a true self-propelled torpedo was his "submarine gun," or "Columbiad," of 1813. "Instead of placing the cannon in a vessel as usual above the surface of the water," he wrote, "I arrange my cannon so low that they will be below the surface. The bullets [sic] will pass through the water instead of through air, and through the side of the enemy's vessel below the surface, which letting in water will sink the vessel."[21] It is not clear, however, whether Fulton actually built such a weapon although it was intended to be part of the armament of the submersible *Mute*, which was still on the drawing board when he died. By September 1813 he had already moved on to diagrams of a spar torpedo similar in design to the weapon developed around the middle of the nineteenth century. Although a number of Fulton's torpedoes were used against the British by the United States Navy in 1813, no successes have been recorded and the premature death of the inventor in 1815 sadly ended any further torpedo developments.

Shortly before he stopped experimenting he wrote: "The question naturally occurs whether there be within the genius and inventive faculties of man, the means of placing a torpedo under a ship, in defiance of her resistance. He who says they are not, and that consequently torpedoes can never be made useful believes he had penetrated to the limits of man's inventive powers and that he had contemplated all the combination which ingenuity can devise to place a torpedo under a ship."

Fulton's optimism and faith in man's genius was not misplaced, and it fell to Robert Whitehead to push "to the limits of man's inventive powers" by creating his self-propelled "fish" torpedo some fifty years later. Before Whitehead produced his version of the torpedo weapon, however, many other inventors, often brilliant in their own fields of engineering achievement, had tried and failed. One such was Colonel Samuel Colt, creator of the world-famous revolver, who demonstrated a static torpedo mine in New York Harbor in 1829. His interesting device was a pioneer version of the modern observation mine—a static cannister of explosive, which, lying submerged, can be detonated as a ship passes over it by means of an electrical firing circuit operated from the shore.

He first exploded the mine successfully in New York Harbor in June 1842 and a month later, to the accompaniment of considerable publicity, sank a small boat below Castle Garden. He also publicly exhibited the mine on the Anacostia River on 13 April 1844, when he blew up a 500-ton vessel which was being towed at 5 knots. Colt's experiments were partially financed by the Navy Department but he seriously exceeded the appropriation and, following a long wrangle with Congress over funding, further development foundered through lack of finance. But aside from the question of money Colt's observation mine was not the answer. For although ingenious in concept the target had to steer towards the explosive device rather than the preferable alternative of having the explosive device move towards the target as Fulton had envisaged.

For the next twenty or so years there was an epidemic of torpedo devices all of which, according to their inventors, were the ultimate weapons of maritime warfare. Although all were known as torpedoes they fell into two distinct categories: stationary devices, which might, on occasion, be given an impetus of movement by drifting with the tide or current; and moving devices, which depended on the close proximity of a control vessel. The former were later classified as "mines" and can, accordingly, be omitted from this brief survey of torpedo development as they were neither guided nor self-propelled although, admittedly, they operated mainly below the surface of the water and thus had the true torpedo's advantage of invisibility.

As for the second category of torpedo development—devices that moved towards their victims rather than moored or free-floating mines—there were two major inventions in use by the world's navies before the advent of Robert Whitehead's famous "fish" torpedo.

The first of these was the spar torpedo—a development of van Drebbel's water petard—so called because the explosive charge was carried on the end of a long spar fixed to the bows of a small launch similar in form to the jousting lance of a medieval knight. The concept was taken up by Robert Fulton but the spar, or outrigger, torpedo did not have its first taste of combat until the American Civil War, when it was used by both belligerents. The spars were usually pivoted and "could be raised up or lowered until the charge was 19 feet under the water," the charge itself consisting of a copper case filled with between 50 and 150 pounds of gunpowder.[22] Detonation was by contact either by means of a percussion cap or by breaking a special glass horn filled with acid.

Following the inevitable pattern of naval development the spar torpedoes quickly resulted in the production of special vessels designed to carry them—a sequence of events that was to follow hard on the heels of Whitehead's own torpedo. Little more than launches in size and powered by small steam engines, they were often given rudimentary protection by the addition of iron plates, while in some advanced designs, the entire boat was built from boiler plate and shaped like a cigar so that it could run awash. It was a fearsome combination. "Its suddenness and an undefined fear of its annihilating effects when the attack is delivered," one American naval officer observed, "creates a moral impression on the assailed, which adds to its effectiveness and diminishes the chance of successful resistance."[23]

But despite the spar torpedo's many disadvantages—its visibility during attack and the vulnerability of the control vessel, which

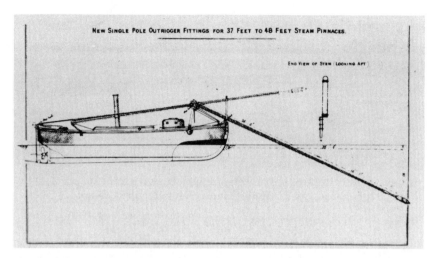

A contemporary diagram (ca. 1870) of the spar torpedo.

needed to approach within thirty feet of its victim—it remained in service for many years even after Whitehead's "fish" torpedo had exposed its inadequacies. Experiment and development admittedly produced a more sophisticated weapon, electrical firing circuits, for example, replacing the primitive percussion detonator, but nothing could overcome the inherent disadvantage of bringing the torpedo boat to point-blank range in order to make physical contact with the spar and, gradually, the weapon fell into disuse. Its last recorded use in combat was on 23 August 1884, when three French launches sank the Chinese ships *Yango* and *Fosing* at Foochow during the struggle for control of Indo-China.

The other form of nonstatic torpedo in service when Whitehead's invention made its first appearance was a towed explosive charge developed by Captain John Harvey, RN, and his brother Commander Frederick Harvey, RN. This particular weapon had sprung from the fertile mind of Robert Fulton some fifty or more years earlier and the Harvey brothers had merely updated and refined the concept. Although in many ways as primitive as the spar torpedo the Harvey weapon had one important advantage. The control vessel could stand off and deliver its attack from a range of 150 yards.

Resembling the modern minesweeping paravane in operation, the Harvey torpedo relied on the often observed phenomenon that an

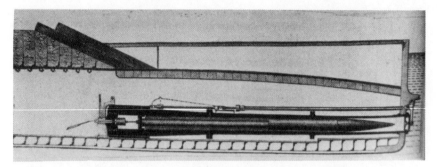

A contemporary drawing (ca. 1880) of John Ericsson's torpedo.
(Photograph courtesy of the Radio Times Hulton Picture Library.)

object towed from the bows of a ship usually diverges from the vessel's
course at an angle of 45 degrees. Thus objects towed on each side of
the bow take up an arrow-shaped formation in which the ship forms
the central shaft with the objects streaming at 45 degrees from either
side of the bow. It was a nasty weapon and detested by nearly all who
had the misfortune to be involved in its use. The attack speed was
found, in practice, to be limited to a maximum of 10 knots and
various chemical fuses were used to detonate the 33-pound gunpowder charge—later increased to 66 pounds of wet guncotton. In its final
and most sophisticated form the Harvey torpedo could be fired electrically by remote control, but as Commander Peter Bethell has observed, this was always assuming that it "had not [already] prematurely exploded, fouled the screw, or parted its tow."[24] But in its
desperate search to obtain a weapon capable of exploding below the
enemy's waterline the Royal Navy closed its eyes to such obvious

The Cunningham rocket torpedo.

imperfections and purchased the design, bringing the Harvey into service in 1870 *after* Whitehead had already demonstrated the overwhelming superiority of the "fish" torpedo.

As noted in the previous chapter the British Admiralty had learned of Whitehead's new weapon within three weeks of the first Austrian trials in December 1866; but, unimpressed, the Director of Naval Ordnance (DNO) Rear-Admiral Astley Cooper Key took no action to investigate Hill's report and the papers were pigeonholed and forgotten. Key's interest in the self-propelled torpedo was reawakened in August 1868, however, when Vice-Admiral Lord Clarence Paget, the C-in-C Mediterranean, wrote to the Admiralty and confirmed that the Austrian government had bought the nonexclusive rights of Whitehead's weapon for £20,000. His letter included a description of both the torpedo and the underwater discharge tube used in the final Austrian trials and he also indicated that he had been in touch with Robert Whitehead.[25] The latter, Paget explained, was anxious to offer *The Secret* to the British government.

The following month Paget and Her Britannic Majesty's ambassador in Vienna, Lord Bloomfield, visited Fiume to inspect the weapon at firsthand and while at the Stabilmento Tecnico Fiumano works they took the opportunity to watch a series of demonstrations that Whitehead had organized for the benefit of other foreign visitors. The admiral noted in his journal: "Another very formidable engine is in process of development which bids fair to surpass even the ram— the torpedo. The importance of the invention may be assumed from the fact that the Austrian Government is said to have awarded £20,000 to Mr Whitehead, the inventor. The French also sent an official to negotiate and I have advised the British Government to do likewise"—this latter being a reference to his August letter to the Admiralty.[26]

Although Key was clearly more impressed by Paget's letter than by Hill's earlier report, he remained skeptical and on 17 September he minuted: "This is not a new idea. I much doubt the possibility of the machine making a straight course for even a cable's length, but it is easily tested and I recommend a trial of it when Mr Whitehead makes his proposition."[27] According to Ruddock Mackay, Key apparently met Whitehead in November 1868.[28] Their discussions led the former to minute: "I consider that if the results are confirmed— and he produces very conclusive evidence regarding them—the invention is one of the *very highest importance* to any Maritime power."[29] But despite this change of heart, and the disquieting interest of France, who was regarded at the time as a potential enemy, some further eight months were to pass before Key, in his capacity as director of naval ordnance, authorized the C-in-C Mediterranean to appoint a committee of gunnery officers to visit Fiume and submit an official report. Indeed it was a matter of sheer good fortune that no other major naval power preempted Britain by signing an exclusive contract with Robert Whitehead in the interim.

In his summary of events leading up to the British Admiralty's acquisition of the Whitehead torpedo Commander Peter Bethell—whose admirable series of articles in *Engineering* constitute probably the best technical history of the weapon so far written—attributed the "singular rapidity" of the Admiralty's decision to buy the nonexclusive rights of the Whitehead torpedo to the fact that Commander John Fisher "was lurking and snorting in the background," and that he "was already a formidable figure [who used] his ruthless fist-shaking methods to overcome [the Admiralty's] inertia and opposition."[30] It is a pity to destroy such colorful illusions, but contemporary evidence exposes the falsity of Fisher's repeated and exaggerated claims that he had been primarily responsible for Britain's acquisition of the Whitehead torpedo. In view of Fisher's later achievements when he dominated all aspects of British naval policy and, in the critical years before 1914, brought the Royal Navy kicking and screaming into the twentieth century, his unfounded yet widely believed assertions require examination in detail.

Fisher's interest in underwater warfare dated back to November 1866, when he was appointed as a member of the instructional staff of the Royal Navy's gunnery school, HMS *Excellent*. It was here that he made his first acquaintance with "torpedoes" and, once bitten by the bug, had thrown himself heart and soul into the subject with typical enthusiasm. The word "torpedo" was, however, misleading for the Royal Navy had none in the modern sense of the word and most of the experimental and instructional work was concerned with sea mines and underwater explosive devices in general—the latter extending to include the spar torpedo.

At the time of the Austrian trials in 1866 defensive mining was the responsibility not of the navy but of the army's Corps of Royal Engineers—an odd arrangement to say the least. In that year, however, Frederick Abel, the chief chemist of the Royal Laboratory at Woolwich, suggested that naval personnel should participate in the instructional courses organized by the Royal Engineers. But the Admiralty, piqued by the tardiness of the replies it received from the War Office, refused to write to the army in support of Abel's eminently sensible suggestion and the initiative came, instead, from the War Office itself, which in February 1867 suggested that the navy should enter some officers in the next class.

Lieutenant Henry Kane was selected for the course beginning in March 1867 and others followed at intervals. Fisher attended the course that began in October—the last time, in fact, that members of the Royal Navy were sent to Woolwich, for Rear-Admiral Key, the DNO, satisfied that he now had sufficient qualified instructors of his own, broke the army's monopolistic grip on torpedo training and, in late 1867, organized the Royal Navy's own torpedo courses at *Excellent* and also at the Devonport gunnery establishment, *Cambridge.*

Fisher came to prominence as a "torpedo" expert with his *Short Treatise on Electricity and the management of Torpedoes*—a work that had been originally started by his predecessor Henry Kane. This slender 128-page volume was privately printed in January 1868 with Admiralty approval and the navy agreed to buy copies for use in the *Excellent* and *Cambridge* plus a further two copies for every ship in commission.[31] It is tempting to speculate just how much of the original text of the *Treatise* was written by Fisher and how much was the work of Henry Kane. For if the book was ready for printing in January 1868 and Fisher only attended the Royal Engineer's instructional course in October 1867, he certainly had little time in which to become either an "expert" in the subject or even to put pen to paper, bearing in mind his demanding range of duties as first lieutenant of the *Excellent.* Kane, on the other hand, had been on the March course and would have thus had some nine months in which to draft the *Treatise,* leaving Fisher with only the task of editing and tidying up. It is not without interest that Admiral Arthur Wilson—another future first sea lord—was under the impression that Kane had been directed to compile the Navy's first torpedo manual and that Ruddock Mackay had been unable to trace supporting evidence of this in the Kilverstone Papers. It is difficult not to wonder whether Fisher, typically, had stolen another man's thunder for his own advantage.

Nevertheless, the word "torpedo" in the title of the *Treatise* is, again, misleading. Most of the book is devoted to the principles and practice of electricity, with a section on the construction, firing, and testing of electrically detonated mines, and a "short account" of experiments with spar or outrigger torpedoes. The appendix, which is undoubtedly Fisher's work, is concerned with the use of electricity to fire a ship's guns—an aspect of gunnery in which Fisher was greatly interested. Many of Fisher's biographers have been misled by his remarks in the preface to the 1868 edition of the *Treatise*, including the late Arthur J. Marder, the respected naval historian and expert on the Royal Navy in the Victorian and Edwardian periods:

> "The first efficient locomotive torpedo—one that could be steered from a ship or from shore—was developed by the Scotsman Robert Whitehead at Fiume in the early 1860s," he wrote in volume one of *Fear God and Dread Nought*. "The early Whitehead torpedoes . . . were primitive weapons which travelled under water at 7 knots for a few hundred yards and carried but 33 to 55 pounds of guncotton. But Fisher had foresight and imagination and could see the terrible possibilities of the weapon even in its early, unpromising, stages. As he wrote in the preface to the first edition of the *Treatise: 'There can be no doubt that the electric torpedo is destined to play a most important part in future wars. . . .'* "[32]

Whitehead, of course, was not a Scotsman and neither was his torpedo developed in the *early* 1860s—he did not meet de Luppis until 1864. It could *not* be steered from either ship or shore. Its course was determined on launching and the weapon had no facility to deviate from its preset straight line of direction. The technical details and performance figures also lack accuracy and appear to be an amalgam of various early patterns. The worst error, however, is the attribution of Fisher's statement in the preface of the 1868 edition to the Whitehead torpedo—a mistake unfortunately perpetuated by Richard Hough in his authorized biography of the admiral.[33]

Fisher was, of course, referring to electrically detonated sea mines—a fact readily apparent from an examination of the contents of the *Treatise*. Indeed he refers to electric torpedoes—a phrase that would immediately exclude the Whitehead. It is also virtually certain, on the basis of his correspondence and other evidence, that he knew nothing of the Fiume weapon when he wrote the Preface at the end of 1867 or in early January 1868. And even when he finally became acquainted with Whitehead's torpedo he showed little enthusiasm for it. As late as August 1869, in his report on the Kiel mining demonstration, he stated quite categorically: "Harvey's divergent torpedo [is], all things considered, apparently far superior" to the Whitehead weapon.[34] Fisher made a brief reference to the Fiume torpedo in the April 1870 preface to his revised *Treatise on Electricity and the Construction and Management of Electrical and Mechanical Torpedoes*, and it was not until the preface to the *Addenda*—dated January 1873 but probably not completed until the end of February 1873—that he gives any details of the Whitehead torpedo and comments favorably upon it.

Somewhat surprisingly the documentary evidence of Fisher's correspondence suggests that he was not personally initiated into the "Secret" of the balance chamber—the torpedo's holy-of-holies—until February 1873. The date can be pinpointed by a letter he wrote to Captain Henry Boys on 18 February 1873: "I think I shall finish the book [the *Addenda to the Treatise*] about Monday or Tuesday at the latest, and then Captain Hood proposes I should go with Singer to be initiated into the Whitehead secret."[35]

So much, then, for Fisher's alleged "foresight and imagination." Perhaps even more revealing, the future first sea lord showed so little appreciation of the Whitehead weapon's potential that from the early part of 1870 until at least June 1872 all of his surplus time and energy was devoted to the development and improvement of the towed torpedo—the device first pioneered by Robert Fulton and already, in the shape of the contemporary Harvey weapon, clearly obsolescent. All this, however, lay for the moment in the future . . .

Fisher's thrusting promotion of his own cleverness and the favorable publicity engendered by the first edition of the *Treatise* served its purpose and in June 1869 he took over charge of all torpedo instruction work at the *Excellent* in succession to Henry Kane, who had been appointed as gunnery officer of the ironclad *Caledonia* with the Mediterranean Fleet.[36] Torpedo in this context, of course, still referred only to sea mines or, at best, the spar weapon. Even Fisher himself seemed confused by the ambiguity of the word in his old age and he embroidered a highly misleading account of his role in the torpedo story in his autobiographical *Records*, published in 1919:

> A First Sea Lord [probably a reference to Admiral Sir Sydney Dacres] told me on one occasion that there were no torpedoes when he came to sea, and he didn't see why the devil there should be any of the beastly things now! This was *a propos* of my attracting the attention of his serene and contented mind to the fact that we hadn't got any torpedoes in the British Navy and that a certain Mr Whitehead (with whom I was acquainted) had devised an automobile torpedo costing only £500 that would make a hole as big as his Lordship's carriage (then standing at the door) in the bottom of the strongest and biggest ship in the world, and she would go to the bottom in about five minutes. Thirty-five years after this last interview, . . . the ironclad *Belleisle* having had several extra bottoms put on her and strengthened in every conceivable manner that science could suggest or money accomplish, was sent to the bottom of Portsmouth harbour by this very Whitehead torpedo in seven minutes. (177)

Taking Fisher's dates as accurate his "acquaintanceship" with Whitehead would have gone back to 1868 and this is not supported by any known evidence, although of course, Fisher may have heard of the Fiume experiments at secondhand and intended the word to have a less personal connotation. But if he did meet Whitehead, and knowing Fisher's inclination for self-advertisement, it is surprising that he made no mention of the Fiume weapon in his official reports or private correspondence before August 1869. His mention of a cost price of £500 also confirms that his memory was playing tricks, for the 1868 torpedo was priced at around £300.

Fisher's first biographer, Admiral Sir Reginald Bacon, made another cardinal error by claiming that, in 1872, Fisher "was sent to Fiume to inspect and purchase a Whitehead torpedo, *the first possessed by our Navy.*"[37] [Author's italics] This, of course, is complete nonsense. Fisher made his first official visit to the Fiume works in November 1876—the Royal Navy acquired its first Whitehead torpedoes in 1870. The dates, alone, are sufficient comment!

Even Fisher's references to the *Belleisle* are misleading for she was not an ironclad but a former armored ram, later reclassified as a coast defense ship. She displaced only 4,870 tons and, completed in 1878, had never been regarded as a seagoing ship or able to stand in the line of battle.[38] Neither was she strengthened in "every conceivable manner that science could suggest or money accomplish,'' for according to Dr. Oscar Parkes she was sunk on 3 September 1903 during tests with an 18-inch torpedo to determine the effectiveness of coal as a protection against an underwater explosion. A cofferdam was built around the vessel—which had already been serving as a target ship for several years—and this was packed with bunkers of coal. The torpedo blew a hole 8 feet by 12 feet in the hull, the coal failed to protect the ship, and the *Belleisle* settled in the water. She was later salvaged and sold.[39]

Fisher, now regarded as the Royal Navy's leading expert on "torpedoes," was promoted to commander on 2 August 1869 at the exceptionally early age of twenty-eight, and nine days later he arrived in Kiel at the invitation of the Prussian Navy to observe mining experiments and demonstrations of underwater explosives after which he proceeded to the Spandau arsenal and the Tegel gunnery establishment near Berlin. Fisher was unimpressed with what he saw and considered that his own work on electrical detonation was of superior merit to the German preference for a chemically induced explosion. While in Berlin, however, he struck up an acquaintance with Captain Louis Hassenpflug, a former member of the Austrian Navy, who had served on the Torpedo Commission that reported on the December 1866 trials at Fiume, and who was now an officer in the Prussian Navy. Fisher quickly became friendly with the Austrian with the result that Hassenpflug not only told him all about the first Austrian trials but also unofficially loaned him his technical papers on Whitehead's torpedoes, which Fisher copied verbatim and enclosed with his 21 August report to the Admiralty about the Kiel mining experiments.[40]

The Committee of Gunnery Officers, which had finally been authorized by Rear-Admiral Key after a delay of many vital months, arrived in Fiume at the beginning of August 1869. The three officers making up the committee—one of whom was Lieutenant Henry Kane—were extremely enthusiastic about the new weapon and on 7 August they submitted a report to this effect to Vice-Admiral Sir Alexander Milne, who had succeeded Paget in command of the Mediterranean Fleet. It is significant that this particular report was completed four days *before* Fisher arrived in Kiel and two weeks before the latter's own report on the mining experiments with which Hassenpflug's papers had been enclosed. Thus Fisher only learned the details of Whitehead's torpedo *after* the committee. Nevertheless his report reached the Admiralty *before* that of the committee because Milne did not forward the Mediterranean Fleet's recommendations to London from Gibraltar until 2 September.

In sharp contrast to the committee's favorable report Fisher's comments were lukewarm and hedged by reservations:

> Although this torpedo has been said to prove effectual as far as 2,000 feet in any required direction, it must be remembered that Mr Whitehead's successful experiments have taken place in:
>
> Smooth water
> Without any tide
> At a fixed object
> From a stationary vessel
>
> and that, once started, his Torpedo is beyond control and will blow up any one it comes across. In addition to this it is extremely delicate to handle and manipulate and requires extreme care to prevent any clogging of the Pneumatic Apparatus. But at the same time it must be conceded that it is a wonderful invention.[41]

Taken together with his assertion that the Harvey towed torpedo was "far superior" to the Fiume weapon—a statement that appears in the selfsame report—it becomes increasingly difficult, despite the final concession that "it is a wonderful invention," to justify Marder's contention that Fisher had been an enthusiastic supporter of the Whitehead torpedo in its early days.

Admiral Dacres, the first sea lord, dutifully impressed by the committee's findings, was favorably disposed to the new weapon and advised the first lord, Childers: "This is a most excellent report on Whitehead's torpedo."[42] But Rear-Admiral Arthur Hood, the new DNO in succession to Astley Cooper Key, appeared to share Fisher's misgivings—possibly because, as the former captain of the *Excellent*, he had been in daily contact with him and regarded him as a man whose opinion was worth listening to. Indeed many of the comments in his Minute of 1 October 1869[43] echo the exact words of Fisher's August report and many of the counter arguments he advances are culled directly from Fisher's own observations.

Unlike Fisher, however, Hood showed a prophetic insight into torpedo warfare and visualized the need for small high-speed ships to fire the weapon in battle, which, he concluded, " would be most formidable in action with ironclads."[44] He also made no disparaging comparisons with the Harvey towed torpedo and concluded, like Key two years earlier, that further experiments were needed to evaluate the Fiume weapon. And he took matters another step forward by suggesting to Dacres that Whitehead should be invited to England to demonstrate his torpedoes.

Both the United States and France were by now showing a growing interest in events at Fiume, and *The Times*, quoting a report from the *Army & Navy Gazette*, stated that the U.S. frigate *Franklin*, flying the flag of Rear Admiral Radford, was lying at Trieste while the admiral himself had gone to Fiume

> to study the effects of [the] torpedoes. These engines, it may be said *en passant*, make a great noise in the maritime world and lately even the Prussians have convinced themselves of the efficacy of this new invention, originated by M. Lupis [sic], a retired captain of the Austrian Navy, and brought to perfection by Mr Whitehead, an English engineer, and proprietor of a machine manufactory at Fiume. The Americans are greatly interested in these torpedoes and entertain a serious idea of making them the base, so to speak, of naval warfare, not only for defence, but for attack. (6 September 1869)

The Americans, however, balked at the asking price of £20,000 and found various reasons for losing interest before finally leaving Fiume without signing a contract. But Whitehead was not unduly worried by this loss of potential business, for both France and Prussia were showing keen interest and he was, of course, aware of the Royal Navy's favorable report. He waited patiently for the unhurried procedures of the Admiralty to run their course and in due time he received the long-anticipated invitation to bring his weapons to England for testing.

This sudden surge of enthusiasm by the Royal Navy boded well for the inventor, who, so it was said, had already sunk £40,000 of his own money into development work on the torpedo. Although this figure is probably a wild exaggeration, Whitehead must have been a relatively wealthy man by 1870 with an income commensurate with his status as an Austrian baron. The £40,000 is, however, more likely the total amount spent on development up to 1875, most of which would have come from the reinvestment of the sums received from the

British, Austrian, and other contracts effected before that date.[45] Nevertheless, once the world's greatest navy had accepted the weapon there was little doubt that every other fleet, large and small, would climb on to the bandwagon and Whitehead would reap the reward of his investment one-hundredfold.

He also now had the advantage of no longer working single-handed. His daughter, Alice, had married Count Georg Hoyos at Fiume on 30 March 1869, and his new son-in-law was on hand to share the burden of the fast-growing business. John Whitehead, by this time almost sixteen years old, was able to make his own contribution when problems arose, although Robert sent him to the Zürich Hochschule for a formal technical education as soon as he was old enough.[46]

The British trials, completed in October 1870, proved more successful than Whitehead's wildest dreams.[47] In April 1871 he signed a contract with the government under which he received £15,000 plus trials' expenses of £2,500 in return for a nonexclusive licence to build the "fish" torpedo in England on a royalty basis and a right to purchase models direct from the Fiume factory. In addition "a select number of officers" were to be trained "in the then jealously guarded secrets" of the weapon—a condition applied so vigorously that the secrets were "not to be revealed even to admirals commanding fleets"[48]—while Whitehead also agreed to keep the Admiralty informed of all improvements and granted them the privilege of "using all such innovations."

The Secret was by no means misnamed for Robert firmly insisted, in modern parlance, on a full security clampdown on its details with the result that the excessive desire for secrecy often degenerated into wild Victorian melodrama. The ritual of initiation into the mysteries of the balance chamber—into which Fisher was admitted in February 1873—were described by Lieutenant G. E. Armstrong in somewhat ironic terms: "The pains taken to preserve this secret were as elaborate as they were futile. The room where the great mystery was unravelled was closed with locked doors, with sentries on guard outside, and every porthole and window carefully screened or closed."[49]

An article by the same officer in the *Cornhill Magazine* was couched in similar vein: "The 'secret' of the balance chamber was kept from the common herd and when at length it was divulged to the budding sub-lieutenant, all the hocus-pocus of closed doors and a signed pledge of secrecy was gone through before this ingenious but simply contrived portion of the apparatus was revealed.''[50]

But although the pendulum mechanism and balance chamber were, in hindsight, simple and straightforward they were, none the less, the unique key to the torpedo's success. And in view of the long years of work which Whitehead had put into his invention, it was hardly surprising that he intended to keep the mechanism a secret for as long as he could.

Fisher was appointed to the *Donegal* on 25 November 1869 and left England for the China Station shortly afterwards, where on his arrival, he was to take up duties as commander of the *Ocean*. He did not return home until the *Ocean* was decommissioned on 22 June 1872 and was thus many thousands of miles away cruising in Far Eastern and Australian waters throughout the critical period of the Medway trials and the subsequent contract negotiations. And, far from showing any interest or even acknowledgment of the Sheerness experiments, Fisher's egotistical letters indicate only his personal preoccupation with various types of towed torpedoes and assorted methods of electrical firing.

In a letter to Captain Henry Boys, commanding officer of the *Excellent,* dated 22 August 1871, he wrote: ''I hope shortly to send home a paper containing the results of numerous experiments I have been making, both from the ship [*Ocean*] herself and from our steam launch, with towing torpedoes of different shapes and sizes— somewhat after the Harvey in principle but differing essentially in shape and size and the mode of firing, which is by electricity.''[51]

As Boys had carried out the final tests on the Harvey torpedo as recently as February 1870, it seems that Fisher had been kept informed of current developments in this particular field of underwater weaponry. Yet his failure to mention the Whitehead weapon in any of his letters suggests that either Boys and his other friends at home remained silent over the Sheerness trials, leaving Fisher in complete ignorance of the Medway trials so that he wasted his time working on an obsolete concept or, equally, that Fisher—already aware of the Fiume weapon following his meeting with Hassenpflug in August 1869—had still failed to grasp its potential superiority.

Public knowledge of the Whitehead torpedo in Britain was virtually nonexistent. Between 1865 and May 1872 *The Times* only mentioned the weapon on two occasions—once in 1869 when it had reported Admiral Radford's visit to Fiume and, again, on 22 May 1872 when a news item was published concerning the tests of the first Whitehead to have been built under licence in the Royal Laboratory at Woolwich Arsenal. Between these dates there was silence although the newspaper continued to print reports of experiments with the Harvey torpedo in some detail. There was also reference to War Office trials at Chatham of a self-propelled weapon designed by a certain George Quick of Southsea that, so it was claimed, could cover 2,000 yards in 30 seconds. This phenomenal 150-mile-per-hour projectile was not reported on subsequently, so it presumably failed to live up to the promise of its inventor's name.[52] There were, however, a number of items on the Whitehead in the specialist and technical press, especially *The Engineer.*

Other countries appeared to be similarly in the dark for it was reported in July 1870 that Russia had just bought no fewer than twenty Harvey torpedoes from Britain. As it is difficult to believe that the Admiralty in St. Petersburg could still be unaware of the Fiume weapon by this date it can only be assumed that the tsar's admirals shared Fisher's lackluster enthusiasm for it. And in fact six full years were to pass before the Russian government belatedly exchanged contracts with the Whitehead Company.

Having obtained the full manufacturing rights from the inventor the British authorities took immediate steps to build their own version of the Fiume "fish" torpedo. A section of the Royal Laboratory at Woolwich Arsenal was set aside for the purpose and work began, without delay, on the first British-built Whitehead—the 16-inch Mark 1* RL. The advantage of fresh minds uncluttered by the weary years of trial and error was soon apparent and Woolwich quickly broke fresh ground. The most important modification was the introduction of twin contrarotating propellers, which gave the weapon greatly increased thrust and pushed the speed up from the 7 knots of Whitehead's original Austrian model to an ambitious 12 knots—and all this despite an increase in total weight from 346 pounds to 530 pounds. It is interesting to note that this particular innovation, which Whitehead himself approved and adopted, sprang from the brain of one of the foreman mechanics employed at the

Royal Laboratory rather than one of the engineer scientists working on the project—but unfortunately his name was not recorded for posterity.

Speed, of course, was also linked with increased air pressure, and the use of improved metals for the air chamber permitted the use of much higher pressures to feed the engine. There were also numerous other alterations to Whitehead designs.[53] Although retaining the Fiume model's sharply pointed nose section, the Royal Laboratory made a significant change to the tail end of the torpedo and the Mark 1* RL featured propellers placed abaft the rudders in contrast to the reversed layout of Whitehead's design. This revised configuration remained the main distinguishing characteristic of the Woolwich and Fiume patterns for more than fifty years.

A letter written by Robert to his brother James which has recently come to light reveals that the inventor's eldest son, John, produced a layout similar to that of the British weapon in 1891: "John has schemed a new kind of tail for the torpedo which is very promising. The rudders are before the propellers and the speed is much increased and the steadiness also. We will probably patent the arrangement in other maritime countries."[54] Exactly how John's design differed from the British pattern is not clear, but although it met with his father's approval, it was not apparently proceeded with. It is interesting to note that informed opinion today regards Robert Whitehead's positioning of the rudders and propellers as the more hydrodynamically efficient layout. It was also at this stage, incidentally, that the Woolwich scientists discarded the circular propeller guard fitted to the early Fiume torpedoes.

The final results were a striking improvement on the Fiume 16-inch weapon, and Whitehead was astute enough to incorporate most of the modifications into his own torpedoes at an early date. The agreement to keep the British advised of all improvements and alterations was proving to be an unforseen reciprocal advantage—to Robert Whitehead.

By this time, too, the original engine with its two eccentric cylinders and single sliding vane had been replaced by a sturdy little Vee-twin air engine of Whitehead's own design, which again improved performance and reliability.[55] But this was soon replaced by the British-designed Brotherhood three-cylinder radial unit which

was destined to remain the standard torpedo engine until the introduction of "heaters" in the early 1900s.[56]

The Royal Laboratory completed its first weapon early in 1872
and in May *The Times* reported:

> The new fish torpedo has been privately tested in the canal at the
> Royal Arsenal, Woolwich, in the presence of a number of officers
> connected with the Royal Laboratory Department and the result is
> understood to have been satisfactory, but nothing is known in refer-
> ence to these experiments as great care was taken to exclude any but
> authorised officials from witnessing them. This torpedo when fully
> rigged with the explosive chamber at its head and the propelling
> screw and steering apparatus at its tail is quite 20 feet long, the iron
> fish-shaped body, which forms the middle portion, being simply the
> vessel which carries the motive power, an atmospheric engine worked
> by compressed air, with a pressure of 1000 lb on the square inch.
> This is the first of these torpedoes made in England but it is under-
> stood that a similar system has been tried in Austria with great suc-
> cess. Certain improvements have, however, been made in the design
> at the Royal Laboratory which it is believed and expected will prove
> highly advantageous. The explosive charge will be 160 lb of gun cot-
> ton fired by percussion on striking a ship . . . but in the experi-
> ments at Woolwich the charge was dispensed with. About thirty tor-
> pedoes of the same description are in the course of manufacture at
> the Royal Laboratory Department, Royal Arsenal, Woolwich, in ad-
> dition to others of different construction. (*The Times*, 22 May 1872)

It was, on the whole, a remarkably uninformative report with no
mention of *The Secret* and a delightful vagueness in its reference to
the middle section as "being *simply* the vessel which carries the
motive power." In many respects, too, it was inaccurate for, so far as
can be ascertained, the Mark 1* RL was only 14 feet 6 inches in
overall length and the warhead contained a charge of certainly not
more than 67 pounds of explosive and probably considerably less.
But perhaps the most significant feature of the report was its total
omission of Robert Whitehead's name as the inventor.

Whitehead's childlike faith in the truth of newspaper reports,
however, remained unshaken by these inaccuracies and he was probably more relieved that no mention had been made of *The Secret* than
he was offended by the failure to mention his name. And, in any case,
by 1872 he had more than enough on his plate than to worry about
news items, accurate or otherwise, in *The Times*. Stabilmento Tecnico Fiumano, his previously secure base, had been forced into bank-

ruptcy by the cutback in naval construction following the financial difficulties of the Austrian government in the wake of the Seven Weeks War of 1866, and having at last produced his revolutionary weapon, Whitehead was faced with the prospect of having nowhere to build it.

Convinced, however, that his new torpedo meant the change in his fortunes for which he had worked night and day since his first arrival in Marseilles over twenty-five years earlier, and aided by his son-in-law, Georg Hoyos, Whitehead bought the factory premises at Fiume from STF and set up in business on his own account under the style of Silurificio Whitehead.[57]

He had finally arrived at the threshold of success. From now on he was too committed to turn back.

The Offer Was of Course Declined

France was almost certainly the first major European nation to show an interest in Whitehead's weapon after the successful Austrian trials. And when Admiral Lord Clarence Paget visited Fiume in September 1868, he noted in his journal apprehensively that "the French [had] also sent an official to negotiate."[1] These original negotiations collapsed, however, presumably due to the £20,000 price-tag that the inventor had placed on his torpedo. But soon afterwards, in August 1870, the French came perilously close to obtaining the secrets for nothing when Whitehead was detained in Paris while on his way to the Royal Navy trials at Sheerness. "It was a near thing whether we were to be first in the field or not," Admiral Edward Bradford observed some years later, "but, thanks to the [British] Ambassador, we were."[2]

Once the French learned that England had bought the manufacturing rights from Whitehead they wasted little time in equalizing the advantage. And although still reeling under the shock of their defeat by the Prussians in the last of Bismarck's wars of German unification two years earlier, they promptly reopened negotiations with the Fiume factory. Within twelve months of the British agreement France, too, had signed contracts with Whitehead for an undisclosed sum under which a licence was granted for the construction of ''fish'' torpedoes at a government establishment in Toulon.

From a financial point of view Whitehead was now getting the best of both worlds. In addition to the lump sums he was receiving for the manufacturing rights he was also being paid royalties *and* supplying ready-made torpedoes from his own factory in Fiume to the British and French navies, plus, of course, the Austro-Hungarian fleet. The catalog price of the Fiume weapon was, at that time, approximately £300 and with production increasing daily a steady and welcome flow of cash began to trickle into the new Silurificio Whitehead. Within a few years the steady trickle was to become an almost embarrassing torrent.

In 1873 both Italy and Germany joined in the queue of anxious customers and, beyond all doubt, the Whitehead torpedo had arrived on the naval scene. There were still, however, many influential people with doubts as to the wisdom of this mad rush to acquire the new weapon. Grand Admiral Alfred von Tirpitz, for example, despite his admission that ''my rise [was] bound up with the development of the torpedo arm,'' was one such critic.

> Stosch [head of the German Navy Department of the War Ministry from 1871 to 1883] had introduced the fish torpedo over-hastily and had bought large numbers of them before they were really serviceable for war. The use of the torpedo still constituted ''a greater danger to the man who launched it than to his enemy.'' People were too optimistic about it and, as is often the case with new weapons, had anticipated the change before the new idea was really practicable.[3]

Others did not, however, share his stringent views. The British admiral Sir W. Tarleton noted in his diary on 3 October 1873: ''In my opinion the torpedo had a great future before it.''[4] And speaking in the House of Commons, Lord Charles Beresford, later to become Fisher's hated rival and enemy, told MPs: ''We may manufacture guns and build very powerful ships, but the nation with the best torpedoes will win the next war. The invention of this terrible engine of destruction has revolutionized naval warfare within the last twelve months.''[5]

Despite the tremendous success of his invention Whitehead still obstinately refused to take out patents to protect his designs and preferred to rely on the security precautions of the various navies which had bought the torpedo to safeguard *The Secret.* This time, however, his lack of patent protection was to boomerang against him. "The fact that Mr Whitehead, having made the construction of his torpedo a secret, instead of the subject of a patent, has been the cause of the many attempts that have been, and are being, made to devise a similar but superior weapon."[6] In many ways, in fact, Whitehead was fortunate that only one firm had sufficient expertise to pirate his design successfully.

Not unexpectedly the facts of the matter were, and still are, obscure. Whitehead by that time had become an important figure in the world of engineering, and the emperor's recognition of his skills had also opened the door to the higher spheres of Austrian society. It had become the practice of the Whitehead-Hoyos families to hold regular dinner parties for influential businessmen and visiting naval purchasing commissions and, on occasion, to invite them as guests for a week or more so that Hoyos and his father-in-law could use the opportunity to obtain further sales. One such guest was a Berlin engineer, Louis Schwartzkopff, the proprietor of a thriving machinery business in the German capital. On the last night of his visit there was a mysterious disturbance in the drawing office—the Whiteheads at that time were still living at the *Casa Rossa* inside the perimeter wall of the torpedo works—and, in the morning, Count Hoyos was horrified to discover that someone had broken into the offices and stolen a complete set of plans. It had not been Schwartzkopff for he was known to have remained in his room all night, and in any case, it would have been quite unthinkable to suspect a respected and important guest of such things. Privately Whitehead and his son-in-law concluded that the burglary was probably the work of a foreign government anxious to obtain the design drawings and details of *The Secret* for its own use. The United States, for one, was suspect, for despite a number of approaches the American navy seemed strangely reluctant to do a deal, and of course, there was always Russia, the proverbial black sheep of European politics.[7]

Precisely who stole the plans was never discovered, but within a year of the burglary, the Berlin engineering firm of L. Schwartzkopff & Company was offering its own "fish" torpedo for sale, which, according to the torpedo expert Captain E. P. Gallwey, was "almost an exact copy of Mr Whitehead's."[8] The pirated version, which the less knowledgeable "experts" were still referring to as the Whitehead-Schwartzkopff torpedo six or seven years later, had, however, one overwhelming advantage over the Fiume weapon. It was constructed entirely from "a special material called phosphor bronze, the composition of which is kept secret"[9] whereas Robert Whitehead's weapon was made from steel.

The superiority of phosphor bronze was enormous, for the alloy was immune to rust—an important characteristic for a metal that was in constant contact with sea water. It was said that the Schwartzkopff torpedo "may be kept in a state of perfect adjustment for many weeks,"[10] whereas the Whitehead needed stripping and cleaning after every immersion in salt water. And in those days tests were frequent, for, without the aid of a gyroscope, every torpedo had its own personal deflection and numerous runs were necessary to arrive at an optimum average—the angle of deflection being a completely individual quotient peculiar to each particular torpedo. In addition, as Commander Murray Sueter pointed out, "these German torpedoes are of the first workmanship and compare favourably with those of other nations."[11]

Schwartzkopffs offered their weapon for sale at £450, somewhat higher than the contemporary Fiume model, which was listed in the Whitehead catalogue at £320, but despite the discrepancy there was no lack of orders. Italy supplemented her supply of Whiteheads with the German-built weapon and China ordered a substantial number for her growing Europeanized navy as did Russia, Japan, and Spain. The special properties of phosphor bronze made the Schwartzkopff design more attractive to the smaller navies and was, in their view, worth the extra cost, for the Whitehead required constant, continual, and delicate maintenance—and time meant money. A further factor in the success of the German torpedo was one of supply and demand. Although production at the Fiume factory was increasing every week, Whitehead and his men had to work flat-out just to keep up with the orders from their original contracts, and there was little spare capacity to build weapons for wider markets at this stage. In fact, there was a worldwide famine in torpedoes which, as will be seen later, reached a dramatic peak in 1885.

Contrary to most accounts the German Navy did not use the Schwartzkopff weapon immediately after it was produced. The Navy

Department in Berlin had negotiated an agreement with Whitehead in 1873, and all their service torpedoes for the next seven years were built in Fiume. According to Grand Admiral von Tirpitz the German Navy did not approach the Berlin company for weapons until after 1879, when plans were already in hand for State Torpedo Workshops.[12]

Espionage, it seems, was rife in the early days of Whitehead's new career as a torpedo maker. But, apart from Schwartzkopff, no one else succeeded in the piracy game. "While it is well known that several drawings, said to be complete and to scale, of the Whitehead have been offered for sale from time to time, and though many attempts have been made to *imitate* this weapon at private yards, yet all have ended in failure."[13] Only one other instance of industrial treason has survived the passage of the years.

The United States had, by 1874, rejected at least three approaches by Silurificio Whitehead to sell their torpedo—mainly because the American navy was tackling the problem along different lines as will be seen in later chapters. But seeing an easy way to fortune a foreman mechanic from Woolwich Arsenal stole a complete set of plans of the British-made Whitehead and offered them to the chief of the bureau of ordnance. "The offer," Lieutenant F. M. Barber, USN, commented piously, "was, of course, declined."[14]

Nevertheless, the competition from Schwartzkopff & Company, plus the rigorous specification demanded by the German Navy—a minimum performance of 16 knots over 550 meters—sent Whitehead back to the drawing-board again, and by 1875, he had produced a completely new model. The distinctive vertical fins were discarded and so, too, was the Vee-twin engine—the latter being replaced by a British-manufactured three-cylinder radial unit by Peter Brotherhood of Peterborough. This miniature engine, weighing only 35 pounds and with a 4-inch bore and 3-inch stroke, was a design masterpiece and it remained basically unmodified for some thirty years. It was still, in 1939, the basis of most torpedo engines, although by then it had obviously grown in both size and complexity.

This original Brotherhood engine produced a healthy 40 indicated horsepower. It drove a single shaft fixed to the after propeller while an intermediate bevel-wheel gearing operated a sleeve in the opposite direction to rotate the forward propeller in a contramotion—

Whitehead having sensibly incorporated the Woolwich twin propeller layout in his new design. In fact it was the adoption of contrarotating propellers that enabled Whitehead to dispense with the fins for there was an almost complete lack of torque in the Royal Laboratory's twin-screw design.

Another important innovation was the servomotor, which, fitted between the balance-chamber mechanism and the rudders, gave the feeble hydrostatic valve and pendulum linkage sufficient power to control the horizontal rudders more efficiently. Some idea of the ratio of translated power can be gauged from the fact that a half ounce pull or push on the slide rod of the servo unit exerted a lift of 180 pounds at the other end! The internal layout was also changed, and for the first time, the balance chamber containing *The Secret* was placed abaft the air chamber which, freed of its central tube containing the rudder control rod, was increased in strength. Compressed air could now be stored to a pressure of 1,000 pounds per square inch with resulting improvements to both the speed and range of the weapon.[15]

The Fiume Mk (Mark) 1, as the new torpedo was designated, was standardized on a 14-inch diameter and proved so successful in operation that the British Admiralty put in an immediate order for 225, and in 1877, switched production at the Royal Laboratory from the original 16-inch weapon to a new 14-inch pattern closely modeled on the Fiume Mk 1. The service classification of the British version was the 14-inch Mk 1* RL.

The Fiume 14-inch Mk 1, once launched, boosted the fortunes of Silurificio Whitehead to such an extent that Whitehead was able to pay off the creditors of the bankrupt Stabilmento Tecnico Fiumano out of his own pocket, even though, as a former employee and manager of the company, he was under no legal liability or moral obligation to do so.[16]

It was during this period, also, that his daughter, Alice Hoyos, began writing the series of letters which have helped to throw so much light on her father's character. His second son, James Beethom, was being groomed for a career in the British diplomatic service and, in preparation for his entry, was sent to St. John's College, Cambridge, for his final studies—the same college at which his uncle, John Whitehead, had died so tragically in 1851. Alice and James shared a very close relationship and were the greatest of friends. And so, when

James left Fiume for England, his sister wrote to him every week to keep him informed of family chitchat. It was a correspondence that continued, on and off, for over thirty years.

> The *one* subject of conversation in Fiume at present is *Papa*. The dear old man [he was, in fact, only 53 years old at the time] has realized his dream at last, and he paid off *all* the shareholders, except S . . . and M . . . Georg [Hoyos] went to town the day before yesterday to a *seduta* which had been called and told them Papa's proposal, upon which they nearly all howled and were really and fairly overpowered—they have all since been out to him, although Papa begged them not to thank him. Was it not generous of him? because he had *no* real or even moral right to do it, *he* lost as well as they did, but it has been a great great pleasure to him. It is so nice to see how modestly and surprisedly he takes all the fuss they make of it. The whole town rings with it, they have all sorts of proposals to do him honour, the least startling of which are a *monument!* and to make him *Ehrenbürger* [honorary citizen] of Fiume! I hope they will only do the latter. Papa would not like the former. I am very proud of our dear old man. Mama also much pleased.[17]

Business, however, made great demands on his time and Frances was not always quite so pleased when important contracts took her husband away from Fiume for long periods. In 1875 Norway, Sweden, and Denmark all agreed to purchase the rights to the "fish" torpedo and Whitehead and his son John visited the respective state capitals in October 1876 to advise the governments on the care and maintenance of their new weapons.

On 5 October Alice reported to James: "A telegram came from Papa this morning; you know that he and Jack were at Copenhagen and Stockholm? Well, they left today for Norway and seem to be trotting about 'pretty considerable.' " She added, with true sisterly concern, "I am very glad of the change for Jack."[18] Later the same month, however, she noted: "Mama is in very low spirits—Papa has written to her so seldom that she feels quite hurt." It was fortunate that Frances knew her husband well enough to appreciate that it was not a case of "out of sight, out of mind." For, once embarked on business and talking about his beloved torpedoes, Whitehead was prone to forget that anything else existed. But, in truth, he never forgot his wife, who had been such a staunch friend and companion throughout their thirty years of married life, and he never failed to return from a business trip without a carriage load of presents.

On Sunday Papa and Jack came home, safe and sound, after a very
pleasant journey. The dear old Father looks ever so jolly. . . . They
brought lots of toys and Papa bought Mama a glorious opal and
diamond ring and a pair of ear-rings the same. . . . He says he will
complete the set in time. I am so glad as Mama has nothing very
pretty in that way. The set, if complete—tiara, necklace, etc.—would
come to 18,000 fl![19]

It was not surprising that *The Times* should refer to his private life
as being "modest and retiring, but genial, unobtrusively benevolent,
[and] full of courtesy and loving kindness."[20] His grandchildren, too,
adored him and he was known to the entire family as *Nono*—the
Italian diminutive for grandfather. Even today many of his great-
grandchildren still refer to him affectionately by his old Italian family
name.[21]

With the torpedo business booming, life in Fiume was good even
though Alice occasionally referred to it as "this heathen place" and
complained regularly about its "raw and foggy" climate. The Whiteheads, by now, had a full complement of indoor servants plus all the
external trimmings of the successful industrialist. And, of course,
there were the continual rounds of dinner parties at which officers
from visiting buying commissions were entertained royally. "The
other night there were 18 at dinner at Mama's, and 8 different nation-
alities. It was a perfect Tower of Babel."[22]

But Whitehead's torpedo was a valuable and much sought-after piece
of property, and not unexpectedly, the peaceful life at Fiume was
frequently disturbed by attempts to steal or borrow the designs, which
Whitehead was still refusing to patent despite the pleadings of his
son-in-law. One such attempt had all the elements of theatrical farce,
the spirit of which was delightfully captured in a series of letters from
Alice to her brother.

The centerpiece of this espionage extravaganza was the new
Fiume Mk 1 torpedo, which, as noted earlier, combined a large number of important improvements. Like all products of Silurificio Whitehead the new weapon was on open sale and there was keen competition to get hold of it by various interested governments—the Royal
Navy taking up an order for 225 immediately.[23] Some, however,
sought to save their national treasuries unnecessary expense by taking an unofficial peek into the internal workings of the new model so

that the modifications could be copied and then fitted, at much reduced cost, into their obsolescent stockpiles.

"It appears the torpedo was found by a peasant floating just near Vemba. He took it to the Arsenal and they, knowing very well whose it was, kept it three weeks before Papa heard of it. . . ." Georg Hoyos was immediately despatched to Pola, the Austrian naval base near Trieste, to discover what was going on. "The only thing we talk about now is the lost Torpedo, or rather, the stolen Torpedo. . . . On Saturday we received a telegram from [Georg] saying he had got to know it had been opened in the Arsenal and *copies taken.*"

So far it seemed to be an almost perfect crime—except for one small oversight: "The reason for the delay was that they had taken it to pieces and . . . simply could not put it together again. [They] knew then, too late, that they had got themselves into the most awkward possible *mess.*" Whitehead and Hoyos wasted no time in publicizing the espionage attempt and promptly placed the matter in the hands of a Trieste lawyer. There was a tremendous row, for Whitehead was a local hero, and Alice noted: "It is curious to see how the *whole country* has taken it up. No one talks of anything else . . . and popular feeling is much against the Government." The affair finally reached the ears of the emperor himself and

> as we expected that *dear* fellow [Francis Josef] took it up *warmly,* would hardly believe it was the case, and got perfectly *furious* while speaking of it. [He] said he admired Papa so much and, in fact, was the *"galant'uomo"* he always is. He instantly gave orders to telegraph Vienna and demanded a *full* report and explanation of the whole affair, and the day after that, in the evening, Szapary was sitting next to the Emperor at dinner, and the first words he said to him were, *"Can* you believe it? I have *still* no answer about that *dirty trick."*[24]

Thanks to the emperor's intervention a full-blown scandal was averted and, in due course, Whitehead received a formal apology and adequate recompense by way of a substantial order from the Austrian Navy for this blatant and bungled attempt to steal his secrets. Indirectly the affair had other results, for some time later, he finally bowed to Hoyos's demands and took out patents on his various inventions—but it had taken him a very long time to get over the bitter memories of his Milan experiences in 1848.[25]

The market, meanwhile, continued to expand at a dazzling rate.

The two great rivals for control of the Balkans, Russia and Turkey, had both acquired rights to the torpedo by the end of 1876—neither country being prepared to allow the other to gain the upper hand in the accumulation of modern weapons. It was an ugly situation, taut with tension, which to Whitehead's dismay erupted violently the following year. Portugal, too, joined the elite ranks of the "Torpedo Powers" in 1877, followed shortly afterwards by Argentina, Belgium. Chile, and Greece, and by the end of that year Silurifico Whitehead was exporting its deadly products to no fewer than fourteen major nations.

Bearing in mind that full-scale production only dated from 1871 and that the torpedo was a weapon as yet untried in the furnace of war, it was a remarkable achievement. And unlike many other large industrial concerns of the late nineteenth century the rapid growth in productive capacity was happily not due to the exploitation of the workers. Robert had learned wisely from his experience at Philip Taylor and a contemporary German reference book noted: "His striving for welfare, his uprightness, and his fatherly care for his workers made him a model factory owner."[26] Few other industrialists of the period could have successfuly claimed similar virtues—and built up a fortune at the same time. It was not all plain sailing, however, for with a tricky machine like the torpedo, accidents were inevitable.

> There was an explosion of the air reservoir on the *Molo* [the torpedo testing pier] yesterday. Fortunately the [British] Commission had that moment gone up to luncheon at Mama's. Had they been there some of them might have been killed. One man got a bad knock on the thigh, fortunately not serious, and another was thrown into the sea by the rush of escaped air. The pieces of the tubes flew from the *Molo* as far as the Cara Bossa! I heard the explosion—it made the house fairly shake, and I fancied it an unusually strong mine. We ought to be very happy that no one was seriously hurt.[27]

In Britain development of the torpedo continued at a fast and furious pace. Within a year of its birth the new 14-inch Mk I* RL model had been superseded by an improved Mark II with slightly more speed and a heavier warhead. And it is an interesting commentary on the Royal Navy's determination to keep ahead of the world to note that, until the introduction of the 18-inch weapon, the Royal Laboratory models always carried a larger charge of explosive than their Fiume cousins.

Technically, too, the Woolwich engineers were fully equal to their Fiume counterparts and often showed the way. One problem they solved was the inability of torpedoes to take their depth again once they had risen to the surface—a difficulty first encountered in the initial Austrian trials some ten years earlier. According to official records, "a device was borrowed from Mr Whitehead and an additional and very delicate piece of mechanism—controlling gear—was added to the depth gear. This device, at first, could not be divulged generally owing to fear of compromising 'The Secret.' "[28] There was considerable controversy about the effectiveness of the Woolwich control gear and Whitehead himself was by no means convinced that the device measured up to the claims made by the Royal Laboratory. He may have been right for although it remained in use for many years it was finally abandoned soon after the 1914–18 war ended.

Jacky Fisher had now returned to the torpedo scene having accepted an appointment to the *Excellent* as commander (for torpedo duties) "although nearly everyone was dead against it." As Professor Marder has pointed out the appointment made him virtually chief of the torpedo department of the Royal Navy, an enviable position to be in with a weapon that promised so much. But Fisher was not completely satisfied and warned that he would resign "if I find that I am not independent" and there can be little doubt that, even at this stage of his career, he lacked any capacity for self-criticism. Despite the fact that the Whitehead weapon had made all other forms of torpedo completely obsolete at a stroke, Fisher still considered that his experiments with towed torpedoes were of the greatest importance, and only a month after his appointment to the *Excellent*, he wrote to his wife saying, "In my heart I think I ought to be promoted for that new torpedo book."[29] Humility and modesty were not counted among Jacky's virtues.

Fisher, however, was, as ever, a whirlwind of energy and he was soon stirring things up in all directions. For now that he was the officer responsible for the navy's torpedoes he knew he would be unable to rest until he had made it the most important and influential weapon in the Royal Navy's armory. One of his first steps was to extricate the torpedo from the stranglehold of the gunnery experts, who heartily disliked the new weapon and nicknamed it "The Devil's Device."[30] Whether Fisher, by analogy, was the Devil was not indicated.

On 20 November 1873, he submitted a scheme of complement to

the Admiralty, which separated the staffs of the *Vernon*, the navy's torpedo school, from the *Excellent*, the gunnery establishment. His proposals were approved in February the following year but his intentions were thwarted, for although their lordships agreed to separate the two complements, they ruled that the entire establishment was to remain as part of the *Execellent*. Undismayed, however, Fisher continued to devote his entire time to torpedoes and his lectures characteristically reflected his own personal philosophy:

> If you are a gunnery man, you must believe and teach that the world must be saved by gunnery and will only be saved by gunnery. If you are a torpedo man, you must lecture and teach the same thing about torpedoes. But be in earnest, terribly in earnest. The man who doubts, or who is half-hearted never does anything for himself or his country. You are missionaries; show the earnestness—if need be, the fanaticism—of missionaries.[31]

He attracted a good deal of unfavorable attention within the navy by inviting politicians and journalists down to the *Vernon* for a display of all the scientific tricks that the school could produce, but unabashed by criticism, he continued with his self-imposed task of making underwater warfare, for the *Vernon* included mines as well as torpedoes, the most important department in the Royal Navy. The Admiralty apparently approved his piratical methods, for on 30 October 1874, he was promoted to post-captain and reappointed to the *Excellent* for torpedo duties in the *Vernon*, and in the following January his scheme for separating the two schools was finally accepted with the *Vernon* becoming an independent command. Fisher was retained to lecture the officers until the changeover was completed and the *Vernon* was ultimately commissioned on 26 April, 1876—her new commanding officer being Captain William Arthur and her commander the up and coming Arthur Knyvet Wilson—an appropriate choice, for both men had served on the original committee that had tested Whitehead's weapon at Sheerness in 1870.

In his farewell message to the torpedo school Fisher reaffirmed his belief in the torpedo as the *ultima ratio* of maritime war. "It is with the deepest regret that I terminate my connection with the torpedo school. I have done my utmost to develop it, from a conviction that the issue of the next naval war will chiefly depend upon the use that is made of the torpedo, not only in ocean war, but for the purposes of blockade."[32]

Fisher spent the autumn and winter serving as a member of the Torpedo Manual Committee at the Admiralty and he visited Fiume in November 1876 to inspect Whitehead's factory at first hand. The British Commission stayed at the Whitehead's home but Alice was not very impressed by him. "No news . . . except the arrival of the English Commission. Captain Singer, whom I think you know, Colonel Fraser . . . Captain Fisher, and Mr Miller. All four old fogies, except the last, who is an old *old* bachelor."[33] Fisher was only thirty-five years old at the time and fancied himself as somewhat of a ladies' man. He would not have felt very flattered.

Whitehead had always considered the torpedo to be a complete underwater weapon, and from the very beginning, his designs were based on the use of submerged torpedo tubes. The Royal Navy, under Fisher's guidance, wanted more scope, however, and experiments began in 1874 by fitting a broadside submerged tube in the *Actaeon*. The trials showed that there were distinct possibilities in this form of discharge even though, when the ship was traveling at 8 knots, the torpedo had a deflection of 30 degrees from its aimed course. Further experiments were carried out with an improved design of tube on the *Glatton* and it soon proved possible to fire torpedoes while the vessel was steaming at 20 knots with a deflection of only 3 degrees.

Having progressed so far the navy became more ambitious, and in March, 1875, the first attempt was made to launch a torpedo from above water. It was a decidedly primitive affair for no suitable torpedo tube was available and the experiment was conducted by placing a 16-inch RL model on top of a messroom table lashed against one of the *Actaeon*'s ports and giving it a hearty push. The results were encouraging, and before long, the navy was experimenting with a boat's frame apparatus for surface launching.

Whitehead was horrified when he learned what was going on, and Georg Hoyos was constrained to write a letter deploring "the rough manner in which English officers use their torpedoes" and admonished all concerned by observing that "such delicate weapons are not meant to be fired like a shot from a gun."[34] But whether intended or not, the Royal Navy had proved that the torpedo *could* be fired from above water, and having concluded the groundwork, the Admiralty promptly put the new method to practical use.

The frigates *Shah* and *Inconstant*, the last vessels to be classified as such until the 1939–45 war, were fitted with two torpedo-launching carriages forward of the 7-inch-gun battery and a stock of the old 16-inch Fiume weapons were carefully lifted down into the magazines. No firing device had yet been produced to launch the torpedoes from deck carriages and their discharge was effected by means of a pneumatic ram striking the delicately constructed tail a sharp blow. It was hardly surprising that Count Hoyos felt he had just cause for complaint about the Royal Navy's sledgehammer methods.

The *Shah* was commissioned as flagship of the Pacific Squadron on 14 August 1876 and left almost immediately for the eastern Pacific. Unlikely as it may have seemed at the time the *Shah's* torpedoes were to go into action less than nine months later—5,000 miles away on the other side of the world. It was to be the first time a Whitehead torpedo was fired in anger.

CHAPTER 7

Too Much Rough Engine Work

Nicholas de Pierola might have gone down in history as the man who stole a battleship, but unfortunately, very few people beyond the frontiers of Peru have ever heard of him.

The republics of South America are torn apart by revolutionaries with such regularity that only the most successful survive to find fame. And, as a defeated rebel, de Pierola has long since passed into obscurity. Yet his impudent theft of the Peruvian armored turret ship *Huascar* set the scene for an important event in the history of naval warfare.

De Pierola's revolution in the spring of 1877 was as short-lived as it was abortive, and crushed by the overwhelming strength of the government forces, the defeated rebels fled for the coast where it was decided that, having failed on land, they should try their luck on the high seas. Making their way to Callao they found the *Huascar* lying peacefully at anchor in the harbor, and after a sharp surprise attack, they seized the ironclad and immediately put to sea.[1]

Although by modern standards she was a fairly small ship, the *Huascar* was, at that time, one of the most powerful warships in

South America. Designed by Captain Cowper Coles (whose ill-fated *Captain* had brought turret ships into ill repute when she had capsized some seven years earlier) and built by Lairds of Birkenhead in 1865, she displaced 1,130 tons and carried a formidable armament of two 10-inch Armstrong muzzle-loading rifled guns in a single turret forward, plus two 40-pounders and a 12-pounder. Single funneled and with a speed of 10 knots, she was also rigged for sailing and her bows were specially strengthened for ramming.

With their revolutionary fervor still burning strongly de Pierola and his crew began their cruise by bombarding various towns along the Peruvian coast—only sparing them on payment of a substantial ransom. But after a few weeks the lofty ideals of revolution faded and the *Huascar* became a pirate ship searching the seas for prizes in the shape of rich merchantmen. Several British ships were attacked, but as the Peruvian government disclaimed all responsibility for de Pierola and the hijacked *Huascar*, it was quickly apparent that the Royal Navy would have to handle the matter itself.

Rear-Admiral Sir Algernon de Horsey, commander of the Pacific Squadron, was flying his flag in the frigate *Shah*. With the corvette *Amethyst* in company, he set out to look for the pirate ironclad. He found her on the morning of 29 May at anchor in the port of Ilo and demanded her surrender "for piracy on the high seas." On paper the *Huascar* was considerably more powerful than the fast but unarmored *Shah* and de Pierola decided to fight it out. A victory at sea might help to reverse the fortunes of his abortive revolution, and in any event, surrender was out of the question.

Nevertheless, the Peruvian rebel showed a certain respect for the reputation of the Royal Navy, and instead of moving out to fight, he steered the *Huascar* for the shoaling waters of the Ilo estuary hoping to escape from the trap by using the ironclad's shallow draught of 14 feet to advantage. The *Amethyst* skillfully cut off de Pierola's line of retreat, and at a range of 1,000 yards, the *Shah* and the pirate ship opened fire on each other. It was just 3:00 P.M.

Using her superior speed and freedom of maneuver the British flagship steamed up and down, presenting the Peruvian gunners with a difficult target while her own 9-inch and 7-inch guns pounded the rebel ironclad unmercifully. It was, however, so much wasted shot for the *Huascar*'s 4.5-inch armor plating was impenetrable, and in fact, out of the seventy hits registered by the British gunners, only one shell succeeded in piercing her hull.

In the fading light of the dying day de Pierola swung the bows of his cornered ship at the *Shah* and gathered speed to ram. Seeing the maneuver Captain Bedford played his trump card and ordered one of the Whiteheads to be fired. A very old Torpedo School legend has it that the *Shah*'s gunnery officer represented that the order should be confirmed in writing since the Peruvians had shown themselves to be gallant fellows that they did not merit such an appalling fate.[2] Bedford's own report of the historic moment was somewhat more laconic:

> Gatling gun commenced firing.
> Fired Whitehead torpedo. Not seen. Port electric broadside, 400 yards.[3]

In the ensuing *mêlée* the Peruvians lost their nerve, changed course, and made another attempt to escape. No one ever discovered what happened to the *Shah*'s torpedo, but it is generally assumed that the range was too great and its speed too slow to catch the fleeing *Huascar*. But whatever *may* have happened to account for its failure one indisputable fact remained. The first torpedo to be fired in battle had missed its target. And no doubt that pleased the gunnery experts.

HMS *Shah* in action against the turret-ship *Huascar* on 20 May 1877— the first occasion on which a Whitehead torpedo was fired in anger.

Robert Whitehead wearing the
Order of Francis Josef—an honor
awarded in recognition of his work
as a marine engineer. (Photograph
courtesy of Count Hoyos.)

The action was more or less broken off when the Peruvian ironclad turned away and by 5:45 P.M. she was standing in too close to the
town for safety and Admiral de Horsey ordered the British ships to
cease firing. Then, as the crews went to their night stations, he called
Captain Bedford for a hurried conference during which it was decided
to make a further and final attempt to sink the pirate ship in the dark.
Accordingly the *Shah*'s boats were lowered away, and armed with
spar torpedoes and a single Whitehead slung over the side of an oared
cutter, the assault party set off towards the shadowed darkness of the
shore. De Horsey's plan was to launch the Whitehead from a range of
80 yards and, if this failed, to follow up by an attack with spar
torpedoes. But it was not to be. While the British were making their
preparations de Pierola had taken advantage of the *Huascar*'s shallow draught to slip away through the shoals and he finally surrendered to a Peruvian naval squadron the following day at Iquique.

Meanwhile, in Europe, the political situation had taken another
turn for the worse following a revolt in the Turkish Empire, and by
early 1877, it was apparent to all that Russia and Turkey would soon
be at war for control of the Balkan peninsula. England was violently
anti-Russian at that time, a feeling undoubtedly shared by Robert
Whitehead, whom von Tirpitz had once described as "a thorough

Englishman."[4] He was, however, facing something of a dilemma, as only a year earlier, he had signed contracts to supply both belligerents with torpedoes and for a man "who was no lover of war" it was a situation fraught with difficulties. Whitehead's ultimate solution was based more on patriotic than moral grounds. Anticipating Britain's participation on the side of the Turks in the coming war he promptly refused to supply the Russians with any further weapons. As Alice dutifully recorded: "Papa is so fearfully patriotic and enthusiastic— in fact so am I—[and] it seems odd to have all these Russians here."[5]

Whitehead's unilateral action brought swift diplomatic repercussions with the result that the Hungarian administration of the Austro-Hungarian Empire made an order forbidding the export of *all* torpedoes to *anyone*. The ban did not last long for Austria, too, found herself in sympathy with the Turkish cause, but it created a number of problems while it was in force. One country to be affected was Germany and von Tirpitz recorded testily in his *Memoirs:* "The Hungarian Government under Tiza prohibited the export of torpedoes, so we were compelled, on the recommendation of Austrian gentlemen, to try and take the torpedoes which we had already bought across the Austrian frontier, which was only half an hour distant, although they were German property."[6]

It is interesting to speculate whether the "Austrian gentlemen" to whom von Tirpitz referred were representatives of Silurifico Whitehead anxious to circumvent the government ban in order not to lose valuable business. Alice Hoyos's version of the affair was rather less dramatic than that of Tirpitz and suggested that the whole matter was conducted on strictly legal lines. "On Tuesday Georg leaves for Vienna and Pest . . . the reason for the journey is that Austria has suddenly taken it into her wise head to forbid the export of torpedoes. All the Commissions are wild about it and Georg is going up to remonstrate—forcibly!"[7] He was apparently successful for two weeks later "Georg returned from Vienna—he has succeeded in obtaining permission for export of the German and Portuguese torpedoes which were already delivered and the other governments will also doubtless soon receive the same, so *that* difficulty is over."[8] Alice's reference to the fact that the German torpedoes "were already delivered" despite the Austrian government's export ban seems to indicate that some means of getting them over the border had been devised, probably on the lines mentioned by Tirpitz in his *Memoirs.*

But, whatever the truth of the matter, it taught the German Navy Office the drawbacks of buying weapons abroad—a lesson they quickly took to heart—and confirmed the wisdom of the British Admiralty building its own models of the Whitehead design at the Royal Laboratory, Woolwich.

Russia finally declared war on the Sultan's empire in April 1877 and in the early months, fighting was mainly restricted to a land campaign in which the tsar's army, having successfully crossed the Danube, pushed southwards into the Balkan peninsula until they were held by Osman Pasha's troops at Plevna in a bloody siege that lasted nearly eight months.

Turkey maintained a powerful fleet of fifteen ironclads in the Black Sea against which the tsar's admirals could only dispose the two circular freaks designed by Admiral Popov. These unfortunate aberrations, known as Popovska's, were completely circular battleships with no fore and aft line, and no bow or stern. They proved to be utterly useless, for they spun uncontrollably when caught in a current and were quickly relegated for use as floating fortresses. So the Russian Navy was forced back on improvisation. A total of nineteen fast merchant ships was commandeered and these were fitted to carry a number of small torpedo steam launches which had been shipped by rail from the Baltic base of Kronstadt.

They were a motley selection and reflected the Russian government's piecemeal policy of buying a sample of everything. Some carried a spar torpedo over their bows, others were equipped to tow Harvey torpedoes, while a few were fitted with a single torpedo tube of Fiume pattern for firing Whitehead "fish" torpedoes—the tube being placed *under* the hull to economize space. Fiume, in fact, built a special model for the Russians, a 14-inch diameter weapon, 11 feet in length, weighing 435 pounds, with a speed of 20 knots. It was priced at £280—the cheapest model listed in the Whitehead catalogue and no doubt the reason why it was selected by the tsar's buying agents.[9]

The Danube crossings led to the first naval actions and on 25 May four spar torpedo launches, under Lieutenant Dubasov in the *Tsarevitch*, came downriver in torrential rain to attack the ironclad *Seifez* and a group of monitors anchored at Braila. The leading Russian boat had a severe bout of boiler trouble and it took the little flotilla an hour and a half to cover eight miles. The attack was launched from a range of 135 yards and when Dubasov was halfway to his target he was challenged by a Turkish lookout. There was a brief moment of confusion, then a rifle fired and the crew of the *Seifez* dashed to action stations. Fortunately for the Russians the Turkish guns misfired—the crew on board the *Tsarevitch* actually hearing the click of the triggers as the enemy gunners jerked the lanyards—and seconds later, the spar torpedo rammed against the ironclad's stern quarter. Dubasov closed the electrical firing circuit—the spar torpedo having developed into a moderately sophisticated weapon by this time—and there was a tremendous explosion which swamped the Russian launch.

But as the smoke cleared away, Dubasov realized that the enemy ship had not been damaged, and ordering his men to bail, he went astern under a hail of fire from dozens of rifles, the bullets screaming over the heads of his crew as they fought to save their fragile craft. The Russians' second boat, the *Xenia*, taking advantage of the Turk's preoccupation with the *Tsarevitch*, swooped in and exploded her spar torpedo against the enemy ship, causing considerable damage and jamming the turret rotation mechanism just in time to save Dubasov from certain annihilation.

As anticipated by the critics, the point-blank range required for a successful spar torpedo attack proved nearly fatal to the attackers and the *Xenia*, like her flotilla mate, was badly damaged. Her propeller fouled some wreckage, and she drifted helplessly in the current while her crew used boathooks and poles to fend themselves away from the side of the sinking ironclad. The *Djigit*, another of the launches, was also severely damaged, and at daybreak, the Russians returned upriver, leaving the *Seifez* wrecked and broken, slowly settling in the water.

On 10 June another group of Russian torpedo boats, led by Lieutenant Makarov, used both Harvey and spar torpedoes against Turkish ships off Sulina, but the enemy's primitive boom defenses proved an effective deterrent and no successes were claimed. In fact, it could be regarded as a victory for the Turks since one of the torpedo boats was sunk by shell-fire as the flotilla withdrew and Lieutenant Rozhestvensky's boat was badly damaged. We shall meet him again in the torpedo story.

Spar torpedoes were used again at Nikopol on 23 June when two launches attacked a Turkish monitor, but as at Sulina, the net defenses proved too formidable an obstacle and the attack was abortive.

Moving to the eastern end of the Black Sea where the Turkish fleet was supporting troops operating in the Caucasus, the Russians initially used towed torpedoes based on the Harvey pattern. The first attack, at Batum on 11 May, failed when the charge refused to detonate, and although hits were scored in the second attack at Sukkum Kale on 23 August, no damage was done to the Turkish ironclads and Makarov lost the *Torpedoist*, one of the four vessels taking part in the action.

So far the Harvey torpedoes had proved decidedly disappointing while the spar torpedoes, after their early success against the *Seifez*, had been neutralized by the use of booms and net defenses, which prevented them from closing with their targets. Now it was the turn of the vaunted "fish" torpedo. Two of the boats were fitted to carry a Fiume 14-inch; the *Tchesma*'s being slung beneath the keel with ropes and the *Sinope* carrying her weapon in a discharge tube mounted on a raft lashed to the side of her hull.

The first attack, carried out in total darkness after the Turks had blacked out every visible light, was something of an anticlimax. Launched from their mother ship, the *Veliki Kniaz Constantine*, which had been skillfully camouflaged with sea-green paint, the two torpedo boats penetrated the roadstead at Batum and dashed towards the ironclad *Mahmoudieh*, which was lying peacefully at anchor for the night. The *Tchesma* fired first—becoming the second ship to launch a Whitehead in action—but the torpedo missed from a range of only 60 yards and exploded harmlessly against a submerged rock. The *Sinope* followed but her Whitehead also missed the target and stranded itself on the beach where it was captured by the Turks next morning.

One further attack took place on the night of 25 January 1878, during the final stages of the war, when the *Tchesma* and *Sinope* crept cautiously into Batum harbor once more and sank the revenue steamer *Intikbah*, which was acting as guardship. The attack was carried out from a range of 80 yards and the Whitehead torpedoes from both ships scored direct hits with such catastrophic effect that the Turkish vessel disappeared beneath the surface within two minutes.

This Russian success at Batum has always been a matter of controversy amongst naval historians and the Turkish commander in chief, Admiral Hobart Pasha, firmly denied that any of his ships were sunk that night. It is doubtful whether the truth will ever be established now, one hundred years later, but *if* the Russian account of the action was accurate the unfortunate *Intikbah* can claim the unenviable distinction of being the first ship to fall victim to Whitehead's weapon. The war, however, demonstrated one factor that was to be a feature of torpedo actions of the future: "Because their loss of life was small and insignificant [this cannot] be held to detract from the individual bravery of the Russian torpedoists. On going into action there were absolutely no reasonable prospects of such an extraordinary survival."[10] We shall see similar bravery exhibited by torpedomen of all nations many times over before this book comes to a close.

An objective review of the Russo-Turkish War, aside from Hobart Pasha's denial of success in the final attack, showed that honors were about even between the spar and the Whitehead torpedo, while the Harvey towed torpedo was totally discredited. Both had a sinking to their credit yet both had been, to a degree, disappointing—the spar on account of the damage suffered by the attacking vessel when at close range and the effectiveness of net defenses in preventing the necessary physical contact, and the Whitehead because of its failure to hold an accurate course. But whereas the spar torpedo could find no antidote to the new net defenses, there was little doubt that Robert Whitehead, with his usual ingenuity, would ultimately devise some way to improve the steering of the "fish" torpedo.

Von Tirpitz, too, was highly critical of the Fiume weapon and considered that "the Whitehead torpedo was all right as far as the idea went; but it still had too much rough engine work, and consequently lacked the necessary clockwork precision."[11] It is not clear to which model von Tirpitz was referring, but in any event, the criticism seems unduly harsh for the Fiume concern had completely abandoned the old Vee-twin unit in favor of the three-cylinder radial in the new 14-inch Mk 1—a move forced upon Whitehead by the rigorous terms of the German government's specifications. And most other nations using the new 1875 model seemed satisfied.

Nevertheless, von Tirpitz, as a leading member of the Torpedo Department, was not. "In the winter of 1877–78 I was sent to Fiume to deal with Whitehead about the torpedoes which we did not consider [to be of] any use. I succeeded in getting rid of half our order which Whitehead sold elsewhere."[12] Whitehead's outstanding business ability was clearly revealed by this episode for it must have taken formidable negotiating skill to arrive at a fifty-fifty compromise and an even greater sales technique to dispose of several hundred torpedoes which the German Navy had rejected as unsatisfactory. It is hardly surprising that by 1880 he was well on the way to becoming a millionaire.

The up-and-coming von Tirpitz had, in fact, paid an earlier visit to Fiume in May 1877, when Alice Hoyos deliberately confused his name in a letter to her brother: "Since Monday . . . Captain Hensser and another, name of Turpin or Tirpitz, have arrived. They and the Frenchmen look daggers at each other—it is anything but pleasant."[13] Tirpitz, however, was a welcome guest and when he returned to Fiume in February 1878, he stayed at the Whitehead's home for several months. On one occasion he accompanied the vast Whitehead-Hoyos entourage on a cruise in the Adriatic on board Prince Liechenstein's yacht the *Hertha*. Family and guests enjoyed themselves although Whitehead, as usual, was more interested in matters mechanical than social. "Papa, the dear old man, kept pottering about the engines, and reading *The Times*, and falling asleep on every cosy corner in the most lazy and delightful manner."[14]

But although von Tirpitz enjoyed Whitehead's hospitality he continued to grumble and noted, somewhat petulantly, in his *Memoirs:* 'When I gave a demonstration of the Whitehead torpedo before the Crown Prince in 1879, in spite of many weeks of preparation, it was still a toss-up whether they would reach the target or dash wildly out of their course."[15]

Yet, during the same period, the Royal Navy was obtaining a 60 percent success rate according to the official Running Returns—the official summaries of test runs—which suggests that the German Navy's training methods left a lot to be desired. In fact the British were achieving a higher degree of success than their statistics indicated, for the Captain's Report from the *Vernon* added that "in considering the amount of success attained with the weapon it must be remembered that we are actually using it in a manner that other nations are barely attempting and that for which the inventor maintains that they are unfitted, i.e. (by) discharge from above water from a ship at speed."[16]

By 1882 the success rate had increased to 88 percent, but as Commander Bethell has pointed out, "It must be admitted . . . that the criteria of a successful shot was somewhat lax, requiring only that the torpedo should hit a ship 200 ft long from a range of 300 yards."[17] Even so, the British seemed to have been obtaining a better performance from their weapons than the Germans and when, in 1880, the charge of torpedoes was transferred from the Commissary-General at Portsmouth to the Engineer-in-charge of the Torpedo Store—or, in non-service terms, when the War Office handed control over to the Admiralty—the Royal Navy was given a further incentive to develop the weapon in the ways it considered necessary.

Germany, however, was on the point of severing its contact with Silurifico Whitehead and von Tirpitz noted that "the Admiralty next approached the German factory of Schwartzkopff which had been advertising so widely the merits of its gun-metal torpedoes."[18] The German Admiralty wanted to give Schwartzkopff a monopoly in the manufacture of torpedoes but Tirpitz resisted the suggestion on the grounds that "a limited company which has a monopoly easily pays too much attention to its annual dividends and not enough to the development of its product,"[19] and in the end, the German Navy set up its own State Torpedo Workshops. Even so, their weapons continued to be based on Whitehead's original basic design and even Hitler's Reich was building torpedoes that bore more than a remote family resemblance to the Fiume models.

Meanwhile, as the torpedo gained in importance, Whitehead and his fast-growing family reaped the rewards of his unique invention. They moved out of the *Casa Rossa* to the new and luxurious Villa Whitehead on the hill overlooking the factory while Georg and Alice Hoyos settled into the old red brick house with their children.

The Villa Whitehead dominated the hill behind the Torpedo Works and a few years later Count Hoyos built his own villa just below it, the two houses being connected by a communal garden. With Robert and Georg involved in house planning it was inevitable for architectural conventions to suffer a rude shock. Ignoring the fact that such things "were not done" they built a carefully engineered tunnel under the busy Fiume-Abazzia main road, and linked the two villas to the factory so that important guests could commute to luncheon from the *Molo* with the minimum of inconvenience and the maximum of safety. Despite their preoccupation with marine engineering both men had a more than prophetic eye into the twentieth-century world of overpasses and underpasses.[20]

Whitehead and his wife visited England every year to see their friends, and Alice's wish that "it would be much more pleasanter for them to go *home* every summer instead of living in lodgings" was finally realized when Robert bought a delightful Victorian mansion, Springfield House, near Ryde in the Isle of Wight.[21] The fact that it was only a short boat trip from Portsmouth, Britain's premier naval base, was probably not entirely accidental in their choice of location.

James, by now, had graduated from Cambridge with honors and joined the British diplomatic service in 1881, going on to serve in St. Petersburg, Rio de Janeiro, and for a period, Berlin.[22] Back at home Robert acknowledged the engineering skill of his eldest son, John, by making him a partner in the Fiume factory while the youngest son, Bertie, was sent to school in England in preparation for a place at Trinity Hall, Cambridge. They were a happy close-knit family with Georg Hoyos regarded more as another son than a son-in-law. And, standing at the head, the object of all their affection, was their beloved *Nono*, still as "genial, unobtrusively benevolent, full of courtesy and loving kindness" as ever, and seemingly unaffected by his sudden acquisition of wealth and international fame.[23]

Neither was this just the prejudiced view of his intimate family circle, for there were many other people who experienced a similar affection for him. Arthur Wilson, an original member of the 1870 committee and later, in 1889, the captain of the *Vernon*, was a regular visitor when duties permitted. In June, 1881, while commanding the *Hecla*, he was detached to Fiume, where "[he] received a very cordial welcome from Mr Whitehead" on his arrival.[24] After attending an exhibition of torpedo tubes and a demonstration of the latest pattern torpedo which was being organized for foreign buying commissions, Wilson was invited to stay at the Villa Whitehead and, a few days later, he wrote to his brother:

> I am spending my time here very quietly going some time or other every day to Mr Whitehead's works to see what experiments are going on and occasionally getting a game of tennis on a gravel court there after work is over. Last Sunday he and Mrs Whitehead took us for a drive [to Abazzia]. I find the Whiteheads altogether an exceedingly pleasant family to deal with, both socially and in business.[25]

But while Robert and his friends enjoyed the carefree life of Fiume, rival designs of the automobile torpedo were now beginning to

Whitehead's granddaughter
Agathe with her husband,
Kapitänleutnant Georg von
Trapp. (Photograph courtesy of
Baron de Banfield.)

edge into the market. And one of these, the Lay, featured prominently in the war between Chile and Peru which began in 1879. By a strange coincidence the ironclad *Huascar* was the flagship of the Peruvian fleet, and with the support of the ironclad ram *Independencia*, she constituted the fragile backbone of her country's seaward defense force. Chile on the other hand possessed two ironclads, the *Almirante Cochrane* and *Blanco Encalada;* three corvettes; and the sloop-of-war *Esmeralda*, in addition to an assortment of smaller craft.

Peru attempted to redress the balance of power by purchasing two torpedoes of somewhat novel design from a former U.S. Navy assistant engineer, John L. Lay. Lay had been a pioneer of torpedo warfare for many years and was noted for the unnecessary complications of his designs. His spar torpedo of 1864 was fired by an intricate ball-drop mechanism which, in the hands of a Union naval lieutenant, W. B. Cushing, successfully sank the Confederate ironclad *Albemarle* on the night of 27 October—one of the very few occasions when a Lay torpedo worked according to plan. As one historian observed: "If anything more be necessary for the attribution of this torpedo to Lay alone, it is that Lieutenant Cushing had to have four separate strings tied to his hands and feet by which to operate it."[26] It is not difficult to agree with Bethell's conclusion that "it is inventors like him [Lay] that help to avoid dullness."[27]

The torpedo pattern supplied to Peru, however, was based on a totally different conception. Similar in appearance to the Whitehead, it weighed no less than 2,500 pounds and was 25 feet long with an 18-inch diameter. Its radial engine was powered by carbonic acid gas stored under pressure and it was designed to run awash on the surface at speeds of up to 16 knots. But unlike the Fiume weapon Lay's torpedo was not a self-contained unit and steering was controlled remotely by an electric cable that linked the device to its operator like an umbilical cord. Electrical impulses transmitted along the cable also started and stopped the engine, fired the 200-pound explosive charge, raised and lowered small marker flags that indicated its position, and as if all this gadgetry was not enough, controlled the

"The perfect English gentleman"— Robert Whitehead at the zenith of his fame. (Photograph courtesy of Lady John Bowman.)

release of unpowered "slave" torpedoes which were towed behind the parent weapon.[28]

The mere threat of the Lay torpedo was sufficient to break up the Chilean blockade of Iquique and in the subsequent battle between the *Huascar* and *Independencia* against the Chilean *Covadonga* and *Esmeralda*, gunfire and the ram were the main weapons employed while the Peruvians even enlisted the aid of an army artillery battery on shore to increase their firepower. The *Covadonga* escaped the trap but Captain Arturo Prat's *Esmeralda* was rammed and sunk by the *Huascar*. Honors, however, were even for the Peruvians lost half of their ironclad strength when the *Independencia* caught fire and foundered during the final stages of the hard-fought battle.

The *Huascar* scoured the seas to avenge her consort but none of the skirmishes in which she became involved yielded dividends. All attempts to use her ram were thwarted by the skillful evasive tactics of the Chilean warships—a failure noted by many historians as the end of the ram's supremacy as an offensive weapon. But on 27 August Miguel Grau, who had been promoted to Contra Almirante (Rear Admiral) for his success at Iquique, caught up with the corvette *Abtao* outside Antofagasta. Instead of turning to ram, the *Huascar* swung broadside on to its opponent and launched one of the Lay torpedoes from its deck. There was a mighty splash as the 2,500 pounds of steel struck the water and the electric cable paid out at lightning speed as it dashed towards the target.

Suddenly a wail of terror rose up from the Peruvian sailors who were lining the rails to witness the violent end of the *Abtao*. The reason for their dismay was not hard to find. The Lay torpedo had succeeded in reversing course through 180 degrees and was heading back, true as an arrow, towards the unfortunate *Huascar*. The operator sitting at the controls frantically twirled every knob in sight, but nothing seemed to deter the traitorous torpedo and the crew waited passively for the inevitable explosion. One man, Teniente (Lieutenant) Diez Causeco, fortunately kept his nerve, and diving into the sea, intercepted the uncontrollable weapon and managed to divert its course away from the ship.

After this display of temperament Grau lost all interest in Lay's invention and "signified his disgust with the weapons by having them buried in Iquique cemetery"—a by no means inappropriate fate for the mechanical traitors that had nearly brought about the loss of his gallant ship.[29]

The Royal Navy tested Lay's weapon as well but it behaved so badly on its trials that the *Vernon*'s experts had no hesitation in tuning it down. Russia, however, with her predilection for acquiring white elephants that no one else wanted, bought the manufacturing rights and, worried lest her traditional rival had at last got hold of something worthwhile, Turkey quickly negotiated a similar contract with Lay. But like so many other attempts to compete with Whitehead's unique weapon the Lay torpedo failed to achieve success and is now only a matter of historical interest.

Another form of torpedo contemporary with the Lay design was John Ericsson's underwater dynamite gun. The dynamite shell was fired from an underwater gun powered by compressed air and measured 25 feet in length with an all-up weight of 1,500 pounds. It was a promising idea but its ridiculously short range of 300 feet doomed it as a serious weapon of war.[30] It was never a viable proposition although Zalinsky's surface version of the dynamite gun was reasonably successful in the 1890s. Ericsson also built an electric torpedo in 1873 but this, too, failed to achieve maturity. This lack of success by men who had built up tremendous reputations in other fields of original engineering thought helps to underline Whitehead's own genius in creating and perfecting the weapon which bore his name.

The United States Navy, having refused to buy Whitehead's torpedo, pursued its own program of torpedo research and eventually concentrated its resources on the Howell design, which relied for its propulsive power on a large flywheel. Invented originally by Captain J. A. Howell in 1870, it showed considerable ingenuity of thought and had the advantage of operational simplicity. The flywheel, which in the early models spun at 9,000 revolutions per minute, was set in motion by a steam winch prior to launching and a system of bevel gearing transmitted its power to two side-by-side propellers giving it a speed of 8.5 knots for 400 yards—a performance in no way inferior to the contemporary Fiume Standard torpedo.

The Howell was a small and handy weapon. It was only 8 feet long and, with a diameter of 14 inches, it carried an explosive charge of 70 pounds. The properties of the flywheel were similar to those of the gyroscope, which at that time, had not been harnessed for torpedo use, and which gave the weapon "'an inherent directive force.'' It thus had a built-in tendency to maintain a more accurate course than the Whitehead, and in addition, its lack of engine meant no telltale track of exhaust gases or air bubbles on the surface to betray its presence to lookouts. The layout adopted by Howell showed a suspicious similarity to Whitehead's design and incorporated a transverse azimuth pendulum control system linked to the rudders similar, in many ways, to *The Secret* although it did not, apparently, work in conjunction with hydrostatic valves and played no part in depth keeping.

Later versions of the Howell extended the range to 500 yards and increased speed to 15.6 knots for 200 yards, while the overall length grew to 8 feet 11 inches. It proved to be a sound and reliable weapon and succeeded in keeping the Whitehead at bay, so far as the United States Navy was concerned, until 1892, when the speed and range of the Fiume models completely outclassed all rival designs and forced Washington to come to terms with Silurifico Whitehead.[31]

By 1880, except for the Howell torpedo and the Schwartzkopff "pirate" design, Whitehead's weapon could claim an almost complete monopoly of the world market. The spar torpedo was now obsolete, the Harvey had proved disappointing under combat conditions, and the Lay was little more than a subject of wardroom humor. No other designs had even got to the operational stage, and though the performance of the Fiume torpedo had not exactly lived up to its inventor's original hopes, it was still far and away the best weapon of its type in the world. The sales figures from the Fiume factory up to 1881 made this superiority very obvious.

Whitehead had sold 1,456 torpedoes by that date: His customers included Great Britain (254); Germany (203); France (218); Austria (100); Italy (70); Russia (250); Argentina (40); Belgium (40); Denmark (83); Greece (70); Portugal (50); and Chile, Norway, and Sweden (78). The prices varied from £280 for the steel 14-inch torpedo, to £325 for the same model in bronze, and up to £380 for the bronze 15-inch design.[32] Taking a conservatively average price of £300 per weapon the total sale of 1,456 torpedoes meant a turnover of £436,800.[33] To this, of course, should be added the costs of spares and ancillary equipment such as torpedo discharge tubes and air compressors.

The Fiume torpedo was fast becoming the proverbial goose that lays the golden egg so far as Whitehead was concerned.

CHAPTER 8

It Takes a Good Man to Make a Stern

By 1883 Robert Whitehead had the world at his feet. In terms of modern money he was a millionaire and the torpedo business was continuing to expand at a breakneck rate. The young engineer from Bolton who had studied every night at the Mechanics' Institution in Manchester and who had worked on the great iron span of the London Road railway station learning his trade was now an Austrian baron, a respected friend of the emperor, and a business confidant of governments and senior admirals throughout the world. His name was a household word, for no one referred to the torpedo without qualifying the word with the prefix *Whitehead*, and his genius as an engineer and inventor was acknowledged by all. Yet he remained, as ever, "the most modest and retiring of men [and was not] one who sought public fame for himself."[1]

Not that Whitehead was averse to fame and honors. In fact, he clearly enjoyed them provided they were not made *too* public. During a visit to Berlin in 1876 a court official asked Whitehead's son, John, whether his father would accept a German decoration should it be offered to him by the kaiser. According to Alice, "Jack said, 'Try him, that's all,' " and she added, "so there is good hope of the dear old man shining forth again in a new Order. I only trust it will be a good one."[2]

It was. And in the spring of 1877 Robert received the Prenssische Krone III Class. Only a short while later he was awarded a Danish decoration and had his photograph featured on the front page of *Flok* in honor of the occasion. Yet, throughout, he retained sufficient humility to maintain a sense of proportion at his sudden recognition and Alice noted that "he remains modest and simple through it all. Not a word of pride or exultation—only his childish look of delight at every new honour."[3]

But his peaceful and happy world was suddenly shattered by personal tragedy when, on 9 April 1883, while on a visit to Springfield House, his wife died. They had always been a devoted couple and she had been an able and affectionate mother to their five surviving children. But the raw Fiume climate had not agreed with her, and from 1876 onwards she had been increasingly crippled by rheumatism.

Her death left a void in Robert's life and although his daughter, Alice Hoyos, quickly stepped in to act as his companion, the bereavement had a traumatic effect on the lonely widower. Freed from his wife's homely restraining influence he suddenly burst forth as if aware, for the first time, that he possessed a fortune.[4]

Springfield House was sold and, after a short period at Midhurst, Whitehead purchased an enormous estate, Paddockhurst Park, at Worth, in 1885. It was a magnificent sprawling mansion set in 3,000 acres of Surrey woodlands with superb views over the South Downs. The house itself, built in 1862 in mock Tudor style, was a great barn of a place featuring, in many respects, all that was worst in Victorian domestic architecture. But Whitehead, his children, and the Hoyos family loved it and it was the setting for the happiest years of their lives.

The first setback Robert encountered on buying Paddockhurst was the unexpected discovery that he had no furniture to put in it—a problem he solved in grand style by a flying visit to Venice, where he bought up an entire antique shop, lock, stock, and barrel! Much of the furniture was as magnificent as the setting it stood in while other pieces seemed strangely out of place against the forbidding background of neo-Gothic panelling and stained glass windows that were featured in many of the main rooms. The "Big Room," for example, with its enormous marble fireplace and Greek columns contained not only a whimsical minstrel gallery but also a vast organ complete with ranging pipes in serried rows that would have done justice to a medieval cathedral.[5]

Taking advantage of his semiretirement, and leaving his son John and Georg Hoyos in day-to-day control of his torpedo empire, Whitehead launched himself into farming with typical enthusiasm. He could never do anything by halves. Sir Edwin Lutyens, the most famous architect of the Victorian era, was engaged to design the outbuildings and, to Whitehead's undoubted delight, produced henhouses complete with parquet flooring—the purpose of which remains a trifle obscure—and magnificent stables ornamented with equine figures in high relief.

> Everything is modern and up-to-date, but so simple and so full of taste as to be in complete harmony with the natural beauty of the surroundings. . . . There is a model farm . . . the keynote of it all is to be found in three words—cleanliness, comfort, and convenience.[6]

The Times noted that "he took much interest in farming which he carried out in style regardless of expense."[7] But, in a reference to costs, the *Country Gentleman* observed "where cleanliness and efficiency are attained at a stroke, no matter what the initial expense, surely, there too, will be found economy in the long run."[8] According to one visitor, indeed, the farm buildings had cost Whitehead £12,000—a tidy sum in those far-off days—but in Robert's eyes, apparently, a sum well spent.

Life at Paddockhurst was carried on in a style appropriate to its magnificent setting. "We had charades most nights and a dance every Saturday. The Great Hall had oak chests full of costumes for dressing up and we all, men and women, used to enjoy the play-acting." Alice, too, was in her element acting as her father's hostess: "Each night we ladies took it in turn to sit next to the host and Countess Hoyos used to knock on the table with a little silver hammer when she wanted attention." There was, however, a certain pathos in the writer's next few sentences: "The old gentleman [Robert Whitehead] who, by the way, was stone deaf, sat in his chair smilingly watching all of us, only happy to see us happy. He was of stout build and not very tall, with a most lovely crop of silver-white hair and such a kind face."[9]

Honors still continued to shower upon the inventor. On 30 July 1884, he was awarded the Legion of Honor by a grateful French government and this latest order was added lovingly to the Prussian, Danish, Portuguese, Italian, Greek, and Turkish decorations he already held. Yet Britain, his mother country, continued to withhold recognition of his services to the Royal Navy—due, so it was said, to his failure to obtain Queen Victoria's permission to accept his original foreign decoration and title from the Austrian emperor in 1868. *The Engineer*, reviewing his foreign honors, observed: "There is reason to believe that he felt acutely that . . . the country of his birth did not recognize him in the same manner."[10]

Following the death of Frances, the Hoyos and Whitehead families became inseparable and when the two parties set off for their annual visit to England, the famous Orient Express was stopped at the small village station of Loosdorff so that Robert's two private Pullman coaches could be hitched on the rear.[11] Whitehead, as we have already seen, was not a man to do things by halves. His family too, now augmented by the Hoyos children, was growing up rapidly, and he undoubtedly experienced a father's sense of pride as, one by one, they married into the cream of English and European society.

John Whitehead, now technical director of Silurifico Whitehead, had married Countess Agatha Breuner in Vienna on 2 July 1887, and nine years later, James was to marry the Hon. Marian Cecilia Broderick, the youngest daughter of the eighth viscount Midleton—a union that produced two daughters and five sons, one of whom, Edgar, became prime minister of Rhodesia from 1958 to 1962. Robert's eldest child, Frances Eleanor, married, first, Kapitän Louis Hassenpflug, and, then, Captain Charles Drury, subsequently a second sea lord of the British Board of Admiralty; while his youngest son, Robert Boville, was an intimate shooting companion of the emperor and the crown prince and a noted sportsman in Austrian society.[12]

Returning to the torpedo, however, the next major development in design emanated not from Fiume but from Britain when, in 1883, the Admiralty appointed a committee to study torpedo design in the light of the vast experience which the Royal Navy had built up over the years. One of the tasks undertaken by the committee was a series of tests to determine whether the contours of the body could be improved upon in the interests of hydrodynamic efficiency.

Until 1883 all torpedoes were built with sharply pointed noses on the assumption that a spearlike motion through the water was the most mechanically efficient way to cut through a liquid. Dr R. E. Froude of the Admiralty Experimental Works at Torquay discovered, to everyone's surprise, that "a body with an egg-shaped head [and] tapering to the stern" produced a much more efficient shape;[13] and, from the 14-inch RL Mk IV model onwards, the now familiar blunted nose of the modern torpedo was adopted. The Royal Navy's armament experts were more than satisfied with Froude's findings, for the fatter nose section meant that a larger warhead could be fitted—with a resultant bigger bang when the torpedo hit its target. But although Whitehead's original design conception was faulted at the front end of the weapon, his treatment of the stern received the full approval of the theoreticians and scientists. No doubt, when he learned of the committee's findings, Robert was reminded of the old shipyard adage: "Any fool can design a bow but it takes a good man to make a stern."[14]

The bows became increasingly bluff with each succeeding model until, by 1900, the nose was completely hemispherical. And, while considering the business end of the weapon it seems appropriate to look at some of the other modifications adopted at this stage of the torpedo's career.

Whitehead's original model had been fitted with a simple impact detonator incorporating a delay device, worked by a spinner, which prevented the pistol from being cocked until it had run about 60 yards. The 1870 Sheerness Committee had thought this distance excessive and suggested a restricted safety run of only 30 yards—their report noting that "Mr Whitehead states that this can be readily done." But it was still a primitive arrangement, and in 1883, Robert produced a highly sophisticated system by which a safety fan, operating on a spindle, prevented the striker from making contact with the detonator until the weapon had traveled a certain distance through the water. This in turn brought the "whiskers" (i.e., the fan blades) into the cocked position so that the slightest contact would detonate the primer. Whitehead's method involved having the detonator *inside* the primer at all times—a dangerous arrangement that, as will be seen later, was to cause the loss of several ships in battle when a shell struck the exposed torpedo tubes—and later modifications increased the safety factor by keeping the detonator at a distance from the

An early Mark of the 18-inch torpedo.

primer until the torpedo was running and "armed." There were, of course, other safety devices, the most important of which was a locking pin in the spinner fan, which had to be withdrawn before the torpedo was fired. This device, too, originated from Robert's inventive brain.[15]

The Royal Navy's Fairey Swordfish torpedo bomber. Despite its venerable appearance, the "Stringbag," as it was affectionately known, scored many successes in the Second World War.

By 1885 world demand had become so intense that a torpedo famine developed. The Royal Navy, throwing moral scruples to the wind in view of the emergency, turned to Schwartzkopff for additional supplies. The Berlin company had, by that time, built up to a production rate of six hundred weapons per annum[16] and was exporting torpedoes to Italy, Japan, Spain, and China in addition to supplying the needs of the infant German fleet—the average price of its phosphor-bronze pattern weapons having now risen to £450 each. Britain purchased 50 of the German company's 14-inch models for immediate delivery and ordered a further 50 just to be on the safe side. In addition she acquired another 11 Schwartzkopffs from the Chinese government for use by the Far East Squadron based at Hong Kong and, at the same time, increased her order from Whitehead to 220 Fiume Mark IVs, 200 of the new Fiume Mark Vs, and 10 models of the experimental "Baby" 12-inch pattern, which had been designed for use from ships' boats equipped with dropping-tongs—a primitive type of launching gear that dropped the torpedo into the water when its jaws opened.

But even this proved insufficient for the torpedo-hungry Royal Navy. Production at the Royal Laboratory, Woolwich, was stepped up from 120 to 300 weapons per year and, with surprising forethought, the Admiralty extended torpedo manufacturing into the field of private industry by signing a contract with the Leeds engineering firm of Greenwood and Batley Ltd to build 100 14-inch Mk IV RL weapons over the following five years. "Greenbats" responded to the challenge with such precision and efficiency that they remained official torpedo manufacturers to the British government for several decades.[17]

Inevitably, as the torpedo gained in importance as a prime weapon of naval warfare, other inventors attempted to stake their claim for a share of the lucrative profits that awaited the successful. As noted in the previous chapter the Howell flywheel torpedo had achieved considerable success and had passed its final official U.S. Navy trials in 1884. While an undoubtedly efficient weapon capable of running "through to the point at which it was aimed, something which no other torpedo could be depended upon to do,"[18] the Howell could still play unexpected tricks, the most notable of which was an ability to run backwards if the Dow steam winch, the apparatus used to spin the flywheel before launching, was incorrectly assembled—a disconcerting trait to say the least!

Most other designs of the period proved as disappointing, though not quite so hilarious, as John Lay's incorrigible 1-ton monster which we met earlier. Hudson Maxim, brother of Hiram Maxim of machine-gun fame, produced a dirigible torpedo in 1885,[19] which quickly vanished from the scene for reasons unstated but easily guessed, while a similar fate was shared by the Hall steam torpedo[20] in the United States and the Peck steam torpedo designed by Edward C. Peck of the Yarrow torpedo-boat works in Britain.

Several designs solved the problem of depth keeping by suspending the torpedo beneath floats. Both the Patrick[21] and the Wood-Haight weapons were based on this principle, the motive power being supplied from carbonic acid gas as with the Lay torpedo. Nordenfelt, the famous Swedish engineer and ordnance expert, also adopted the float suspension system and used a battery-powered electric motor of 18 horsepower to push it along, although like John Lay, he also used an electric impulse wire for guidance. Rockets, too, were adapted as power units, the two best known being the Cunningham,[22] of which few technical details survive, and the Berdan. The latter was tested by the Turkish Navy without any great success despite its six propellers and its claimed ability to dive beneath anti-torpedo nets.[23]

An expatriate Irishman, Louis Philip Brennan, was the only man to successfully challenge Whitehead's monopolistic grip on the British torpedo market.[24] He also, it should be added, invented the monorail system and pioneered the helicopter long before either Focke-Achgelis or Sikorsky appeared upon the scene. Born at Castlebar, County Mayo, on 28 January 1852, Brennan emigrated to Melbourne with his parents in 1861 and lived in Australia for the next twenty years. Having completed his technical education at Collingwood's College for Artisans, and while still a young man, he produced a number of minor inventions including a window-latch, a mincing machine, and a billiard marker—practical items redolent of Whitehead's own early work in Milan.

The initial concept of the wire-driven dirigible torpedo came to him in 1874 and was patented in London on 1 February 1878.[25] The idea developed from his observation that a cotton reel, if the thread is pulled towards the operator *from underneath*, moves forward and not backwards. Tests with a working model were staged at Hobson's Bay, Melbourne, on 21 March 1879 before an audience of prominent

The last remaining Brennan torpedo, now a museum piece.

citizens, business men, engineers, and service personnel, and proved so successful that Rear-Admiral J. Wilson, the commodore of the Royal Navy's Australian Squadron, reported back to the Admiralty in glowing terms. Brennan quickly obtained financial backing for the venture, including a grant from Victoria's colonial government, and as a direct result of Wilson's favorable report, he was invited to England.

He arrived in London in 1880 with one of his backers, John Temperley, but was promptly handed over to the army by the Admiralty when their lordships realized that the invention was only suitable for use from a shore station. The Royal Engineers, who, as noted earlier, were responsible for Britain's coastal defenses, were impressed with Brennan's weapon but wanted further development to be carried out. And having settled the financial terms, one of which, for some reason, gave the Admiralty an option to purchase, the army erected an experimental station at Garrison Point Fort near Sheerness in 1883 where the work was to be carried out under Brennan's personal supervision—a task for which he was paid a retainer of about £1,000 a year.

Meanwhile Brennan and Temperley formed the Brennan Tor-

pedo Company, and when the new improved weapon had been successfully tested it was again offered to the Admiralty under the option
clause of the 1883 agreement—the price being set at £100,000 for
the exclusive rights or £30,000 for a nonexclusive contract; figures far
higher than those asked for by Whitehead in 1868.

The torpedo itself was similar in external appearance to the
Fiume weapon but was much larger, with a diameter of 24 inches, a
length of 24 feet, and a total weight of 3.5 tons—twelve times that of
the contemporary Royal Laboratory 14-inch Mark III of 1882. Nevertheless, its 200-pound warhead of wet guncotton and maximum
range of 1.5 miles at 30 knots made it vastly superior on paper to both
the RL and Fiume models of the period. However, unlike Whitehead's free-running and self-steering torpedo, Brennan's monster
was steered *and driven* by 18-gauge piano wire, running over two
drums inside the body of the torpedo, which was operated and controlled from steam-powered winding-engines ashore. "The drums
were connected through a differential gear to twin in-line propellers
arranged to rotate in opposite directions. If one drum were rotated
faster than the other then, although the propellers continued to rotate
at the same speed, the rudder was operated. . . . These twin
[winding-engines ashore] were so arranged that their respective
speeds could be varied within fine limits, thus providing sensitive
control for the steering of the torpedo."[26] There was, in addition, a
pendulum compensator for regulating the running depth.

It was an ungainly and awkward weapon typical of Victorian
technology and totally unsuited to the fast-moving tactics of modern
torpedo warfare. But for some obscure reason the British government
fell head-over-heels in love with the contraption—possibly because
they would not be required to share its secrets with other naval powers
as was the case with Whitehead's weapons. A contract was signed
and sealed on 18 January 1887 that provided for a total tax-free
payment of £110,000 in six installments to the Brennan Company in
exchange for the British government's exclusive ownership of the
patents and other secrets. It also affirmed that brick-built winch
houses were to be erected along the banks of the Medway river in Kent
and on the coast of the Isle of Wight as part of the outer defenses of the
Chatham and Portsmouth naval bases while Brennan himself was
appointed as the full-time superintendent of the Brennan Torpedo
Factory at Gillingham at a salary of £1500 per annum—a post he

held until 1896. He continued working as a part-time consultant until 1907, however, but finally, apparently tiring of his unlovely brainchild, he moved on to more interesting, if less rewarding, fields of invention and engineering research.

Brennan's torpedo remained in operational service for upwards of twenty years, and there have been unsupported claims that it was adopted by several other countries. Martin Nasmith, the commander of the submarine *E.11*, thought that "a Brennan" had been fired at his boat when he attacked shipping in Constantinople harbor in May 1915.[27] It is probable, however, that he confused the Brennan weapon with the Berdan torpedo which Turkey had tested many years earlier and there appears to be no reliable evidence to support the claim that Britain sold the device to a foreign government. Admiral Penrose Fitzgerald recalled a Brennan being in active employment as part of the defenses guarding the eastern entrance to Hong Kong harbor in 1898 and stated categorically: "I saw several runs with it."[28] But Hong Kong was, of course, a part of the British Empire and not a foreign country.

On another and more memorable occasion the weapon was reduced to the ignominious status of a royal plaything when King Edward VII—while still Prince of Wales—watched a demonstration of the Brennan off the Isle of Wight during which Princess, later Queen, Alexandra operated the controls. She made, so we are told, a "remarkably good shot . . . at the target."[29]

Improvements in the performance of the Whitehead weapon following the introduction of the heater engine together with the army's decision to mount batteries of 9.2-inch guns along the banks of the Medway finally spelled the end of the Brennan although many writers attribute its demise to the fact that it depended on wires for its propulsive power and steering. Ironically history has come full circle—a not unusual occurance in the development of the torpedo—and most of today's heavyweight weapons are now wire-guided, current examples being the British 21-inch Mk 24 TIGERFISH; the German SST-4; and America's Mark 48. Perhaps Louis Brennan's torpedo was not quite such a technological anachronism as some modern experts would have us believe.[30]

By a strange coincidence both Fisher and von Tirpitz gained control of their respective torpedo departments in 1886, and under the influence of their powerful energies, the torpedo gained even further importance as a weapon of naval warfare. Tirpitz became inspector of torpedoes for the Imperial German Navy but many of his schemes were frustrated by the new minister, Count Monts, who was strongly prejudiced against the weapon. The first time he inspected the torpedo flotilla he told Tirpitz that "the whole thing was a mere show which would be useless in battle."[31] It was a fortunate thing for the German Navy that the count did not remain in office for more than a few months.

On his appointment as director of ordnance on 1 November 1886, Fisher promptly added "and Torpedoes" to his new title to ensure that he had complete control of all naval armament.[32] In point of fact, at the time of his appointment, control was something of a misnomer for authority for all items of naval and military ordnance still rested with the War Office. This state of affairs had existed since the end of the Crimean War and one oddity produced by this extraordinary arrangement was that the cost of the Royal Navy's guns and ammunition formed part of the Army Estimates rather than those submitted to Parliament by their lordships of the Admiralty.

Fisher led the fight to restore Admiralty control of naval armaments and it is to his eternal credit that he succeeded. Had the army still retained authority when war broke out in 1914 it needs little imagination to visualize the chaotic results of such an arrangement.

He celebrated his success by appointing Arthur Wilson as assistant director of torpedoes in March 1887—a wise choice, for Wilson had been involved in torpedo work since the Sheerness trials of 1870, and as a close friend of Whitehead, he had been kept apprised of all developments as well as making his own contribution in the shape of various inventions allied to the practical use of the weapon.

On 1 January 1889, Wilson was appointed captain of the *Vernon* and was soon embroiled in a first-class row over the new 18-inch torpedo which Whitehead had recently developed at his Fiume factory.[33] It was a big step forward and, at 1,236 pounds, it weighed nearly twice as much as the then current 14-inch Royal Laboratory weapon. It was faster, had a greater range, and most important of all, its warhead carried a charge of explosives very nearly four times greater than the standard pattern 14-inch model. And, naturally, the Royal Navy wanted it.

Wilson entered into the negotiations when they had been in progress for some months, but unfortunately, he was not fully aware of the facts. Discovering that the Admiralty was about to order 150 of the new 18-inch pattern torpedo without consulting him in his capacity as chairman of the Torpedo Design Committee, he flared into a temper and lodged a bitter protest. In his view the 18-inch had many disadvantages due to its weight and size, and as a new design, there was the added probability of teething troubles. With the true conservatism of the senior naval officer he wanted the Admiralty to give the matter further consideration or, at least, to only order a limited number for trials and experiments at the *Vernon.*

But time could not wait for either Wilson or the Admiralty for there were other buyers in the market. Captain Edwin P. Gallwey, "an expert in torpedo work second only to Mr Whitehead himself," had already been to Fiume and seen the 18-inch tested at the factory.[34] Finding himself completely satisfied with it his report urged the Admiralty to place an immediate order. Whitehead, too, demonstrated his old business acumen by letting it be known to Gallwey, when he visited Paddockhurst, that several other nations were also interested in the weapon and explaining that "while giving the British government the first refusal [he] could only undertake an early delivery on condition of an order for a large number, failing which, delivery was very indefinite."[35]

It is evidence of Whitehead's unique position at that time that he could bring pressure to bear on the British government by the use of quite legitimate commercial blackmail. It is even more symptomatic of his power that his threat was successful. Captain Jeffreys, Wilson's successor as assistant director of torpedoes, pushed the contract through, and as a result, Britain became the first nation to operate the 18-inch torpedo. By 1890 the Royal Gun Factory, which was to take over production of all torpedoes from the Royal Laboratory three years later, had also produced its first RGF 18-inch Mk 1 weapon and this size of torpedo (its diameter was strictly only 17.7 inches) was the mainstay of the Grand Fleet when war broke out in 1914. For once Arthur Wilson's judgment had been wrong. But even the best of people make mistakes on occasions.

Nevertheless it was not an especially happy period for Robert Whitehead despite the success of his new torpedo. The Paddockhurst estate was proving an expensive investment, his children were costing him money, and he was feeling the loneliness of life without Frances.

Whitehead's love for his children grew even stronger as, on growing up, they moved away to continue their education and set out on their own careers. Without the companionship of his wife he felt very lonely and he awaited their letters with almost pathetic eagerness. "Papa got your dear letter . . . and was greatly pleased. You must write to him oftener—a letter from you makes him perfectly happy and you should *see* the beaming face with which he brought it to me."[36]

Overriding everything, however, was the tremendous cost of Paddockhurst. And to make matters worse, Whitehead exhibited an irritating lack of concern. Inefficient agents and advisers were leading the estate to the doors of the bankruptcy court, but despite her pleadings Alice could not persuade the old man to take any positive action.

> Papa was as sweet and amenable as possible and told me everything
> . . . I asked Papa to call A——— then and there and tell him, but
> he said, oh no, better leave it until P——— comes, and went on
> reading his paper calmly! It is desperate sometimes!
> For example in all those years there has been no stock-book
> kept! And A——— confessed that he would be quite unable to show
> how much stock had been bought and sold since '85. Can you
> *imagine* it? A stock-book was begun then but never continued, there
> was "no time". All this strikes P——— as perfectly *inconceivable* on
> Papa's part.[37]

Alice's concern at the way Paddockhurst was eroding the family fortune was understandable. And such was her dismay that she even brought herself to write: "The real fault, although perhaps we ought not to say it, lies with Papa in never taking advice and allowing this dreadful mess to go on."[38] Indeed it *does* seem inconceivable that he should have allowed the management of the estate to get into such straits when he had demonstrated such an aptitude for business with his torpedo. The problems of Paddockhurst, however, show just how much he owed to Georg Hoyos for the success of Silurifico Whitehead, for the count was a shrewd and hard-headed business man. Robert, in contrast, was a kindly, genial, and rather naive engineer, too reliant on other people's honesty, and capable of being taken for a ride by unscrupulous men intent on lining their own pockets at his expense. Precisely how much money was swallowed up by Paddockhurst and its vultures cannot be established but "[Papa] showed us a paper at last, poor old dear, in a rather shamefaced way, showing that in '85 he had paid . . . £29,000 and some hundreds, in '86 £32,000, in '87 £31,000 and odd hundreds, this merely . . . and *only* for the estate. The Laundry Cottages etc are all separate. And this year he says will be much heavier, probably about £40,000 when all is paid.[39] Bearing in mind the relative value of money in those days it is clear that Robert was losing a veritable fortune with nothing to show for it.

> Papa spoke with much melancholy about his expenses and said [that] in justice to his children he could not keep this place up and would sell it if possible. He declared he was living on his capital. Georg succeeded in comforting him by proving that he did *not* spend half the interest of his capital every year, and that the Vienna and London houses *completely paid the yearly expenses of Paddockhurst.*[40]

The count's statement certainly indicates how much Whitehead was earning from his torpedo by this time and suggests that his income, at a minimum, was £40,000 per annum from property investments plus a further £80,000 interest on capital. And £120,000 a year in 1888 was not exactly peanuts! But the closing up of Paddockhurst at the end of the season disclosed more unwelcome figures, although fortunately, by then, matters were under strict control: "All went well and Papa I think saw that the house is a far smaller item than any other expense. The sum now in [the] book, fully paid up to the end of November '88 is £20,418 - 8 [shillings] - 10 [pence]. This includes *all.*"[41]

The whole sorry business was getting Whitehead down and the financial worries were seriously depressing him. "Papa, in his heart of hearts, dislikes the change [i.e., leaving Paddockhurst for Europe and the new management arrangements] because it means a certain amount of decision and energy also on his part."[42] Yet although Robert lacked energy over domestic problems he continued to show his usual eagerness for anything to do with the torpedo, and despite an ostensible holiday in Brussels, he and Georg Hoyos spent many hours discussing a new torpedo defense battery with the Belgian authorities. "Most satisfactory . . . the order will probably be given to Fiume."[43]

And then, as if the financial excitements were not enough, Whitehead and the family had a narrow escape from physical disaster while on their way to Germany. Just outside Coblenz the couplings of their private Pullman car broke a spring and the fault was only discovered in the nick of time. 'The stationmaster here said it was a merciful escape from a most terrible accident—the whole train might have slipped over into the river.''[44]

Resilient as ever Robert seemed to suffer little ill effect from the incident for Alice was able to report that same evening: "Papa [who] had been eating happily all day . . . did ample justice to his supper—is extremely cheery and bright, and had *quite* forgotten his Paddockhurst worries.''[45] He had not, however, been quite so cheery a few days earlier when his youngest son's first university bills arrived for payment. "Papa was simply in a passion about it and I was *afraid* to show him the bills for fear that he might have a fit or something. So T—and I looked at each other and calmly lied saying they were not ready.''[46] But, as usual, Robert proved to be the indulgent father and he paid up—although Bertie was strictly warned to economize in future.

It had been a worrying period with trouble coming from all directions. And, even when he was back in Fiume, Whitehead was unable to forget the problems hanging over his head despite immersing himself yet again in further development work on the torpedo. Alice and her husband did all they could to help him, but once involved in work, Robert was often difficult to approach. "Georg says Papa was much cheered after his talk. I wish he would speak oftener to Georg who knows how much he broods during those long hours of work. Georg says the work he has done lately is beautiful . . . Mr Hill was full of admiration and said he had a Master hand!"[47]

But there were big things in the wind, and in 1890, Silurifico Whiteheads opened their own branch in England at Portland—usually referred to as "the Weymouth factory"—and Captain Gallwey, the man responsible for the Royal Navy's acquisition of the 18-inch, resigned his commission and joined the company as its English manager.

"Georg says the Weymouth business is certain to succeed and the expenses are far lower than he expected. £50,000 will cover *all*, machines included, and the place will be as big, as useful, and as important as the Fiume one.''[48] Among the features of the new factory was a 1,000-yard pier built out into Portland harbor for test-firing torpedoes from rafts and the increased range of the new models also led the Royal Navy to building a fresh testing ground at Horsea Island firing range, which came into service in 1888.[49]

But for once Robert Whitehead and Georg Hoyos had miscalculated. In 1894 the Royal Navy decided that its own production facilities were sufficient to meet all British needs and, after twenty years, its connections with Fiume were severed. This unexpected decision left the new Weymouth factory high and dry without its anticipated main customer on the doorstep and there was a mad scramble to find fresh buyers for its products. Fiume by now was producing nine hundred torpedoes a year and yet, such was the phenomenal demand by the navies of the world, that despite prices rising to an average of £450 per weapon, all production was sold and little spare capacity was left lying idle. When it came to the crunch, world demand proved so insatiable that, right from the beginning, Weymouth was working at full stretch to meet its orders.

Even so there was a question mark poised over the future of Silurifico Whitehead. Both Germany and Britain, the two fastest-growing naval powers in the world, had switched entirely to home production, cutting Whitehead completely out of their markets, although, fortunately, the loss was partially balanced when Holland, in 1885, and the United States, in 1891, added their names to Fiume's list of customers. Whitehead, however, was undismayed and he answered the unspoken question with a gesture of defiance by having the old Fiume factory completely rebuilt on modern flow-production lines with an even greater capacity than ever.[50]

Whitehead was still a fighter. The torpedo was now the most important weapon in the naval armory. And if the world was going to use torpedoes then he intended to ensure that they would be *Whitehead* torpedoes.

CHAPTER 9

I Am Asking You to Sacrifice Your Lives

Although Whitehead had produced his first torpedo in 1866 more than ten years passed before naval architects came to grips with the type of ship best suited to exploit the potential power of his unique weapon. And the result was the birth of an entirely new class of warship, which, with its low and rakish lines, was to exercise the same romantic fascination as the graceful frigate of Nelson's era.

Not unexpectedly the American Civil War had produced the first pioneer torpedo boats, as indeed it foreshadowed nearly every other modern development in naval armament and warship construction, but credit for the systematic evolution of vessels designed for the sole purpose of launching torpedo attacks rests with a small group of British shipbuilders: J. Samuel White, Alfred Yarrow, and John Thornycroft.

Initially built for use with the spar torpedo the first torpedo boats were little more than steam pleasure launches similar in every detail to the smartly painted, brass-funnelled craft that cruised the rivers, estuaries, and coasts of Victorian England, but hastily stripped and converted to carry in their bows the lowering gear for an unwieldy

45-foot-long spar. The suicidal range necessary to successfully explode an outrigger torpedo against its victim required a handy, fast-moving attack craft, and these small steam launches were the only vessels immediately suitable for the purpose without the expenditure of vast sums of money in designing a special warship to carry out this one specific task. And, of equal importance, they were expendable.

The first torpedo boat was constructed in 1873 and although some authorities credit its creation to Alfred Yarrow, whose works were at Poplar in the center of London's dockland, it seems probable that John Thornycroft's yards at Chiswick, several miles upriver from Poplar, was the true originator of the design. Thornycroft's first boat was the *Rapp*, built to the order of the Norwegian government. Weighing only 16 tons, the little steam launch was 57 feet in length, with a speed of 14.5 knots, and an armament of two *towed* torpedoes similar to the Harvey-type weapon described earlier.[1]

Yarrow entered the lists in the same year when he mounted a spar torpedo in the bows of one of his pleasure launches, and once planted, the idea of the torpedo boat caught on with surprising rapidity. France, Austria, Greece, Italy, and Chile all scrambled to purchase the new vessels, which in the eyes of most Continental experts, would spell the doom of the ironclad battleship at economy prices. Some of the early boats displaced as little as 5 tons and many failed to achieve more than 12 knots even when fully extended. In appearance they resembled an admiral's steam pinnace of the mid-Victorian era with a brass funnel set well forward, rakish lines, and an exposed steering position—ideal for a day's pleasure cruising in peaceful sunshine but scarcely suited for close-range attack against heavy defensive fire. Yet, as seen in chapter 7, these graceful little vessels fought many a bloody battle against daunting odds. And to the eternal credit of their gallant crews they often succeeded.

But although these new boats originated in England, almost five years were to elapse before the Royal Navy awoke from its slumbers to realize their existence, and it was not until 1876 that the Admiralty ordered Britain's first torpedo boat. The *Lightning* was built at Thornycroft's Chiswick works and delivered in May 1877.[2] Her overall length was 84 feet and she displaced 28.7 tons, but her 460-horsepower steam engine could drive her along at 19 knots, which gave her a distinct advantage over the plodding 12-knot ironclad of the period. Designed originally to operate a spar torpedo, she was taken in hand in 1879 and refitted to carry a single abovewater discharge tube containing a 14-inch Whitehead torpedo, and from her basic scantlings all subsequent torpedo craft have evolved.

The Royal Navy had not, however, selected Thornycroft's design by a flash of uncanny prescience. The building of torpedo boats had been forced upon a reluctant Admiralty by the rising pressures of public opinion alarmed by the sudden expansion of rival European fleets, and the British government had only discovered the answer to the problem of finding a vessel suitable for torpedo warfare the hard way and, even then, only after a considerable amount of bitter experience. And, needless to say, they started off by making two costly and futile mistakes.

The first ship which the Royal Navy designed and built for the specific purpose of firing Whitehead torpedoes[3]—as opposed to the conversion of existing ships, like the *Shah*, by the use of deck launching carriages—was the 245-ton *Vesuvius*. Launched in 1874 and constructed of iron, this strange vessel was typical of the freak warships produced during this transitional period of naval architecture, but, while undoubtedly unusual to the modern eye, she was no less of an oddity than dozens of other strange warships built in the 1860s and 1870s. She was designed without a funnel, and to prevent smoke, her Maudslay engines used coke rather than coal for fuel, the fumes being carried away by a series of exhaust ducts vented along the side of the vessel's deck. Twin screws gave her a speed of 9.7 knots—slower than most of her intended victims—and fitted with a single 16-inch tube in the bows, she carried no fewer than ten Whitehead torpedoes. The *Vesuvius* was intended to be noiseless so that she could creep up on her target at night undetected and it was partially for this commendable reason that the funnel was omitted. But to ensure that no telltale sound should escape and betray her presence to the enemy her designer thoughtfully provided for the engine room to be completely battened down when she went in to attack. It need hardly be added that the *Vesuvius* failed to revolutionize naval warfare.

The success of Tegethoff's ramming tactics at Lissa had convinced many experts that the ram was to be the supreme weapon of the future, and a number of ships were built solely for the purpose of ramming the enemy. The birth of the torpedo, however, brought certain doubts and in the Royal Navy, at least, designers attempted a compromise. The result was the *Polyphemus*, described by the first lord of the admiralty as "of a kind as yet unknown in any part of the world but which had been much talked about."

Nathaniel Barnaby originally designed the *Polyphemus* as an ironclad ram—a vessel in which every feature was secondary to the prime function of striking the enemy with the 12-foot steel spur built into her specially strengthened bows. But the professional head of the Navy, Admiral of the Fleet Sir George Sartorius, had other ideas. Despite the fact that this veteran sailor was eighty-eight years old he was still sharp enough to realize that the torpedo had brought to an end the short-lived supremacy of the ram, and on his insistence, Barnaby had to amend his design to incorporate five torpedo tubes and a number of light guns with which to repel enemy torpedo launches. One discharge tube was mounted below the ram in the bows, two submerged tubes were fitted on the broadside—one to port and one to starboard—and two more were placed above water on the hurricane deck. With a speed of 17 knots and a displacement of 2,640 tons the *Polyphemus* was a formidable ship but she was undoubtedly too slow and unwieldy for the duty for which she was designed. In the end result she was a complete failure.

The sudden proliferation of torpedo boats caused the British Admiralty serious misgivings, for by sheer weight of numbers it was quite possible for a swarm of small craft to overwhelm the defenses of a large ironclad and occasion her doom with the aid of a single well-aimed Whitehead. Initially a form of defensive netting was evolved, which, draped from booms along the side of the ironclad, acted as a safety skirt and prevented torpedoes from reaching her vulnerable belly. But the nets were heavy and cumbersome and could really only be used when the ship was at anchor or steaming slowly. Clearly some other means of thwarting the torpedo boats had to be found.

Thoughts at first moved in the direction of torpedo cruisers, the first of which, the *Leopard* and *Panther*, had been built by Armstrongs of Elswick for the Austrian Navy in 1885. These, as their title suggests, were larger ships than the *Lightning* and her successors, and carried a heavier armament. But their speed proved insufficient to intercept or pursue the rapidly improving torpedo boats and they were soon obsolete—although not before the Royal Navy had climbed on the bandwagon with the *Fearless* and *Scout*. But as the torpedo boats themselves grew in power and strength it became apparent that the answer to the problem could well rest in a parallel development along similar lines.

The initial antidote, the torpedo-boat catcher, unfortunately failed to live up to the promise of its name. In the 1887 Spring Exercises at Portland the first, the *Rattlesnake*, was matched against eighteen torpedo boats and failed to catch a single adversary—nearly blowing up her boilers in the attempt. For a while both torpedo boats and "catchers," the latter now reclassified as torpedo gunboats, developed side by side, each striving to obtain a superior margin of speed over the other. But in the end the solution proved to be an amalgamation of the two types into a single hybrid which incorporated the necessary elements of defence and offence in a skillfully balanced combination of guns, speed, torpedo tubes, and seaworthiness. And such, very briefly, were the origins of the modern destroyer.

Torpedo boats and destroyers were not, of course, the only ships to carry Whitehead's formidable weapon. By 1880 no fewer than thirty-three warships of the Royal Navy had been fitted to fire torpedoes, and by 1900, nearly every major warship had its tally of torpedo tubes, either mounted on deck or fitted below the waterline for submerged operation. The first British battleship to be equipped with Whitehead tubes as an inherent part of the original design was the 11,880-ton *Inflexible*, laid down at Portsmouth Dockyard in February 1874 and completed in October 1881. Two 14-inch torpedo carriages were mounted at deck level above water and two submerged tubes were fitted at the bows. In addition she carried "a peculiar scoop down which a torpedo ran when released" on top of her bows plus two 60-foot 2nd class torpedo boats on skids on her poop.[4] It is clear from these design details that the Royal Navy had taken the torpedo seriously even as early as 1874.

But despite all the modifications and improvements that had gone into the torpedo, it still suffered, even in 1890, from a certain amount of directional instability that even the genius of its inventor had been unable to overcome completely. The British navy professed itself satisfied with the steering properties of the RL and RGF pattern torpedoes, but much of their vaunted reliability came from continual test running—with resultant high wear and tear—which enabled their operators to compute a precise average deflection that reduced directional error to 3 percent or less. Even so, as ranges increased, even a 3 percent error was sufficient to miss a target, and as battle distances lengthened the degree of accuracy demanded from the torpedo became more and more critical.

The gyroscopic effect of the giant flywheel in Howell's torpedo already pointed the way towards stabilization of steering control, but at that time, scientists had not yet appreciated the special properties of the gyroscope and no one seemed interested in following up this line of thought. No one, that is, except Whiteheads.

Family legend attributes the first suggestion of gyroscope control to Alice Hoyos, who, while reading a children's book about that favorite Victorian toy, the spinning top, pointed it out to her husband, Georg.[5] Robert was by this time living in semiretirement and control of the technical side of the factory rested with his eldest son, John. And it was to John that Georg Hoyos took the first smatterings of the idea suggested by Alice. Robert was brought in for consultation, and the three men got down to theoretical discussions in which, no doubt, Howell's flywheel figured prominently. The idea was clearly promising but to design a form of gyroscope from scratch was a trifle too ambitious even for the technical talents of the Whitehead family, and so, although they continued to examine the proposition, they also kept their ears close to the ground for rumors of other scientists probing into the same problem. Early in the 1890s, the exact date is not known, one of their Russian contacts brought news of the Petrovitch—a primitive form of gyroscope on which more experimental work was still needed. John was immediately dispatched to Russia to collect a sample unit, and once it was safely back at the Fiume factory, he set to work first to perfect the device and, at the same time, to incorporate it into the torpedo's guidance mechanism.[6] But the Petrovitch was very crude and development seemed likely to be measured in years rather than months. And while John and his father struggled to solve the problem they had set themselves their torpedoes continued to gain further combat experience on the high seas.

The scene was again set in South America, where in 1891, another revolution had broken out, this time in Chile, where the Balmacedist faction were struggling for power against the Congressionalists—the latter having thoughtfully gained control of the Chilean Navy to improve their chances of victory.[7] The atmosphere of confusion was complicated by the arrival of two new torpedo gunboats, the *Almirante Lynch* and *Almirante Condell*, at the rebel held base of Punta Arenas. The *Lynch* and *Condell* were identical ships, built to the pattern of the new torpedo gunboats, the successors to the catchers described earlier. They displaced 750 tons each, carried three 14-pounder quick-firers, four 3-pounders, and five 14-inch torpedo tubes; their 4,500–indicated horsepower engines gave them a speed of 21 knots. The Balmacedists looked at them enviously, convinced that with such modern machinery at their disposal the enemy's control of the main Chilean fleet could be neutralized. And within a few days of their arrival pressure was being brought to bear on their officers and men to espouse the rebel cause.

After a good deal of wheeling and dealing the two gunboats agreed to sail under the Balmacedist flag, and following a short period of shakedown exercises, they set off from Punta Arenas on a do-or-die mission against the main strength of the federal fleet, which, according to intelligence reports, was anchored in Caldera Bay.

When they arrived in the early hours of 23 April they were disappointed to find that only one enemy ironclad was berthed in the anchorage—the 3,500-ton *Blanco Encalada*, which we last encountered during the Peru-Chile war of 1879. Another familiar name, the ex-Peruvian *Huascar*, now serving in the Chilean Navy following her capture at Angamos, was expected to be in company with the *Blanco Encalada*, but by the good fortune that contributed to her long life, she had not made her intended rendezvous and so evaded the trap. The moon was obscured by drifting clouds as the two torpedo boats closed in on the bay, and just before dawn, they dashed into the landlocked harbor on their daring mission. Capitan de Navio (Captain) Carlos Moraga led the attack in the *Condell*, and steering straight at his target, he fired his bow torpedo tube before swinging round in a wide arc to discharge his two beam tubes. There was a soft splash as the three Whiteheads struck the water and three bubbling white wakes fingered towards the slumbering *Blanco Encalada*. But the old problem of directional stability reared its head, and veering slightly from their aimed courses, all three torpedoes ran wide of their target.

Aroused to action by the unexpected attack the *Blanco Encalada*'s crew dashed to their battle stations and opened up on the *Condell* with an assortment of quickfirers, machine-guns, and rifles.

Capitan de Fregata (Commander) Fuentes, following close behind Moraga in the *Lynch*, witnessed the failure of the first attack and altered course to launch a second strike, unobserved in the confusion. He loosed his bow tube at a range of 150 yards and, when this missed, approached his target even closer. The *Lynch* heeled sharply as Fuentes swung his ship broadside on to the ironclad and two more Whiteheads leapt from the beam tubes. This final gesture was sufficient. One of the two struck the *Blanco Encalada* and there was a tremendous explosion. Within six and a half minutes the Chilean battleship had completely disappeared taking with her 11 officers and 171 of her ship's company. It was the first *real* success of the torpedo in action and it demonstrated, once and for all, what could happen when its lethal potential was translated into stern reality.

Less than three years later, the torpedo was again to prove its worth in battle. The political background to the Brazilian uprising that provided the setting for this next test is irrelevant to the context of the Whitehead story, and it is sufficient to note that the regular navy supported the Melloist rebel party leaving the government forces under President Floriano Peixoto to improvise a fleet from whatever resources they could lay their hands on.[8] The leader of the revolt, Contra Almirante (Rear Admiral) Custodio José de Mello, assembled his ships—the battleship *Aquidaban*, the cruiser *Republica*, a half completed corvette the *Tamandare*, and several other units, including the *Javry*, "an antique turret ship"—in Rio harbor where the insurgents controlled the fortress island of Villegagnon and several other small islets at the head of the bay.

The revolution had broken out in August 1893, and exchanges of fire between the shore batteries and the rebel ships continued throughout the winter while rumors, gaining credence with each passing day, indicated that the government was trying to build up an entirely new navy with which to confront de Mello and the revolutionaries. The rumors proved to be correct, and before long, Peixoto had assembled a force consisting of the *El Cid*, a converted merchantman carrying the dreaded Zalinsky dynamite gun, a British-built torpedo gunboat the *Gustavo Sampaio*, and three smaller torpedo boats built by the German Schichau Company of Elbing. The British-built ship carried 16-inch Whitehead torpedoes while the German vessels were equipped with the equivalent-sized Schwartzkopff weapons.

The attack took place in April 1894 when the rebel flagship, the *Aquidaban*, took refuge in a secluded anchorage in the lee of Santa

Catherina Island. The four ships of the attack force came into the bay in line abreast but lost touch with each other in the darkness with the result that each boat operated independently. Numerous torpedoes were fired in the *mélée* that followed but all apparently missed until the *Gustavo Sampaio* finally located the target. Even then there was an element of farce about the affair:

> The captain went full speed towards his enemy and brought the bow tube to bear and gave the order to fire, but the officer in charge had previously fired thinking the order had been given before; therefore the shot was lost. The captain, exceedingly chagrined at such an opportunity being thrown away, swung his ship round the battleship's stern and, when abreast of her funnel, gave the order to fire the beam tube at a distance of 450 feet—but nothing happened. The Second Officer, hearing the order, rushed aft and fired the torpedo by hand, which hit the *Aquidaban* forward under the port bow.[9]

The insurgent battleship, which, up to that moment, had been hotly engaging the torpedo boats with her Nordenfelt quick-firers, suddenly stopped shooting and struggled towards the shoals inshore where she finally grounded in 22 feet of water. But despite the torpedo's success in disabling its mighty opponent there remains some confusion regarding the manufacturer of the victorious weapon. Peter Bethell credits the success to a 16-inch Schwartzkopff although he agrees that the relevant torpedo was fired from the British-built *Gustavo Sainpaio*.[10] Because of their similarity in design either manufacturer's weapon could be fired from a standard torpedo tube and it is always possible that, although nominally equipped with Whiteheads, the *Gustavo Sampaio* shipped the German model at the time of the action. On balance, however, it seems more probable that the torpedo used originated from Whitehead's company, for the Brazilian government was an official customer of his Weymouth factory. But no matter which firm manufactured the weapon that disabled the *Aquidaban* one fact remained beyond dispute. A ''fish'' torpedo had crushed the revolution and given victory to the government.

Japan's attack on China in 1894 proved to be the last occasion when torpedoes were fired in anger during the nineteenth century, and it presented the experts with a welcome opportunity to see how the weapon would perform under conditions of modern warfare. The only major fleet action of the conflict was the Battle of the Yalu River on 17 September 1894, when China's five ironclads and supporting craft met up with Japan's seven armored cruisers and their five obsolete escorts. On paper the two fleets looked evenly matched, but China appeared to have one overwhelming advantage—her fleet was augmented by four torpedo boats while her enemy had none. In the circumstances, could China's use of the torpedo swing the balance?

The action opened at 12:50 P.M. when Admiral Ito's highly disciplined ships attempted to "cross the T" of the Chinese squadron, which was steaming in a line abreast formation similar to Tegethoff's van division at Lissa. The fighting quickly developed into a big-gun slugging match in which the Chinese were clearly seen to be getting beaten. Ito's cruisers gradually outflanked the enemy fleet, forcing the starboard wing to fall back, but in the rear of the Japanese line, the situation was deteriorating so rapidly for the Chinese that the *Hiei* dashed straight through the enemy fleet to join the head of the Japanese line now moving around behind Admiral Ting's ships in an encircling maneuver. "The Chinese guns flamed at him from both quarters and torpedoes could actually be seen jumping from wave to wave, but the *Hiei* got through undamaged."[11] Most of the Chinese torpedoes were released from too great a range to ensure accuracy and the strange antics of the weapons "jumping from wave to wave" suggests that the Schwartzkopffs' depth-keeping mechanism had not been well maintained.

As the battle reached its climax the Chinese torpedo flotilla made a half-hearted attempt to close the enemy but Captain Togo in the *Naniwa* drove them off without difficulty with machine-gun fire, and joining up with two cruisers, the flotilla turned its attention on the Japanese auxiliary *Saikyo Maru*. The converted merchantman fought her way clear, but not before she had seen a Chinese torpedo, fired at point-blank range of 40 yards by the *Fulung*, pass harmlessly beneath her keel—further evidence that the Chinese Navy was not setting the depth regulators with the accuracy demanded of such delicate weapons.

Smashed and pounded by Japanese shell-fire and with five ships already sunk Admiral Ting led the remnants of his fleet towards the mainland at high speed and by dawn the following day the defeated force was safely inside the harbour of Weihaiwei. Ting's vaunted torpedo boats had made no useful contribution to the battle and every single torpedo fired by the Chinese had missed its target. The Admiral's misfortune, however, provided an unexpected bonus for the local fishermen. Several Schwartzkopffs ended their headlong run on the shore where enterprising fishermen picked them up and proceeded to sell them back to the Chinese government for $100 apiece![12]

Throughout the bitter winter of 1894–95 the Japanese Navy stood guard over the entrance to the Chinese refuge at Weihaiwei while the army gradually encircled the town from the landward side. Ting was called upon to surrender with honor but he refused and in February the Japanese made their preparations for a torpedo strike on the cornered fleet. Three flotillas of torpedo boats were picked for the raid, and on 3 February, Admiral Ito addressed the following message to the captains of the boats:

> Your orders are to sink the enemy ships in the harbour forthwith. No such operation has ever hitherto been undertaken by any navy in the world. I am asking you to sacrifice your lives for your country and to earn undying fame for yourselves.[13]

It was a stirring signal. And the import of the message was one that was to become cruelly familiar to several generations of torpedo-men in future wars. Success with the torpedo could only be achieved by sacrifice. And success was all that mattered. The men were expendable.

On the evening of the third, in the face of a raging storm, Torpedo-boat No. 6 smashed its way through the heavy seas and shattered the boom that had closed the harbor entrance to all comers. At 3:00 A.M. four more torpedo boats, under the control of Captain Togo, staged a dangerous diversionary attack on the western entrance to the harbor, braving the boiling seas, the shrieking winds, and the razor-sharp reefs to distract the enemy's attention from the eastern entrance. They succeeded well in their task, and initially, the ten boats launching the main attack had only the sea to contend with as they dashed for the harbor entrance. It was bitter cold and ice formed a variety of grotesque patterns on the guns and superstructures of the tiny boats as they sped through the darkness. Two were thrown headlong onto the treacherous rocks that bordered the entrance and one failed to launch its weapons, which were found to be frozen solid inside the exposed torpedo-tubes. But the remaining three boats let loose a total of eight Schwartzkopffs, one of which struck the *Ting Yuen* under her stern quarter forcing the ironclad to beach herself to prevent total loss. Recovering from their initial surprise the Chinese gunners hit back hard and all the Japanese boats were damaged by shell fire, although all succeeded in making their way out safely.

The following morning five torpedo boats, split into two divisions, launched a second raid on the base. Three skirted to the east of the shattered boom while the other two smashed through another obstruction near Channel Island. Ignoring the enemy searchlights and scorning the hail of shell fire that plunged all around them the five boats pressed home the attack. One let go three torpedoes, the others were content to fire two each. But it was enough. The *Wei Yuen, Sai Yuen,* and *Chen Yuen* were all sunk—the *Sai Yuen* turning turtle and trapping her unfortunate crew inside the hull where they could be heard crying out for help several days later. Admiral Ting's fleet was no more.

Admiral Ito's final success had been brought about solely by the gallantry of his torpedomen, plus, it must be added, the excellent maintenance the Japanese gave to their Schwartzkopff torpedoes. As Commander Murray Sueter observed: "The attacks were carried out in the coldest weather, many of the men being frozen to death at their posts. We have no hesitation in saying that the heroism displayed by these torpedo-boat officers imbued the Japanese . . . with that spirit of emulation which is so valuable an asset for an admiral to possess in his torpedo-craft flotillas."[14]

The attack on Weihaiwei ended the war in a single stroke and started Japan on her aggressive program of expansion. And that victory had been determined, finally, by the Schwartzkopff torpedo. Yet, with typical inscrutability, the Japanese rendered their thanks to the Berlin company by switching their future orders for torpedoes to Silurifico Whitehead in that same year—1895.[15]

CHAPTER 10

I Answer for Our Success

Whatever Ludwig Obry produced his gyroscope in 1895 he set
the torpedo on the right path in more senses than one.

Although the principle of the gyroscope had been established on
a theoretical basis early in the nineteenth century no real progress had
been made in either putting the theory into practice or in finding a
working use for its unique properties. And because of the advanced
techniques required no inventor had succeeded in producing a functional model although several had tried. Robert Whitehead and his
son John, in fact, were probably the first engineers to realize that the
properties of the gyroscope could be harnessed to solving the problem
of stabilization, but as already noted, their initial experiments with
the Russian Petrovitch apparatus were beset with difficulties caused
by the inherent imperfections of its basic design.

Obry's gyroscope, however, was a precision-built instrument,
machined to the finest tolerances, which operated perfectly and could
achieve the required rate of high rotation necessary for both accuracy
and duration. According to the torpedo expert G. J. Kirby it consisted
of "a 1¾ lb wheel some three inches in diameter . . . held in gimbals

with its axis along that of the torpedo and the wheel was spun up to a maximum of 2,400 rpm by means of a pre-tensioned spring."[1] Bethell records that the energy exerted in this first unit was in the nature of 20 foot-pounds. This wheel, the vital key to the gyroscope, was utilized by the Whiteheads to control a supply of pressurized air to the controls of a vertical rudder at the stern of the weapon. And thus any deviation from course was immediately corrected by the relative inclination movement of the gyro, which released a measured amount of air to a valve controlling the rudder mechanism.[2]

It was an ingenious solution to a problem that had bugged the torpedo ever since its birth in 1866 and, in its basic simplicity, bore all the hallmarks of Robert's genius. Certainly no one else had found a practical use for the gyroscope before 1895 and Whitehead's success, once he had got hold of a reliable instrument, was yet one more tribute to his grasp of applied mechanics. Today the gyroscope is used in the solution of many stabilization problems including those of space travel. Yet even the gyrocompass, the most important adaptation of the principle, was not perfected until well into the 1900s. And Sperry, the acknowledged leader in gyroscope development, did not begin manufacture of his own device until 1896. With no evidence to the contrary it seems reasonable to claim that Robert and John White- head's adoption of Obry's apparatus and their earlier experiments with the Petrovitch model was the first example of the gyroscope principle being applied for practical use.

One result of Obry's apparatus was an increase in the accuracy of the torpedo's course by reducing the deviation angle (i.e., the amount of deflection from its line of aim) to a mere 1/2 degree over a distance of 7,000 yards. It was, however, only a theoretical advantage, for in 1895 few Whiteheads had a range of more than 1,000 yards and, at maximum speed, even less. But by solving the problem of directional stability the experts were now able to concentrate their energies on increasing the range and power of the weapon.

Other improvements soon followed. Faced by a similar situation to that encountered with *The Secret*—the transmission of high energy from a low energy thrust—Whitehead invented a small relay valve which, acting as servomotor, enabled the sensitive gyro-wheel to exert more power on the rotary valve controlling the admission of air to the steering engine without increased effort, and step by step, further refinements were added to keep the delicate gyro spinning for longer periods. Initially the wheel only functioned for five minutes before it finally tilted over and lost its equilibrium. But this was rapidly improved upon until, within the confines of its own inherent limitations, the gyro was able to maintain its functional life for the entire period required by the torpedo's engine.[3]

Obry's rights were promptly bought up by the men at Fiume, but the Royal Navy, conservative as ever, at first refused to adopt the new system on the grounds that its Woolwich-built torpedoes were sufficiently accurate for all likely operational requirements. As a claim it was quite valid for the Royal Navy had made a fetish of recording and averaging the results of hundreds of trial runs so that the characteristics of each individual torpedo could be calibrated and analyzed. Perfection, indeed, had been carried to such lengths that from 1883 onwards each torpedo had its own logbook in which was entered details of every test run and all the relevant data on deflection angles, rates of speed, strengths of wind, and directions of tidal flow.[4] Some admirals noted for their mania for perfection took the thing too far. Sir Robert Arbuthnot, for example, ordered a Court of Inquiry whenever a torpedo was lost during exercises. In retaliation, and behind the rear admiral's back of course, the flotilla officers under his command instituted a Court of Inquiry Cup, which was held by the wardroom of the ship with the highest score.[5]

It was soon apparent that the Obry gyroscope gave an even greater degree of accuracy than all the logbook data and Courts of Inquiry findings put together, and by 1898 Britain had reversed her decision by agreeing to manufacture her own gyros on payment of a £25 royalty to Whitehead for each unit built.[6] Although the Admiralty had divorced her torpedo production from Fiume a few years earlier, it was apparent that she could not afford to sever her links with Whitehead completely.

The United States Navy was, in this instance, one step ahead of her British cousin, for Washington had purchased the Obry rights from Whitehead two years earlier in 1896. The reason was not hard to discern. Having entered the conventional torpedo field late the United States Navy possessed a stock of only 200 Whiteheads and it was no great problem to call in and modify each weapon to incorporate the new Obry steering device. The Royal Navy, on the other hand, possessed more than 4,000 Fiume and Whitehead-based torpedoes, many of which were on board ships serving in the farthest corners of the world, and the organization required to carry out the necessary alterations and additions was, to say the least, a slightly more difficult problem.[7] Even so the complex process was completed by the end of 1900—an achievement that mirrors the efficiency of the Royal Navy at the turn of the century.

Before leaving the gyroscope it remains only to record that Schwartzkopffs, too, adopted the device when it was realized the advantages which their Fiume rivals had obtained from Obry's apparatus. And with Obry's rights bought out by Whiteheads they had to search for another design, which by good fortune they found fairly quickly. Chasing close behind Fiume's coattails Schwartzkopffs, too, were soon marketing a gyrostabilized model using the Kaselowski unit as an alternative to Obry's instrument.[8]

Having solved the steering problem, energies were now released in other directions—mainly towards increased speed and longer range. Quadruple-bladed propellers were tried out successfully but it was soon apparent that little further progress could be expected along these lines for the propellers only transmitted power and did not create it. Even so the four-blade unit was standardized in 1898 with the Mk IX and Mk X RGF 14-inch weapons.[9] Next the scientists turned their attentions to power units. The turbine, already used successfully by the Americans and well publicized on this side of the Atlantic following the *Turbinia's* flamboyant excursion during the Royal Fleet Review in honor of Queen Victoria's Diamond Jubilee, looked a likely answer, and experiments were carried out between 1897 and 1899 using a Parsons's cold-air turbine in a Woolwich 14-inch torpedo.[10] It failed to match the performance of the contemporary Brotherhood air engine, however, and although interest revived in 1900 when trials were held with another cold air impulse unit, this too proved disappointing and the Royal Navy lost interest in torpedo turbines leaving the field clear for the United States, where the Bliss-Leavitt design looked promising.

Recently discovered correspondence reveals that Whitehead was investigating the potential of turbine propulsion many years ahead of his rivals. And although he ultimately decided against developing the technology for torpedo use it is now apparent that he was experimenting with turbines as early as 1891—only five years after the first steam turbine had been invented by Charles Parsons. In a letter he reported: "I am working at the application of Dow's turbine engine to the driving of the torpedo. We have made a small turbine on his system which promises well but, on account of its greater velocity, 20–40,000 revolutions per minute, it requires gearing down tremendously."[11] By a strange coincidence Whitehead's American rival, Howell, was also using one of Dow's products, a steam winch, to spin the flywheel of his torpedo on launching.

Frank McDowell Leavitt used a Curtis turbine—also tested without much approval by the British[12]—and by November 1903 his weapon was sufficiently advanced for the U.S. Navy to order three hundred. It is interesting to note that Whitehead's original rights to manufacture in the United States, which he sold in 1891, were purchased, not by the government, but by Leavitt through his Brooklyn-based company Bliss & Williams—later known as E. W. Bliss & Company.[13] So it was not surprising that, aside from the Curtis propulsion unit, the Bliss-Leavitt torpedo contained all the standard features of the Fiume design, which, of course, may well have accounted for its rapid success. It is true to say, also, that all U.S. Navy torpedoes up to at least the Mark 48 can trace a direct line of development from these first Whitehead-based Bliss weapons.

Having discarded the turbine the Woolwich scientists turned back to the tried and tested radial engine. The three-cylinder Brotherhood had, by now, been developed to produce 50 horsepower and the pressure inside the air vessel increased to 1,400 pounds per square inch. In 1899 a four-cylinder radial unit was introduced by the Peterborough company which boosted the power output to 53 horsepower and a nickel-steel air vessel, fitted into the RGF Mk V 18-inch allowed air pressures to climb to 2,200 pounds per square inch.[14] But although each design modification incorporated some small additional improvement the experts were still only tinkering with existing ideas. What was needed was a breakthrough but no one knew in which direction the required breakthrough would lie.

The first glimmerings came, as such discoveries often do, quite by accident. In 1901 the Woolwich torpedo factory chanced to find that the warming effect of sea water on the cold air supplied from the compressed air chamber increased the speed of the weapon by half a knot.[15] It was a miniscule improvement in performance but it was highly significant. What it led to, and how it happened, will follow later in the torpedo story. For the moment the importance of the discovery must be regarded as more negative than positive for it marked the first major step in torpedo development in almost forty years that had not sprung, initially, from the brain of Robert White-head himself. It was an inevitable progress with the passing of time, but, nevertheless, there was a certain sadness in the fact that other hands were now taking over the control and development of the weapon he had nurtured for so long.

Whitehead's heyday gradually faded as the century drew to its close. The wild extravagancies of Paddockhurst, where, so it seemed, unscrupulous men and social hangers-on sought to part the old man from his money, proved too much for even his almost unlimited financial resources, and reluctantly he was forced to sell it and move to a smaller house at Leweston near Sherbourne in Dorset. From Leweston House he moved to Beckett Park, an old country house near Shrivenham in Berkshire, which he leased from Lord Barrington. And it was here that he lived out the rest of his days of retirement.[16]

Due to his deafness Robert was forced to lead a restricted social life but he never allowed his disability to interfere with his responsibilities as head of the family, and in 1892, he traveled to Vienna, where on 25 June, his twenty-year-old granddaughter, Marguerite Hoyos, married Count Herbert Bismarck at the Helvetian Reform Church. It was a splendid affair with an international guest list drawn from the very cream of European society and received considerable publicity.[17]

The Times noted the arrival in Vienna of Prince Otto von Bismarck—the old chancellor himself, driven from office by the young Kaiser Wilhelm II some four years earlier—father of the bridegroom; Mr. Robert Whitehead; Count Georg and Countess Alice Hoyos, the bride's parents; and many other notabilities. Two days later readers were informed that "the wedding breakfast [is] to be at the residence of Count Palffy and later on the bride and groom [will depart] for Schonhausen, the Bismarck residence, in Berlin which (is) to be their permanent home."[18]

Whitehead's health, however, was now slowly failing, although on occasions, he was still capable of demonstrating his old stubbornness. When the doctor limited him to one cigar per day and extracted the old man's solemn promise to obey the instruction, Whitehead promptly ordered a supply of enormously long cigars, which he proceeded to cut up into convenient lengths, and which, by coincidence, were exactly equal to that of an average cigar. He then impressed upon everyone that he was obeying his medical adviser's instructions to the letter and was, quite truthfully, only smoking one cigar per day.[19]

His addiction to cigars was said to have been responsible for an operation carried out on his mouth in 1890, and there was considerable concern in the family when, in 1893, further trouble occurred. "For some time past he had felt a little worried by a slight swelling and hardness under the tongue, and we were anxious also, as you may imagine, after that operation on his lip three years ago. But, thank God, Billiotti at once pronounced it to be nothing—a slight swelling of the salivary gland produced by irritation, or smoking—and added that Papa looked particularly healthy."[20]

Like most notabilities of the period, however, Robert took "the cure"—his choice of spa being Giesshubl. Whitehead clearly treated it all very seriously but Alice, as usual, could see the funny side of it. "I have been up at six every morning to go with him to the springs, a regulated little ceremony, where Pompeo [his personal manservant] walks in the queue and fills Papa's glass, and then brings it back to him gravely, after which Papa walks for 20 minutes with equal gravity, and the operation is (then) repeated."[21]

Despite the hard-learned lessons of Paddockhurst Robert continued to show a mania for buying large houses and Alice, in alarm, dashed off a hurried letter to James telling him that "he frightened Bertie and myself by saying he might buy a larger house in Dorset if he liked the county. But I thought it better to say nothing."[22]

This particular alarm passed and the family settled into Leweston House with a sigh of relief. But at Christmas 1893, Robert's hankerings for another place were renewed much to the consternation of his children. "Imagine—he told me on Christmas Day that he fully intends to buy another place—a much smaller one—if he can find one to suit him. I put it to him strongly that his losses over places in England [Springfield, Midhurst, Paddockhurst] had been, so to say, considerable. But any opposition makes him more obstinate so I left it. It is a curious mania."[23] Indeed Robert's urge to be always on the move, first exhibited in 1846, never left him—not even when he had found fame and fortune at the end of the proverbial rainbow.

Business worries, general financial problems connected with the disposal of Paddockhurst, and his continued loneliness made Robert more and more morose and he spent hours and hours just sitting in his favorite armchair reading novels and newspapers. Once again Georg Hoyos came to the rescue. Realizing that work was the only thing that could revive the old man's interest in life he found various jobs and projects that required plans and blueprints and persuaded Robert to help him with them. "Happily he has almost given up reading novels and now works all day—we have to drag him away from the drawing-board, which he has now placed in the window next the fireplace and finds much more comfortable. Georg had persuaded him that these drawings were absolutely necessary to the works. So he is very busy and looks all the better for it."[24]

Whitehead's engineering drawings were still of exquisite quality even though he was now well into his eightieth year and even *The Times* was constrained to comment that, despite his advanced age, "it was said that some of his [engineering] drawings . . . were of quite exceptional beauty and skill."[25] His deafness and other disabilities now acted as a restraint on his usually active mode of life and, apart from his continuingly keen interest in torpedo development, his pleasures were few and simple—a good book, a handful of choice cigars, and a game of cards. And, when the ever-faithful Georg was there to pit wits with him, his over-riding passion, dominoes.[26]

The unexpected death of his eldest son, John, in 1902 came as a terrible shock, for his work on the gyroscope showed that he had inherited much of his father's brilliance in engineering and applied mechanics. Georg Hoyos took over the day-to-day management but the extra burden of work on a man who himself was no longer young led to a breakdown in his health as well.

John's death, following so shortly after that of Whitehead's eldest daughter, Lady Frances Eleanor Drury, in 1900, took its toll and, a few months later, he suffered a severe stroke that left him semi-paralyzed and a permanent invalid. Alice Hoyos did her best to cope with the burdens thrown upon her but it was an onerous task trying to look after her aging father and an ailing husband at the same time. And it is testimony to the determination of the Whitehead character never to admit defeat that she succeeded in tending both patients in addition to all her other activities.[27]

But, while the two men most responsible for the successful creation of the torpedo lay sick behind the drawn blinds of an English country house, ten thousand miles away on the other side of the world, another group of equally determined men were planning to exploit the lethal power of Whitehead's weapon in a do-or-die clash with their hated enemy, imperial Russia.

Japan had won an overwhelming victory over the Chinese in the war of 1894. But, fearful that the rapidly growing empire of the new Japan might upset the balance of power in the Far East, the major European nations with interests in China intervened in the peace settlement and, in Japanese eyes at least, robbed her of the fruits of victory. The chief culprit was Russia, who by an astute piece of double-dealing, secured control of the valuable ice-free naval base of Port Arthur, a strategic dagger pointed at the heart of Japan, and despite continual diplomatic activities and long negotiations the To-kyo government was seemingly making no progress towards loosening the Russian's grip on the port.

Since her victory over China, Japan had been rapidly expanding her navy, and her switch from Schwartzkopff torpedoes to White-head's products was symptomatic of her determination to have the very best ships and weapons that money could buy in readiness for the coming conflict. In sheer weight of numbers the Russian fleet was greatly superior, but for reasons of geography the tsarist navy had to be divided three ways—in the Baltic, the Black Sea, and the Far East. Providing that the Japanese could achieve a complete victory against the Far Eastern fleet before the rest of the Russian Navy arrived in Asiatic waters there was a strong chance that the war could be won. But if victory was delayed and the Russians could mass their full naval strength, Japan stood no chance at all.

Surprise was therefore an essential part of the plan worked out by Admiral Heihachiro Togo—surprise to the point of treachery. And to achieve that surprise and to ensure the wholesale destruction of the Russian Far Eastern Squadron before the Baltic fleet could come to the rescue the Japanese decided to rely, not on gunnery but on torpe-does, Whitehead's torpedoes.

To put their enemy off guard the Japanese government had opened negotiations with Moscow in June 1903 with the express intention of solving the problem of Russian expansion in China and the rest of Asia by diplomatic means. The talks dragged on through the winter, until suddenly, on 5 February 1904, the leader of the Japanese delegation at St. Petersburg, Shin-ichiro Kurino, asked for his passport. Clearly something was in the wind, but in its accustomed state of lethargy, the Russian Navy made few preparations. A state of readiness was ordered at Port Arthur and two destroyers were instructed to patrol the seaward approaches to the anchorage. But their commanders were hamstrung by a warning not to open fire in any circumstances but to return to harbor and make a report if anything suspicious was observed.

On the same day, 5 February, Togo called his captains on board the *Mikasa* and briefly told them the Japanese war plan, adding: "We sail tomorrow and the enemy flies the Russian flag."[28]

The First, Second, and Third Torpedo-boat Flotillas were allocated for the assault on Port Arthur while the 4th and 5th headed for the Russian base at Dalny. On each boat the Whitehead torpedoes were checked with loving care while the combat crews carefully went through their firing drill.[29] The tubes trained slowly through a prescribed arc while crewmen Numbers Two and Three spun the handles to line the sights on the imaginary target.

"Stop!"

The tubes pointed towards their target.

"Starboard tube. Up port!"

The small door at the nose was triced up while crewman Number Four inserted the pistol through the opening and checked that the pistol was well screwed in. Then, removing the safety pin, he ensured that the cocking fan was running freely. Number One, the leading torpedoman (LTO), took the safety pin and closed the pistol door. As it snapped shut he shouted:

"Port tube—launch in!"

The four-man crew slid the Whitehead into the empty tube and pushed it home until its tail clicked against the side stop. The LTO removed the propeller clamps and checked that the propeller blades were in the starting position while Numbers Two and Three closed the rear door of the tube—the former having inserted the firing cartridge ready to blow the weapon from the tube on receipt of the executive command. He then checked that the electromagnet was in gear and that the port-locking gear was free. Then, and only then, the safety pin of the firing lever was withdrawn.

"Ready."

"Stand-by valve open."

The leading torpedoman cast his eyes quickly over the apparatus to confirm the shouted reports. Long hours of training made it automatic. Then he, in turn, reported back to the torpedo officer on the bridge on the internal telephone or, on the older boats, the voice pipe.

"Starboard tube, Ready!"

"Fire!"

The torpedo officer's thumb stabbed the firing key, his spoken command intended only to instruct the crew for manual firing should the electrical circuit fail, and there was a disciplined scramble to prepare for the next shot as the Whitehead hissed from the tube. Number Two replaced the safety pin in the firing lever, Number Three closed the standby valve, Number Two lowered the port and, with the aid of Number Three, secured it. The rear door was swung open and the crew closed up to manhandle another 716-pound, 14-inch weapon into its hollow womb. And then, in strict drillbook sequence, the whole firing procedure was repeated.

Only long and tedious hours of practice could produce the efficiency necessary for success in action. Only tight discipline could ensure that no matter what happened the torpedo crews would perform their functions like machines. Shells might explode over their heads, one of the crew might be cut to pieces by shrapnel in front of his comrade's eyes, but never once must a single step in the drill be overlooked. The smallest mistake could spell disaster for the torpedomen, the ship's company, and even the ship itself. But even that was of little account in comparison with the greatest sin of all. One minor error or one split-second fumble and *the torpedo might miss its target.*

A few hours before the final attack was due Togo called his young torpedo-boat commanders on board the *Mikasa* for briefing. One by one the little ships stopped, a boat was lowered, and the captain, sitting stiffly erect in the sternsheets, was whisked across to the massive hulk of the flagship to be piped aboard with the same deference and ceremony as that accorded to the commander of a 15,000-ton battlewagon.

Assembling the officers in his day cabin Togo quickly ran through the operational orders—orders which wisely left tactical initiative in the hands of the divisional commanders on the spot—and concluded his brief oration with a few pungent phrases that sum up, even today, the essence of torpedo warfare:

> Let me remind you that your attack must be delivered with the greatest possible vigour. For this is war and only those who act

without hesitation can hope for success. Our task, gentlemen, is quite simple. And all I ask of you is, be worthy of the trust I am putting in you, and for which I am responsible to His Majesty the Emperor.[30]

Champagne was brought in by the battleship's stewards, an effete touch that contrasted strangely with the austerity of the Japanese Navy, and toasts were exchanged between admiral and men. Then, after shaking hands with each commander individually, Togo watched them take to their boats and return to the waiting torpedo craft. A few hours later, in the early evening of 8 February, the executive signal fluttered to the *Mikasa*'s masthead.

Proceed to attack according to plan. I wish you success.

The ten torpedo boats swung away in the direction of Port Arthur. And, before the twilight mist swallowed them up, Captain Shojiro Asai, the commander of the First Division, signalled his reply from the *Shirakumo:*

I answer for our success.[31]

CHAPTER 11

His Fame Was in All Nations Round About

Seaman Bolovdin at the forward lookout position in the bows of the destroyer *Rastoropni* was the first man in the Russian fleet to spot the Japanese approaching. It was a pitch-black night with temperatures below freezing and there was a thin glaze of ice on the steel-plated deck where the sea spray had hardened and frozen.

The officer of the watch swept the sector with his night glasses as Bolovdin made his report. The dark shapes—he counted ten of them— were veering away, for Captain Asai, too, had spotted the Russian sentinels and was cautiously taking avoiding action to maintain the element of surprise. Hesitating for a moment the Russian officer gnawed his lip with indecision as the mysterious shapes vanished into the darkness. Then, flipping the lid of the speaking tube, he reported to the *Rastoropni's* captain. The *Beztrashni*, their running mate, had also spotted the intruders and a shaded signal lamp flashed from her bridge. Then, in strict obedience to orders, the two Russian destroyers reversed tracks and headed back towards the anchorage to report what they had seen.

Although the element of surprise still remained with the Japa-

nese, their brush with the Russian scouts and Asai's sudden altera-
tion of course had broken their tightly disciplined formation. And in
the pitch black of the February night they stood no chance of linking
up again. From that moment onwards it would be every captain for
himself. It needed little more than an hour to moonrise. And in that
time they knew they must get in among their enemy if surprise was to
be maintained. Any form of warning and the attack would be doomed
to massed suicide as the little torpedo boats came face-to-face with
the might of the Russian Pacific Fleet.

Fortunately for the men of Nippon the Russian Navy was as
inefficient as the Russian Army. Despite the sudden cessation of the
St. Petersburg negotiations and all the other tiny, yet significant, signs
of Japan's treacherous intentions, the Russian ships slept snugly at
their anchors. Antitorpedo nets were still secured, there was no ammunition broken out alongside the guns, the ships still carried their
normal peacetime lights, and their crews slept easily in gently
swinging hammocks. Only the guard-ship *Pallada* showed any signs
of life, but even then, there was a lack of purpose and cohesion in the
silvered beams of her searchlights sweeping fitfully across the black
rim of the horizon. Not even the arrival of the two destroyers with their
alarming reports of unidentified ships approaching the harbor
aroused the *Pallada* to readiness, for observing the strict etiquette of
the tsarist navy, certain procedures had to be followed before the
junior officers commanding the destroyers could deliver their urgent
warning to the majestic importance of a full-blown post captain.

But by then it was too late!

Captain Asai's First Division, led by the *Shirakumo*, had managed to hold its formation and now fired at the guard ship from a
range of 700 yards. One Whitehead took the *Pallada* in the belly on
her port side, smashing into her midships coal bunker with a tremendous explosion that set the coal on fire. Following close behind their
leader the other three ships of the First Division wheeled into position.
A salvo of Whiteheads splashed into the water, quickly picked up
their running depth, and arrowed straight and true at the anchored
ranks of Russian ironclads.

The explosion on board the *Pallada* woke the sleeping Russian
sailors with surprising speed. Grabbing whatever clothing came to
hand they rushed to their gun and searchlight stations and, within
minutes, the air was torn with the whining screech of shells. Others

ran towards the booms holding the antitorpedo nets and the winches screamed as they were swung out. From the forts on shore the gun batteries opened up and the loud boom of their heavy calibers joined the sharp crack of the quick-firers aboard the ironclads.

Two more explosions shattered the night. The battleship *Retvizan* shuddered as a Whitehead struck her on the port side just forward of the mast and, moments later, the *Tsarevitch* rolled violently as an exploding torpedo ripped open the magazine bulkhead and flooded the steering compartment. Lurid flames lit the sky as the torpedoes struck home and the Russian gunfire doubled in intensity. Captain Asai's First Division, their task well done, swung away in a wide arc and raced back to the safety of the main Japanese fleet prowling the horizon a few miles away.

The light of the rising moon made things more difficult for the boats of the subsequent divisions. Thrown out of formation during the approach to Port Arthur they dashed in singly or in pairs, braving the gunfire until they were close enough to discharge their torpedoes at point-blank range. But sheer bravery was not enough.[1] The net cutters fitted to the Japanese weapons proved inadequate to pierce the Russian defenses and most of the torpedoes ended their careers with their noses strangled in the formidable meshes of the ironclad's nets like fish trapped in a trawl. Of the nineteen torpedoes fired that night only three found their marks. The remaining sixteen either missed altogether or tangled in the net defenses. And although three of the Russian ships had been hit and severely damaged none had been sunk. As the reports trickled back to the *Mikasa* Togo must have begun to wonder whether, perhaps, Whitehead's wonderful weapon had been somewhat overrated.

Despite the lack of material success, however, the torpedo had done its job. The attack on Port Arthur so shattered Russian morale that, from then onwards, the issue of the war was never seriously in doubt. With three ships crippled and imaginations distorted by the sight of the exploding torpedoes, the Russian fleet was frozen into immobility at the precise moment when the strength of seapower was needed to stem the Japanese troop landings in Korea. Imperial Russia still had sufficient ships at Port Arthur to sail out and, given a modicum of luck, defeat Togo's fleet. But the torpedo had broken her resolve and her will to win.

The torpedo, however, could also turn traitor. In one sortie from

Port Arthur on 8 March 1904, the Russian destroyer *Steregustchy*, detached from the main squadron, found herself cut off by Togo's Third Squadron. She fought like a cornered animal until her decks were littered with the dead and dying. Only her forward quick-firer remained in action. Then a chance shell landed square on her torpedo tubes and the Whitehead inside detonated with such force that the destroyer was literally torn apart.

There was considerable disappointment among naval experts over the relative lack of success shown by the torpedo in these early stages of the war. But experience in the use of the weapon under conditions of modern combat was sadly lacking and the tactical use of torpedo boats was also still in its infancy. From a technical point of view the weapons were mostly of the older Fiume, or even old Schwartzkopff, patterns and few were fitted with gyroscopes. And it was probably this lack of directional stability that contributed to their failure to hit moving targets. Several apologists tried to explain away the poor results by blaming the Japanese for failing to operate their weapons properly. For example, in one instance it was said that many of the torpedoes caught in the Port Arthur net defenses during the first attack still had their safety pins in place and could not therefore detonate their war-heads. Later investigation, however, showed that the so-called "safety pins" were, in fact, part of the net cutting device fitted over the nose of the torpedo and that, in all instances, the detonators were correctly primed.[2]

Admiral Sir Cyprian Bridge was one such critic. "Perhaps nothing stands out more clearly in the campaign," he wrote in 1905, "than the insignificance of the results effected by locomotive torpedoes."[3] And even a modern historian, Peter Bethell, was moved to comment: "The subsequent course of the Russo-Japanese War did not reveal the torpedo in a favourable light."[4]

Writing in 1907 Commander Murray Sueter, one of Britain's pioneer submarine commanders and, later, flag officer of the Royal Navy's aviation branch, advanced numerous reasons for the torpedo's failure—adjustments were insufficiently accurate; firing took place at too great a range; the flash of the powder impulse used to discharge torpedoes from deck tubes gave the Russians sufficient warning, during night attacks, to turn away; water leaking into the warhead through the net-cutter gland made the explosives wet. And apart from these alleged technical faults there were a number of instances where the torpedo froze inside the tube and could not be fired. British sailors added a further theory—that Japanese torpedoes were built to run sideways!

By a strange quirk of fate it was the mine—the static underwater weapon that had been known as a "torpedo" in pre-Whitehead days—that had most success, and both moored and floating mines claimed many times more victims than the "fish" torpedo. Admiral Makarov was lost when his flagship the *Petropavlovsk* struck two mines while setting out on a sortie from Port Arthur on 13 April, and Togo saw his own battleship strength reduced by 30 percent when the *Hatzudze* and *Yashima* both sank on the same day—15 May—after running into an uncharted minefield. The disasters of the day were completed later that evening when the destroyer *Akutsuki*, a veteran of the first Port Arthur attack, suffered a similar fate. In many ways the evidence of war seemed to indicate that mines were a more effective way of blowing holes in enemy bottoms than torpedoes.

After an abortive sortie on 23 June the Russian Pacific Squadron finally put to sea on 10 August with the intention of forcing a way through to Vladivostock where it could await the arrival of Rozhestvensky's fleet, which, incidentally, had still not left the Baltic and was not destined to do so until the following October. Togo swooped after the Russians and the early stages of the battle comprised a long drawn-out stern chase in which an ability to stoke the boilers faster than the enemy was of greater consequence than fighting power.

The battle, when it was finally joined just before sunset, resolved into a gunnery duel in which torpedoes played no part at all. Admiral Vitheft's force was badly beaten—the Russian commander being killed by a direct hit on his flagship, the *Cesarevitch*, which, when the smoke and confusion had cleared, left only his leg behind on the shattered deck—and Togo appeared to have his demoralized enemy at his mercy. But the threat of the distant fleet still being prepared in the Baltic meant that he must continue to husband his forces, and rather than face the chance of incurring losses to gain a victory, he allowed the scattered Russian ships to scurry for shelter. Some retreated back to Port Arthur, others were interned by the Chinese and the French. A few escaped northwards only to be run down and destroyed by Japanese cruisers. The Battle of the Yellow Sea was over. And, yet again, the torpedo had failed to exert any influence over its result. It was beginning to look as if the critics of "the Devil's device" were correct in their contempt for the weapon.

On 15 August, less than a week after the battle, in the peaceful calm of Beckett Park, Count Georg Hoyos died—worn out from the exertions of the previous few years during which, since John's death, he had virtually run the Whitehead empire single-handed. It was a trying time for both the family and the company. The disappointing results achieved by torpedoes in the war that was still raging on the far side of Asia meant that Silurifico Whitehead was about to face a crisis of confidence. And its fate rested in the hands of the first and last of the triumvirate, Robert Whitehead himself, now over eighty years of age and a permanent invalid following a stroke three years earlier. Indeed he was so ill that, on medical advice, he had not been told the conflict between Russia and Japan in the Far East.[5]

Captain Edwin Gallwey, the general manager of the Weymouth factory and acknowledged as "second only to Robert Whitehead" in his knowledge of the torpedo and torpedo warfare, assumed virtual control of the company under Robert's nominal chairmanship, and aided by a brilliant young Scottish engineer, A. E. Jones, who had been a close engineering associate of the Whiteheads since 1886, he pressed forward with a research program the results of which, he hoped, would answer the growing band of critics.[6]

There was still one final battle to be fought in the Far East, however, a battle in which, at last, the torpedo could claim a modicum of success. But before it took place there was a further series of raids on the remains of the Russian fleet still bottled up in Port Arthur. In the course of five consecutive nights in December, Japanese torpedo boats stormed the defenses with consummate skill and courage. Yet of the 150 torpedoes fired only *four* found their target. And although three of these successful shots finished off the tsarist battleship *Sevastopol* it cost Togo two more of his precious torpedocraft.

This time it was not wholly the fault of the torpedoes. In the eternal struggle between offense and defense the scales, at that point of time, were tilted in favor of the defenders and the Russian torpedo nets undoubtedly saved many of their ships. Two attacks were made on 11 December without success and the next night another flotilla, under the command of Lieutenant Commander Chugo Arakawa, launched six Whiteheads. Three struck the nets of the *Otvazhi* but failed to explode, two more lost depth control and sank, while the sixth was discovered next morning trapped impotently in the protective netting.

Just before dawn a second flotilla dashed in with a similar disappointing lack of success, and as the sun was rising, a third attack was mounted using two tiny picket boats reminiscent of the pioneer torpedo boats of the 1870s. Both got to within 100 yards of the *Sevastopol* under very heavy fire and two torpedoes were launched—one exploding against the bows of the battleship and the other tangling itself in the nets with negative results. A mass attack on the thirteenth yielded no joy to the Japanese either, and the next night Togo sent in no fewer than twenty-five torpedo boats in an effort to overwhelm his enemy by sheer weight of numbers. Over sixty torpedoes were fired of which only four came anywhere near the battleship and only one caused any damage. Even more disconcerting was the fact that sixteen Whiteheads ended up on the beach without detonating.

The final attack, spearheaded by Lieutenant Commander Seki's Fourteenth Flotilla, was launched in the early hours of 16 December. One torpedo struck the destroyer *Storoshevoi* and damaged her so badly she had to be beached, while the remainder streaked towards *Sevastopol*. The first torpedoes blew enormous holes in the net defenses and the Whiteheads following in their wake passed straight through the gaps. Two more explosions echoed across the harbor and the *Sevastopol* began to sink.

But despite this deserved success a number of the torpedoes again failed to explode and there certainly seemed to be something amiss with the Japanese weapons. Their directional stability appeared to be satisfactory for there were many instances of torpedoes striking the nets surrounding the targets, and yet, over and over again, they failed to detonate. As on previous occasions a number of reasons were advanced for the failure of the Whiteheads—bad maintenance, frozen tubes and release gear, a seepage of water into the warheads via the net cutters, or simply a failure to remove the safety pins. Even Togo, in his official report on the first assault on Port Arthur, was forced to concede: "The torpedo is an uncertain weapon at best."[7] And it was this very uncertainty that largely contributed to the problem.

Togo had told his torpedo-boat captains repeatedly that success at Port Arthur *must* be obtained before the Baltic reinforcements arrived. During the initial attacks the torpedo vessels had, in most cases, fired at long range—and missed. As a result it is highly probable that the Japanese torpedo boats approached their targets *too* close in order to guarantee a hit. As one officer wrote to a friend shortly before the torpedo flotillas attacked the Russian fleet at Tsushima six months later: "We ought to be able to close within twenty yards of the target before she is sunk. . . ." One result of such deliberately suicidal tactics was to reduce the running distance of the torpedo and this meant that the safety fans had insufficient time to spin down and prime the warhead thus leaving the weapons uncocked when they struck the enemy's ships. Such a theory—and it is admittedly unproven—would account for the numerous reports of the safety pins still being in place. The suicidal bravery of the Japanese sailor is an accepted fact today following the experiences of the Second World War. But in modern technological warfare such bravery can, on occasions, be a disadvantage.

The final great sea battle of the war, Tsushima, was fought on 27 May 1905, when Togo's ships met up with Rear-Admiral Zinovi Rozhestvensky's Second Pacific Squadron, which had spent nearly six months steaming halfway round the world from the Baltic.

Togo's brilliance wrested victory from the Russians in the very earliest stages of the action, and for most of the day, the battle was limited to a merciless gunnery duel that smashed and battered the Russian fleet into a collection of useless hulks and it was only in the later stages of the fight that the torpedo was allowed to show its paces.

Fire opened at 2:08 P.M. and by 3 o'clock the battle was virtually over. The Russian formation was completely broken and Togo's ships circled for the kill. At 3:10 P.M. the battleship *Oslabia* turned turtle and sank while both the *Alexander III* and *Borodino* were flaming wrecks. Rozhestvensky's flagship, the *Suvorov*, was also in a bad way with her steering gear destroyed and out of control. Two attacks by Japanese torpedo boats were, however, successfully driven off for the Russian warship still had sharp teeth despite her wounds. But the end was not long delayed. Commander Fujimoto's flotilla dashed in for a third attack. "Although reduced to a still-burning cinder, and although she had endured so many attacks and had been a target for our whole fleet; although, finally, she could now fire only one small gun, this proud vessel continued firing. . . . In the end, at about 7:22 P.M., and after being attacked twice more by our torpedo-boats, she began to settle and, majestically, sank out of sight."[8]

This last attack, carried out by the Eleventh Flotilla, scored at least two torpedo hits and these, coupled with earlier damage, proved fatal. Rozhestvensky, however, had not gone down with his ship.

Seriously wounded and unconscious he had been taken off the flagship some time earlier by a Russian destroyer.

The *Ural*, too, was finished off by a torpedo fired from one of Togo's battleships and by dusk both the *Borodino* and *Alexander III* had gone down as a result of the devastating destruction wrought by Togo's big guns. As darkness fell upon the sea the remains of the Russian fleet fled northwards, scattered and demoralized, seeking the safety of their northern base.

Deciding that a night action involved too many risks for his battleships, Togo sent his torpedo boats off in hunting packs to ride down and sink the pathetic remnants of the short-lived Second Pacific Squadron. It proved a rewarding chase and a complete, if late, justification of Robert Whitehead's torpedo.

The 8,889-ton battleship *Sisoi Veliki* was torpedoed and so seriously damaged that she had to be scuttled next morning; the 8,500-ton armored cruiser *Admiral Nakhimoff* was also hit and sank the following morning, the tsar's ensign still proudly flying from her forepeak; the battleship *Navarin*, struck by four torpedoes on both port and starboard beams, sank with the loss of all but three of her crew; and the armored cruisers *Vladimir Monomakh* and *Dmitri Donskoi* also succumbed the next day after being struck by Whiteheads during the night actions. "The officers commanding the Japanese torpedoboats, aware of the day's results, were afire to do deeds of prowess in their turn. They hurled their ships upon their wounded prey, launching their torpedoes, returning time after time to the attack, and charging straight into the beams of the Russian searchlights."[9]

In exchange for these overwhelming successes the Japanese lost three of their torpedo boats, Numbers 34, 35, and 69, all falling victim to Russian gunfire. The Battle of Tsushima, indeed, was proof to the world that the Whitehead torpedo was a fearsome weapon which, when properly used, could destroy the mightiest of ironclads. And the little torpedo boats, often numbered and not even honored with a name, could, in the right circumstances, take on and sink an opponent many times their own size. As Lieutenant Armstrong put it:

Only a number, not even a name,
How shall posterity hear of my fame?
Perchance it may still live, after the grave,
In the name of an ironclad under the wave.[10]

Getting a quart into a pint pot—the interior of a Whitehead torpedo in 1904.

Togo's victory at Tsushima virtually ended the war. Russia had been annihilated at sea and her armies beaten on land. Japan, too, was nearly bankrupt by the cost of the war, and so when the United States intervened and suggested peace talks on 9 June 1905, both sides acceded willingly and the war was ended, in Japan's favor, by the Treaty of Portsmouth, signed on 23 August 1905. The torpedo, that device of the Devil, had played a substantial part in securing the Japanese victory. And the emperor's admirals took careful note of its offensive power for future reference.

Just a few months later, on Tuesday, 14 November 1905, Robert

Robert Whitehead at Paddockhurst—the dream that nearly bankrupted
him. (Photograph courtesy of Mrs. Mary Fletcher.)

Whitehead died at Beckett Park. The man who hated war and yet who had created one of its most potent weapons had lived just long enough to see his invention vindicated by Japan's ruthless exploitation of its capabilities. But the knowledge did not make him happy. To him the torpedo was a masterpiece of scientific creation, engineering skill, and Man's mechanical ingenuity. That it had been responsible for the deaths of thousands of men in the Russo-Japanese War grieved him. It was neither a pose nor an attempt to assuage a troubled conscience for Robert Whitehead sincerely believed that his torpedo would be a deterrent to war and not a means of making it more frightful.[11]

His gross estate was valued for probate purposes at £452,407 (£268,339 net)—several millions of pounds in terms of today's money—and in addition to gifts and other settlements made *inter vivos*, and the assets mentioned in earlier chapters, the Probated Will also revealed that Robert owned two properties in the City of London, 57½ Old Broad Street and 7 Austin Friars, as well as a landed estate in Austria-Hungary, the Campagna Zandonati.[12]

His funeral was held at Worth's beautiful old parish church only a few yards from the gates of his former home at Paddockhurst, and a large congregation of mourners led by his two surviving sons, James and Bertie, and his devoted daughter, Countess Alice Hoyos, followed the cortege to the grave. Surmounting the coffin was a torpedo made from white flowers.[13]

His death was reported in almost every newspaper and journal in the world, and in Britain especially, attention was drawn to the fact that he had died without being honored by the country of his birth. The comments in *The Times* were typical of the nation's feelings:

> Singularly enough, we would even say quite unaccountably, [his invention] has brought him no public recognition in the form of honours or distinctions conferred in his native country. Of foreign decortions and distinctions he received abundance, but he must have felt, as we believe he did, that the neglect of his own country was thereby rendered the more conspicuous.[14]

But Robert Whitehead did not need the gaudy baubles of civic honors to make his name endure. As the inscription on his tombstone at Worth states in all truth:

His fame was in all nations round about.[15]

This Insidious and Somewhat Sneaking Weapon

Whitehead's death placed the company in a precarious position. Until then it had always been a family concern with Captain Gallwey, the general manager of the Weymouth factory, the only outsider with any form of executive responsibility. Now Gallwey was the only one left of the team and it was clear that, sooner or later, the firm would have to pass into the control of other hands. The key question was—*whose?*

The old Silurifico Whitehead, founded in 1872 by Robert and Georg, had been a partnership. The two men had run the affairs of the torpedo works personally for more than twenty years until, when Robert's health began to show wigns of deteriorating, his eldest son, John, was admitted to the partnership. By 1905 both John Whitehead and Georg Hoyos were dead, and mindful that Robert was also seriously ill it was decided to incorporate the firm as a limited liability company under Hungarian law. The issued share capital amounted to 7,350,000 Austrian crowns, each share having a par value of 10,000 crowns, and the entire holding was vested in Robert Whitehead and other members of the family.[1] Robert's death did not affect

176

this position, for Captain Gallwey had the technical expertise to maintain the firm's high standards of engineering, and to help share the burden of responsibility, Georg's eldest son, Edgar, gave up a promising career in the Austrian diplomatic service to take over as general manager at Fiume.[2]

But then, as if the deaths of John in 1902, Georg in 1904, and Robert in 1905 were not enough, fate struck the company another savage blow when Captain Gallwey died in 1906. In the space of four years the entire engineering brains behind the firm had been wiped out and there was no one left with sufficient technical expertise to keep the company going.

The vultures gathered quickly, for Silurifico Whitehead was a golden goose to the profit-hungry investors in the violent-death business, and the accelerating arms race that was sweeping Europe promised rich dividends to whoever controlled the leaderless company. The Fiume works had been completely rebuilt in 1898 and Weymouth, too, was a new, modern factory. Both were fitted with the very latest machinery and employed the cream of the world's torpedo experts. Even more important, their order books were full. Basil Zaharoff was interested—he held a single share—and so were several other leading European armament manufacturers. So, too, was the British government. They had no intention of seeing so valuable a property fall into unfriendly hands.

According to Sir Trevor Dawson, at that time managing director of Vickers, he received an urgent message late one evening in 1906 to go to the Admiralty at once. On his arrival he was informed that the Whitehead Company was for sale, and a strong hint was dropped that perhaps Vickers might be interested in buying it. There was no suggestion that the government should purchase the shares—even the most profitable of private concerns might suddenly fail and it would not do to risk public money in such a venture—but, as Whitehall saw it, there was absolutely no reason why a patriotic British company should not take the chance.[3]

It was a tempting opportunity and the government's sources of information seemed to be one step ahead of the other parties interested in acquiring the torpedo company—the fact that Robert's second son, James Beethom Whitehead, was working at the British embassy in Berlin at the time may not have been entirely coincidental. Dawson called an extraordinary meeting of the Vickers directors and they had little hesitation in making their decision. Their main rival, Sir W. G. Armstrong, Whitworth & Company Ltd was also interested, having been prodded, no doubt, by the same group of civil servants who had interviewed Dawson and who believed in backing their chances both ways, and the two firms agreed to buy control of the Whitehead Company between them. Each took 184 shares leaving the remaining 367 shares in the hands of the Whitehead family. Control cost them around £400,000 (a considerable figure in 1906) but it proved to be worth every penny.[4]

On completion of the purchase the Weymouth factory was split away from the Fiume concern and registered as a separate company under English law on 1 January 1907 under the style of Whitehead & Company (Weymouth) Ltd and it was soon building weapons for the Royal Navy again in addition to its own fast expanding export market.

The Russo-Japanese War had spotlighted the deficiencies of torpedo design. Depth keeping was satisfactory thanks to the pendulum device which, although now over thirty years old, was still the basic component of the apparatus, and Obry's gyroscope ensured directional accuracy. The drawbacks, and they were important ones, were lack of range and a speed inadequate for modern war conditions. The short range meant a suicidally close approach to the target during an attack while the relatively slow speed enabled the erstwhile victim to take avoiding action. Development was therefore concentrated on overcoming these deficiencies—Tell Jones working on the projects at Fiume with another team studying the problems in England.

The weapon, meanwhile, was continually growing in size. The Royal Gun Factory produced their first 21-inch torpedo in 1908 while the Weymouth factory brought out *its* pattern a year later. The first 21-inch models proved disappointing, however, and the Whitehead Company had to produce a Mark II when the bugs were finally ironed out some months later. The German Navy, too, was seeking a larger weapon and, in 1906, adopted their famous G-type 500-millimeter (19.7-inch) torpedo carrying a 440-pound warhead with a range of 6,560 yards at 36 knots—a formidable rival, indeed, to the Whitehead and Woolwich designs of the period. The 21-inch, though, was not the biggest torpedo to be built up to that time for a few years earlier the Fiume factory had been experimenting with a 27.5-inch weapon for the Japanese Navy although technical problems led to a curtailment of further development. And even earlier, in 1898, they had built a 24-inch model for the Tokyo government. These will be examined in more detail in chapter 15.

The Japanese, in fact, were pioneers of the torpedo in many ways. On one celebrated occasion they fitted an Antoinette internal combustion engine into a Whitehead, which yielded a range of more than 180 miles at 30 knots. But for obvious reasons the idea was not pursued. The Japanese, too, were present when Sir W. G. Armstrong, Whitworth & Company Ltd demonstrated their "Elswick" heater for the first time in 1905—a year before they became joint majority shareholders in the Whitehead Company. The discovery that even the slight warming effect of the sea had an effect on a torpedo's performance has been noted earlier, and following up this line of research, Armstrong took out patents on their heater in 1904.[5] The following year Fiume produced a slightly different system known as the Whitehead heater. Without going into technical details Armstrong's engine used a "dry" heat system while the Whitehead version was based on the "wet" principle. The increased inlet temperatures resulting from the use of heaters—up to 1,000 degrees Fahrenheit—led to the adoption of a new four-cylinder radial engine designed, inevitably, by Brotherhoods of Peterborough.

Even the original Elswick heater, when fitted to a Fiume 18-inch Mk 3 produced an increase in speed of 9 knots and it was obvious to other designers that something on these lines was the answer to the range and speed problems highlighted by the late war. The Royal Navy was not far behind either and in 1908 the Royal Gun Factory introduced their own simplified heater system based on the designs of Engineer Lieutenant Hardcastle.[6] Examination of the appendixes will demonstrate the tremendous leap forward in performance which resulted from the adoption of "wet" heater engines, and for all intents and purposes, this was the final stage of development prior to the commencement of World War One. Unlike its British and Fiume counterparts the Bliss heater, which was developed at around the same time, worked on alcohol fuel and thus fell into the "dry" category—and a similar system was also favored by German engineers.

Vickers, working jointly with Armstrong Whitworths, also injected new life into the Fiume factory when it was decided to use its yards for submarine construction. Vickers, of course, had a monopoly of the Royal Navy's submarine building program at this time as a result of their agreement with the Electric Boat Company of New York and it was only a natural progression to expand these activities to the new branch company in the Adriatic. Whiteheads began by building two boats based on the well-tried designs of the Electric Boat Company,[7] but keeping character with their founder and eager as ever to experiment and break new ground, they also constructed another underwater vessel based on the Koster-Hay pattern.[8]

Three vessels, the *Havmanden*, *Havfruen*, and *Thetis*, were built for Denmark in 1911–12 and the Danes constructed a further eight boats to the Koster-Hay design at Copenhagen under licence from the Fiume concern. Holland, too, adopted the Whitehead pattern submarine and K. M. de Schelde built five vessels at Flushing for the Royal Netherlands Navy. As their first underwater boat had been based on the ubiquitous Electric Boat Company design it must be assumed that the Dutch found Whitehead's vessel superior to the original Holland design which EBC had pioneered.

It was only natural in the circumstances that Austria should also turn to Fiume for submarines. Whitehead's reputation as a marine engineer had never been forgotten and his old admirer, the emperor Francis Josef, was still ruler of the Hapsburg empire. Laid down in 1908, the first two submarines built for the Austrian Navy were based on EBC's Holland design. Numbered the *U-5* and *U-6*, they were completed the following year and carried three 17.7-inch torpedo tubes and were capable of submerging in three and a half minutes—a commendable time in those early days.

Fiume's venture into submarine building, especially the construction of the *U-5*, was to add another strange twist to the remarkable story of Robert Whitehead. Of the many millions of people destined to enjoy the Hollywood musical *The Sound of Music* only a few realized that there was a connection between the music of Rodgers and Hammerstein and the brutal crash of an exploding torpedo. Yet over a span of three generations there *was* a link between the two. And that link was the *U-5*.

In 1908 the Imperial and Royal Austro-Hungarian Navy had assigned a promising young officer, Kapitänleutnant (Lieutenant Commander) Georg Ritter von Trapp, to the Fiume factory to study the design and construction of submarines and torpedoes at first hand. Born at Zara in 1880 Georg was a handsome young naval officer and, like Count Hoyos, soon set the hearts of the Whitehead girls fluttering. Although John had died in 1902 his in-laws, the Breunner family, and his children were still living at the Villa Whitehead overlooking the torpedo works and it did not take long for his eldest daughter, Agathe, to notice the smartly uniformed naval officer. It was almost an exact repetition of her Aunt Alice's whirlwind romance with Georg Hoyos some forty years earlier, and the two young lovers were soon inseparable companions at the parties and balls that made up the social season of Trieste, Pola, and Fiume.[9]

The following year, 1909, Agathe Whitehead performed the launching ceremony for the newly completed *U-5* and, standing close to her on the flag-bedecked platform, was the Kapitänleutnant. They were obviously very much in love, but in those days, betrothals and engagements took an unhurried course and it was not until 1911— when Agathe was 21—that they finally obtained consent to get married. The wedding took place at Fiume, and after a brief honeymoon, Robert's granddaughter moved to her husband's villa at Pola and settled down to the life of a naval officer's wife.

Georg's appointment to the Whitehead factory came to an end in due time and he was sent off to command *Torpedo-boat 52*, where he quickly demonstrated his professional ability. He stood high in the esteem of his senior officers and it was apparent that, barring accidents, the young Kapitänleutnant was destined for a top place in the Austrian Navy. To give him further experience, the Admiralty appointed him as captain of the submarine *U-5*—the boat which his wife had launched before their marriage.

But unfortunately for Georg his promising future vanished like a desert mirage when Austria lost the war and had to surrender her coastal provinces to Italy and Yugoslavia. Without a coastline to defend she needed no navy and Georg found himself out of work in a demoralized and defeated country.

Agathe stood by him valiantly during this difficult period of readjustment, showing that same fortitude in the face of adversity that both her grandmother, Frances Whitehead, and her aunt, Alice Hoyos, had demonstrated at moments of crisis. It was some consolation to the von Trapps that they had a large and happy family even though the multitude of mouths to feed must have caused considerable worry. Then tragedy struck, for in the epidemic that swept across central Europe in 1922, Agathe died of diphtheria at the early age of thirty-two, leaving Georg, deprived of his chosen profession and with few prospects for the future, to bring up their family of five children without the help and comfort of a mother. Georg was at first distraught with grief but he pulled himself together. Faced with the problem of looking after the children he engaged a governess, who, among other things, taught them to sing. Georg ultimately married the governess, Maria Augusta, and she, too, bore him several children. Before long the musical talents of the family brought them worldwide fame as *The Trapp Family Singers* and their unusual story, recounted by Maria von Trapp in her book of the same name, became the basis of the Hollywood film *The Sound of Music*—five of the children being, of course, great-grandchildren of Robert Whitehead.[10]

The launching of von Trapp's submarine, the *U-5*, was one more incident in the frantic scramble of the armaments race that led, ultimately, to the Great War and to the carnage that followed—a carnage in which Whitehead's weapon was to play no small part. The torpedo had, by then, been accepted by the majority of experts as one of the supreme tools of sea power and the addition of the gyroscope and the "wet" heater engine had turned it into a weapon feared by all who dared to venture to sea in time of war. Some, like Admiral Sir Percy Scott, were convinced that the power of the big gun would be the decisive factor in any future war at sea, using the example of the Russo-Japanese War to prove their point. But Scott, and other like-minded critics, had overlooked two important points. Neither side had operational submarines in use and, in 1905, the torpedo was still sadly lacking in performance.

Admiral Sir Reginald Bacon summed up the blindness of the gunnery experts.

> During the interval between the two battles [Tsushima and Jutland] the Whitehead torpedo had, year by year, gained in efficiency. It had extended its 800-yard range of action in 1905 to 10,000 yards and even more in 1916 and its explosive effect had been increased four-fold. This insidious and somewhat sneaking weapon had, in the intervening years altered the whole of naval tactics, for its deadly menace had forced the effective fighting range of ships up from the 3,000 yards or so at Tsushima to some fourteen, sixteen, or even eighteen thousand yards at Jutland . . . this brought about the development of long-range gunnery.[11]

Bacon developed his argument further by claiming that although gunnery would still be the supreme arbiter in a fleet action the "decision had to be obtained outside of torpedo range, otherwise the action would merely have developed into a gamble in which skill and training would have been sacrificed to sinkings by the chance adventures of torpedo attack."[12] History was to demonstrate that skill was just as important as chance in torpedo warfare but, even so, Bacon had made a valid point. Long-range gunnery came about not by the choice of the gunnery experts but because the threat of the torpedo made close-range fighting too dangerous! The chicken may have come before the egg, but in this instance, the egg had the power to keep the chicken at a safe distance.

The British commander-in-chief, Sir John Jellicoe, had a healthy respect for the torpedo and, although himself a gunnery man, admitted:

> The reasons which make it necessary to be more cautious when dealing with under-water weapons than with gun attack are the greater damage which one torpedo will cause, damage which may well be fatal to many ships . . . with the gun it is usually different; a ship which is being heavily hit can—if her own defensive powers will not save her by crushing the fire of the enemy—so maneuver as to derange temporarily the accuracy of that fire.[13]

But unfortunately Jellicoe's tidy mind dwelt too much on the theoretical potential of the torpedo and led him to conclusions which, in hindsight, were at best alarmist and at worst ridiculous:

> In the case of a British line of eight battleships attacked "beam-on" the chances of a hit for torpedoes which reach the British line may be assessed roughly at seven to nine, taking the length of a ship as 600 feet and the distance from the bow of one ship to the bow of her next astern . . . as 1,500 feet, thus giving a total length of *ships* of 4,800 feet and the total interval between them as 6,300 feet.[14]

So much for the theoretical basis of his argument. His conclusions were even more astonishing: "A German destroyer usually carries six torpedoes and at long ranges one may calculate the chances of hits *on the above reasoning as between three and four per destroyer*, provided all the torpedoes are correctly fired . . . and provided that the British ships can take no effective steps to avoid torpedoes."[15] As the German High Seas Fleet had an establishment of eighty-eight destroyers they could, on Jellicoe's calculations and assuming that avoiding action was not possible, wipe out the entire British battle-line in one single attack.

This, then, was the tactical view of the torpedo at the time the Great War broke out in August 1914. If Jellicoe was correct—and as he had been selected and groomed for the post of commander-in-chief by Admiral Fisher himself it must be assumed that he had the best tactical brain in the entire Royal Navy—the Whitehead torpedo had become *the* decisive weapon of naval warfare. And so it proved, although not quite in the way that Jellicoe had envisaged.

There were few technical advances in the final years leading up to the outbreak of war, although each succeeding mark of torpedo introduced some minor improvement in performance as each side's engineers and scientists strove to perfect the weapon. The Royal Navy established its own torpedo factory at Greenock to take over the work of the old Royal Gun Factory, which had, in its turn, swallowed up the even older Royal Laboratory at Woolwich. One reason advanced for the new factory was that it provided the navy with a greater productive capacity. But it was also officially admitted that "owing to the confidential nature of the modern torpedo [it was desirable to] eliminate its manufacture by private firms."[16] When war broke out, however, the Admiralty showed itself to be only too happy to make use of these same "private firms" to boost torpedo production even higher.

Whiteheads, too, were expanding. A French company, *La Société Français de Torpilles Whitehead*, was established at St. Tropez to supplement the demands of the French Navy, which the State Arsenal at Toulon was unable to meet, and in the same year, 1913, an Italian subsidiary was also formed. The De Lucca works at Naples were purchased by this new company, *La Societa Anonima Italiana Whitehead & Company*, and this, like the French concern, was controlled by Vickers and Armstrong Whitworths. Mention must also be made of the Russian branch which it was intended to form by an amalgamation of the Petrograd firm of A. Lessner & Company with a fully equipped works and testing range at Feodosia in the Crimea. However, war broke out before the deal was completed, and as Fiume was situated in an enemy country, there were tremendous complications. The wrangling between Vickers, Armstrongs, and Lessners continued right up until the outbreak of the Bolshevik revolution in 1917, and the already confused situation was made even worse when the German army occupied the factory in May 1918. Realizing that they had backed the wrong horse, Vickers washed their hands of the whole affair, writing off the loan they had made to Lessners in 1914 into the bargain, and the embryonic Russian branch vanished into limbo.[17]

The war naturally brought traumatic changes for the factories. Austria eagerly grabbed the Fiume works when hostilities opened, and in 1915, when Italy joined in the conflict, the factory was evacuated lock, stock, and barrel to a former Dutch-owned textile works at St. Pölten some 40 miles south of Vienna. The Fiume yards were kept in use for torpedo testing and, later in the war, the building slips were requisitioned for the assembly of German U-boats. These boats, destined for operations with the famous Catarro Flotilla, were shipped by rail in prefabricated sections from Germany, put together by civilian technicians and navy engineers at the old Whitehead works, and then commissioned into the German Navy on completion. Irritated by the presence of a U-boat factory on their very doorstep, the Italians made several efforts to bomb the Fiume plant, but most of the raids proved unsuccessful, although there was one spectacular attack on 8 August 1916, when a Caproni Squadron dropped four tons of bombs on the former torpedo works.[18]

In Britain the Weymouth factory took on a new importance and almost immediately after war broke out the Admiralty assumed 100 percent control of the company. Production was augmented in September 1915 when the Caton Engineering Company Ltd was formed to acquire the old railway wagon shops at Caton near Lancaster. The Admiralty put up £240,000 of the capital while Vickers and Armstrongs subscribed the remaining £60,000. The first torpedo deliveries began in October 1916, and the Caton works produced a total of 1,726 torpedoes before it was finally wound up in 1919. At its peak the Caton Engineering Company was producing 22 torpedoes per week and there were more than 850 workers on its payroll. Two years later, in 1921, the Weymouth factory was also wound up when lack of orders forced the company into voluntary liquidation.[19]

Weymouth was too valuable an asset to be wasted, however, and during reconstruction Vickers and Armstrongs acquired the shares held by the non-British members of the family from the Custodian of Enemy Property—a wartime British government department— leaving the rest of the family with only 251 out of a total of 735 shares. This new company, the Whitehead Torpedo Company Ltd, was floated with an issued share capital of £50,000 in £1 shares, of which only 2,510 were held by the Whiteheads. But even this tenuous finger in the factory's affairs was given up in 1928 when Vickers and Armstrongs amalgamated and the new company bought the remaining 2,510 shares from them. The great factory was now Whitehead in name only, and from 1931 onwards, the family had no connections left with the venture that Robert had begun some forty years earlier.[20]

The French branch suffered the same fate and by 1925 most of the holdings were in the hands of a French syndicate. On reconstruction it became *La Société des Torpilles de St. Tropez*—a title that did not even contain a reference to the inventor's name. The company subsequently merged with Schneider of La Londe. The Italian factory, too, achieved independence as *Silurifico Italiano Societa Anonima* and again all connections with Whitehead vanished.

Only the original Fiume concern remained, and situated in a defeated and disarmed country, it stood little chance of survival. Vickers and Armstrongs were, in theory, the controlling shareholders, but when war broke out their control became even more theoretical. No money was ever received from the Austrian government for the 21-inch torpedoes ordered shortly before the war, and in May 1918 a disastrous fire almost totally destroyed the new St. Pölten works.[21]

Defeat brought chaos in its train. Most of the new machinery bought to replace that lost in the fire was taken back to Fiume, and for a while the company attempted to remain in business by taking on light engineering contracts. But, unable to meet its liabilities, it fell into the hands of a group of Austrian financiers, *Wiener Bankverein*, who immediately encountered fresh problems when Fiume was ceded to Italy under the terms of the peace treaties. In 1923 the remains of the once-great torpedo complex passed into the control of the Italian Orlando industrial group backed, so it was said, by Italy's new fascist government.[22]

The factory, however, continued to build torpedoes for Mussolini's navy alongside the now distinct Naples concern and its products still bore the legend *Whitehead, Fiume*. In fact, of the ten patterns of torpedoes employed by the Royal Italian Navy in the Second World War, eight were of Fiume origin while the remaining two were identical in specification to those designed and manufactured at the former Whitehead factory. The Italian company is now owned by Gilardini SpA, a component subsidiary of the FIAT group.[23] but the name of Whitehead remains in use—the current lightweight 12.75-inch antisubmarine weapon being officially identified as the Whitehead A-244/S.

And so, in the aftermath of war, the family interests in the torpedo, which Robert had invented, came to an untimely end. It is ironic that the war that Whitehead always believed would be averted by the devastating nature of his invention should, in the event, demonstrate its complete supremacy as the prime weapon of naval warfare. And yet, at the same time, it should also destroy all family connections with the torpedo. Fate, indeed, can be a fickle jade.

CHAPTER 13

Courage! Nous mourrons ensemble!

I t is the combination of the submarine and the torpedo that is so valuable; but for Whitehead, the submarine would remain an interesting toy and but little more."[1] Such was the verdict of Admiral H. J. May in 1906. And although he made his observation at a time when the submarine as a practical means of undersea warfare was still in its primitive infancy the events of two world wars were to point to the truth of his statement. In the submarine the torpedo found its true role—an unseen weapon fired from an unseen vessel—and the major proportion of the torpedo's success emanated from the submarine. In the 1914–18 War, German U-boats alone sank a total of 11,018,865 tons of merchant shipping and 95 percent of this destruction was achieved by torpedo attack.

One of the prime problems facing the early submarine pioneers, aside from the methods of propulsion to be adopted and the matter of persuading the vessel to rise to the surface after it had submerged, was the type of weapon to be employed. The submarine, in fact, antedated the torpedo by several centuries, with the result that, having constructed an underwater vessel capable of moving and surviving beneath the surface, the erstwhile designer found himself without a suitable weapon.

At first the pioneer submarines used a primitive form of limpet mine. Bushnell's *Turtle* of 1776 vintage was fitted with a wood screw so that an explosive charge could be fastened to the underwater hull of the target ship, and (moving forward almost a century) Wilhelm Bauer's *Der Brandtacher* utilized a strange apparatus consisting of two leather gloves with which to fix an explosive charge on its intended victim. In special circumstances, for example with the tasks performed by the British X-craft midget submarines of World War Two, the use of limpet mines proved an effective and adequate method of attack on anchored shipping, but it was clear that, with moving targets, a more flexible form of attack was required.

The spar torpedo naturally attracted the attentions of the pioneer submarine designers. Van Drebbel had produced his water petard, and it will be recalled, Fulton had a similar weapon on his drawing board at the time of his death. In 1858 a French engineer, de Brun, talked his government into building an underwater boat armed with a spar explosive charge. *Le Plongeur* was 140 feet long with a displacement of 410 tons—a veritable giant by comparison with other early designs—and she began her first running-trials in 1865 while Whitehead was still secretly working inside the locked hut at the STF works in Fiume on his "fish" torpedo. By a strange coincidence de Brun, like Whitehead, also used a compressed air engine as his power unit and it proved a wise choice in both instances.

But although her designer succeeded in making *Le Plongeur* behave, after an unnerving series of trials and experiments, her spar torpedo was never tested in practice—which was probably fortunate for her crew as an underwater explosion in such close proximity to the submarine would have undoubtedly led to her hasty demise. The Confederate Navy in the American Civil War was to discover this fact to its cost. Starting with an awash boat armed with a spar torpedo, known as a *David*, the Confederates progressed to a full submersible fitted with the same suicidal type of attack weapon. On 17 February 1864 one of these new boats, the *Hunley*, poked her spar at the Federal corvette *Housatonic* and both predator and prey were destroyed in the subsequent explosion.[2]

Thorsten Nordenfelt, the Swedish armament king, was the first man to marry the Whitehead torpedo to the submarine. His original boat, steam powered and based in part on the designs of an English clergyman, the Reverend George Garrett, was only 64 feet in length with a displacement of 60 tons, but she proved to be far and away the best submarine to be built up to that time (1885).[3] And in addition to carrying a 1-inch Nordenfelt quick-firer on deck she was also fitted with an external torpedo tube in the bows although it was reluctantly admitted that the Whitehead "could not be launched underwater without placing the crew in imminent jeopardy."[4]

John Phillip Holland, probably the greatest name in the history of submarine development and the true "father of the underwater warship," began his experiments in 1877. His first two boats were unarmed, but in the *Holland III* launched in 1881, he introduced the "submarine cannon," a form of pneumatic discharge tube similar in many ways to the Zalinski dynamite gun. It is interesting to note that even Holland acknowledged his debt to Robert Whitehead and was reported as saying: "The submarine boat is a small ship on the model of the Whitehead torpedo, subject to none of its limitations, improving on all its special qualities, except speed, for which it substitutes incomparably greater endurance."[5] Based on such a fulsome statement a generous person could, indeed, credit Robert Whitehead with more than a minor part in the successful development of the submarine, for in the final analysis, it was Holland's design that became the standard pattern for all future underwater vessels. And on Holland's own admission he had based his ideas "on the model of the Whitehead torpedo."

The *Holland VIII*, the final stage of development and the submarine which persuaded the U.S. Navy to adopt this novel form of underwater warfare, was fitted with both an internal bow tube for a Whitehead torpedo and a Zalinski pneumatic gun firing a dynamite shell. The latter was soon dropped and with the dawn of the twentieth century the submarine emerged resplendent from its cocoon with just one main weapon—the Whitehead torpedo. The two inventions, in fact, complemented each other in almost every way. Brought together they were to prove the most lethal combination ever seen in the history of warfare at sea.

Britain's first submarines, the *Holland* class, were fitted with a single 14-inch bow tube but the next class, completed in 1903, increased the strike power of the submarine by adopting two tubes for the larger and more potent 18-inch weapons. By 1914 the Royal

Navy's standard submarine, the *E* class, mounted no fewer than *five* 18-inch tubes—two in the bows, two amidships firing on the beam, and one in the stern—an armament that, in the right hands, was to yield many successes. The first British submarine to carry the new 21-inch torpedo was the unsuccessful steam-driven *Swordfish*, completed in 1916. She was equipped with two 21-inch tubes plus four 18-inch tubes and was one of the few submarines built to carry a mixed-caliber armament of torpedoes. By 1918 the Royal Navy's underwater boats were all fitted with the larger tube and the famous 21-inch weapon became the primary submarine torpedo, a position it continues to retain even today in Britain's nuclear powered submarines.

Germany's first official U-boat, the *U-1*, was fitted with the 17.7-inch tube and this caliber continued until 1912, when the U-19 design incorporated the 19.7-inch tubes—two in the bows and two in the stern—firing the highly efficient Type G torpedo which was, in almost every way, superior to those produced by either Whiteheads at Fiume or the Royal Naval Torpedo Factory (RNTF) at Greenock. The 19.7-inch, or 500-millimeter, torpedo carried a warhead of 440 pounds and, in its later states of development, could range up to 11,000 yards at 28 knots. During the 1914–18 War, U-boats fired more than 5,000 of these deadly weapons at their victims—usually successfully—and the 19.7-inch torpedo remained standard equipment right up until 1918, although there was a reversion to the smaller 17.7-inch in the earlier types of U-boats which were built for operations in coastal waters.[6]

1912 also witnessed the first instance of a submarine-launched Whitehead torpedo being fired in anger, when the Greek submarine *Delphin* attacked the Turkish cruiser *Mejidieh* and the torpedo gunboat *Berk i Salvet* on 9 December 1912. The 295-ton Schneider-Laubeuf submarine, commanded by Lieutenant Commander E. Paparrigopoulos, was based at Tenedos as part of the squadron blockading the Dardenelles. The Turkish ships emerged at 8:30 A.M., and despite their escort of four destroyers, Paparrigopoulos managed to get within 500 yards of his targets before firing a solitary Fiume 18-inch torpedo from the submarine's single bow tube. It sank before reaching the target.

But although the Type G was probably the best underwater weapon to be produced in the 1914–18 War it was still found that success could only be guaranteed if the submarine approached extremely close to its target before firing. Most attacks were carried out from between 300 and 400 yards with the torpedo set to run at its maximum speed, around 38 knots, and it was generally agreed that a shot outside the 3,000-yard range would be an almost certain miss.[7] Yet despite the superiority of the Type G one British submarine, the *G-13*, actually managed to hit an enemy submarine at a range of more than 7,000 yards with a 21-inch RNTF torpedo in 1917.[8] Even after fifty years of development Whitehead's weapon could still be a capricious animal.

The initial attacks launched by the Royal Navy's submarines produced some disconcerting results and there were numerous instances where the torpedo arrowed at its target but then passed beneath the keel of its victim because it was running too deep.[9] Lieutenant-Commander Godfrey Herbert in the *D-5*, after a hazardous approach run through the destroyer screen surrounding the German cruiser *Rostock*, fired two perfectly aimed shots at close range only to see them pass directly beneath the enemy ship. Ernest Leir, captain of the *E-4*, suffered a similar disappointment when he caught the *U-23* on the surface off Heligoland on 10 September 1914. His 18-inch RNTF Mk VIII streaked straight for the U-boat but failed to hit it, and Leir, always a humorist, noted in his log that the torpedo had presumably run under its intended victim "judging by the gesticulations on her bridge." Martin Nasmith, another of Britain's top submarine aces, also missed a sitting duck when the *E-11*'s torpedoes skimmed below the keel of a German battleship in December 1914, and it was clear that something was seriously wrong with the Royal Navy's weapons—a doubly puzzling problem as they had performed impeccably during peacetime exercises. Vice-Admiral David Beatty, officer commanding the Battle Cruiser Fleet, voiced his dismay in a letter to Flag Officer (Submarines) Roger Keyes: "What has gone wrong? I hear the damned torpedoes dive too deep."[10]

Lord Fisher, by this time back in harness as first sea lord, was characteristically more forthright. "Our torpedoes seemed to be filled with sawdust!!! There's a heavy reckoning coming to everyone connected with *Vernon* [the Navy's torpedo establishment] during the last four years. . . . I hope to get a good many officers disgraced for it!" Continuing in the same vein Fisher expressed the desire to have Charlton, the assistant director of torpedoes from 1911 to 1914 "blown from a gun" and swore to have the senior officers hung or shot; he did not express a preference as to method.[11]

The answer when it was finally discovered, however, justified Fisher's violent strictures. All data issued on torpedoes had been based on practice runs made in peacetime. In making their reports the "boffins" had overlooked the fact that the practice warhead was 40 pounds lighter than the real thing. Thus the settings recommended for a given depth resulted in the torpedo running considerably deeper due to the additional weight of explosives carried in the nose section. And once this problem was recognized and resolved British submarine captains achieved many notable successes.

Torpedoes, by 1914, had become expensive toys costing, on average, £900 apiece, and, even more important, the outfit of torpedoes carried by a submarine on combat patrol was severely limited— usually one weapon per tube plus an equal number of reloads. Not surprisingly submarine captains made great efforts to ensure that none were wasted. Deck guns were used to sink smaller vessels on which it was not worth wasting a torpedo, and whenever possible, submarine crews boarded their victims and destroyed them with explosive charges fitted with time fuses. To miss a target and lose a torpedo was not only a slur on the captain's ability to aim straight, it was also something akin to disaster, for a single lost weapon probably represented about 10 percent of the submarine's total offensive capacity.

Martin Nasmith, the second member of the British submarine service to win the Victoria Cross for his underwater exploits, went to almost incredible lengths to ensure that torpedoes which missed their targets were not, as was usually the case, irretrievably lost. His first attempt to salvage a torpedo for reuse took place on 27 May 1915, when the *E-11* impudently pushed her nose into the heavily defended harbor of Constantinople. Under international law a torpedo had to be rendered harmless at the end of its run and this was achieved by a small automatic valve which opened and admitted water into the body of the weapon thus giving it negative buoyancy and causing it to sink. Had this particular device not been fitted the torpedo would have remained floating on the surface with its warhead primed—an ever-constant danger to any vessel that chanced to cross its unpredictable path.

A few days before his Constantinople adventure Nasmith decided to flout the conventions of international law by taking a deliberate gamble and he ordered his torpedo artificers to adjust the automatic valve so that the torpedo, if it missed its target, would rise to the surface and be recovered. His scheme had its first test when the starboard beam torpedo missed a well-laden enemy ship leaving Constantinople harbor. As soon as the Turkish vessel had passed out of sight he brought the *E-11* to the surface and, after a tedious search, located the 18-inch RNTF torpedo bobbing gently in the swell—its docile fishlike appearance belying its lethal purpose. The next part of the recovery process was, however, deemed too hazardous even for the *E-11*'s eager volunteers, and Nasmith himself, stripping off his uniform and holding a heavy wrench in his teeth, dived into the water and swam towards the drifting torpedo. Clasping its steel body with his left arm, and working with the utmost care, the *E-11*'s captain gently reversed the spinners of the safety fan up the spindle and then cautiously removed the firing pin with the aid of the wrench. Satisfied that the torpedo was now rendered harmless, and pushing it along in front of him, Nasmith swam the weapon back towards the submarine, where the crew had already raised the forward torpedo hatch ready for the 1,500- pound "tin fish" to be lowered back into the submarine. It was a backbreaking task but the sweating sailors set up a new record time for hoisting a torpedo inboard. It was a matter of life or death. Lying surfaced deep inside enemy-controlled waters with the fore hatch wide open, they were completely powerless to dive if they were surprised by a Turkish patrol and until the torpedo was safely inside the bowels of the submarine they could do nothing to reduce the danger.

Fortunately, they were not disturbed in their task and half an hour later the *E-11* was safely beneath the surface again with the salvaged torpedo neatly stowed. Realizing the risk he had taken Martin Nasmith reconsidered the problem. While admitting the danger of recovering a lost torpedo in enemy-controlled waters he refused, however, to give up the idea and decided that next time he would stage the recovery *while the submarine was submerged.*

This novel solution was tested for the first time on 2 June 1915 when a snap shot at a fast-moving Turkish dispatch-vessel missed its target. Once again there was a long and tedious search for the torpedo but, finally, it was sighted rolling gently on the surface. Nasmith brought the *E-11* up to allow his first officer, Lieutenant Guy D'Oyly

Hughes, to dive into the water and waited as Hughes swam across to the torpedo and made it safe. Next, six volunteers from the crew joined the lieutenant in the water, and they helped him maneuver the weapon while Nasmith took the submarine down beneath the surface for the reloading stage.

The empty stern tube was pumped clear of water, the inner door was clamped tightly shut, and the outer door swung open. Delicately, as if threading the eye of a needle with a piece of stiff cotton, D'Oyly Hughes and his six assistants gradually eased the RNTF weapon beneath the surface and pushed it, nose first, into the entrance to the tube. A sharp rap on the steel plates of the submarine's hull signaled that the task was complete and, having closed the outer door of the tube, Nasmith brought the *E-11* back to the surface to pick up the salvage gang. Then the submarine slipped beneath the sea again to complete the job of reloading.

The stern tube was pumped dry for a second time, the inner door was unclamped and swung open, and the torpedo was drawn out of the tube nose first. Making use of the narrow gauge track that ran the full length of the submarine from bow to stern and which was designed to facilitate the movement of torpedoes during reloading operations in harbor, the 17-foot-long monster was then hand hauled down the boat into the fore torpedo compartment, where artificers fitted the firing pin back in position before the weapon was slid into the empty bow tube. Nasmith's careful forethought had ensured that the torpedo entered the submarine nose first so, of course, when it reached the opposite end of the vessel it was already pointing in the correct direction for loading.

Four days later the torpedo which he had taken such pains to recover was fired at a Turkish transport anchored off Panderma, striking its victim in the engine room with such devastating effect that she sank within a few minutes.[12]

A torpedo attack by one submarine, whether British or enemy, is much like another and it would be tedious to describe more than one such episode in detail. It seems appropriate, therefore, to select as an example an attack made by the man who married Robert Whitehead's granddaughter, Kapitänleutnant Georg Ritter von Trapp, commanding officer of the Austrian submarine *U-5*, herself built at the Fiume torpedo works.

At the time of the action the Austro-Hungarian fleet was bottled up at the northern end of the Adriatic while an Allied blockade line sealed off the Straits of Otranto—the only means of exit. And in April 1915 one of the squadrons making up the blockade line was supplied by the French Navy with the armored cruiser *Leon Gambetta* acting as flagship.

Von Trapp had sighted the patrolling squadron early in the evening of the 26th but the slow submerged speed of the *U-5*, a mere 5 knots, meant that it was impossible to keep up with the enemy force. The *U-5*, in fact, could only make 10 knots on the surface while the *Leon Gambetta* could reach 22 knots despite her ungainly appearance and 12,518 tons. Fortunately for von Trapp the Straits were fairly narrow, and despite steering an irregular zig-zag course, he knew that, ultimately, the squadron must reappear on the return leg of its patrol. The sea was calm and the moon was almost full. Standing on the surface and moving gently through the water to minimize the tell-tale phosphorescent glow of her wash, *U-5* quartered the area like a hound searching to pick up the scent of a lost fox. Then, just before midnight, a keen-eyed lookout on the U-boat's bridge spotted a dark smudge on the horizon.

"Object starboard twenty."

Von Trapp swung around, searching the bearing.

"Make ready for diving!"

The lookouts scrambled down the hatch, followed by the watch officer. Von Trapp took a last look at the horizon. The oncoming target was now clearly defined in the light of the moon and he noted with satisfaction that she had four funnels, oddly spaced, one pair well forward just behind the bridge with the other pair grouped awkwardly towards the stern. It could only be the *Leon Gambetta* returning on the reverse leg of her patrol. And she was coming straight towards him!

He ducked down the steel companionway, slammed the hatch shut above his head, and slid the dog catches home. The surface motors had already been shut off at the first warning command and the submarine vibrated softly with the soft hum of the electric motors. Calling off a fresh course to the helmsman he threw his cap on to the chart table and walked across to the periscope.

"Stand by to dive."

"Open main vents."

"Dive!"

The sea swallowed the *U-5* as she angled down, and within three minutes, only the tip of the periscope remained above the surface. Von Trapp watched the cruiser edging closer.

"Make tubes ready."

"All tubes clear and secured, Herr Leutnant."

The watch officer passed the report to the commander and he nodded in acknowledgment. The tubes in the bows, their outer doors open, were flooded and the 17.7-inch Fiume torpedoes were poised for action as the *U-5* swung towards her unsuspecting target.

On board the *Leon Gambetta* the crew were sleeping at their action stations in anticipation of a surface torpedo attack, "submarines not having as yet attempted to operate by night," and speed had been reduced to 6 knots to conserve her coal stocks. Lookouts scanned the horizon in search of Austrian destroyers but no one examined the sea in close proximity to the cruiser and no one saw the stalk of the periscope or the whisper of telltale spray just a few hundred yards away.

Von Trapp allowed the enemy ship to pass square into his sights, holding the *U-5* on course without deviation in order to minimize the vital deflection angle. Then, at 12:20 A.M. precisely, he gave the order:

"Port tube—fire! Starboard tube—fire!"

The Whiteheads shot from their tubes with all the precision that came from fifty years of constant development. The radial engines roared into life, and even before the tails of the torpedoes were clear of the tubes, the gyroscopes were already spinning at the required 2,400 revolutions per minute, which were holding them firmly on course while the swinging pendulums on which Whitehead had labored so long operated the servomotor and swung the rudders to maintain the even, preselected depth.

The first torpedo slammed into the cruiser's port side and exploded in the dynamo compartment, plunging the ship into instant darkness. A moment later the second torpedo penetrated the boiler rooms and stopped the engines as it blew up. The doomed ship drifted slowly forward with the current, settling by the head despite the efforts of her commanding officer, Captain André, to flood the starboard compartments to keep her on an even keel. Then, realizing that nothing could be done to save the cruiser, he ordered the crew to abandon ship.

"To the boats. Be steady, my children. The boats are for you—

we officers will remain. *Nous autres, nous restons!*" An eyewitness recalled:

> There was no panic. Discipline was preserved. The officers were everywhere encouraging and helping the men. The sick and wounded were brought up from the sick-bay. In the lower flats officers with pocket torches were enabling men to reach the deck and endeavour to escape. One officer, possessing great fortitude, stood up to his knees in water—for the cruiser was heeling 30° to port—calmly lighting a cigar to inspire the men. Boats were launched, some were broken against the hull, killing some men, injuring others, casting many into the water; floating material was set adrift and, with splendid order, the ship's company were bidden to save themselves if they could. *"Courage! Nous mourrons ensemble!"* cried the officers to those for whom there was no hope.

Twenty minutes after the two torpedoes had struck home the greater cruiser plunged her bows into the sea and slid gently and gracefully to the bottom. As she went down there "came the cry *Vive La France* which was taken up by the men still on board and by those in the sea." Then, suddenly, there was nothing but a bubbling froth of water to mark her grave and the bobbing heads of the survivors. Not a single officer escaped and of a total ship's company of 737 men only 137 survived.[13]

Such was the power of the Whitehead torpedo when launched by the unseen hand of a submerged submarine. It was a scene to be repeated many thousands of times in both world wars with victims that ranged in size from small coastal freighters to mighty aircraft carriers and battleships.

Go in and Get a Hit

T hroughout his life Robert Whitehead clung firmly to the obstinate belief that heavier-than-air machines would never fly.[1] It seems strange that a man blessed with such a highly inventive brain and with such a genius for solving intractable engineering problems should be so dogmatic, but once his mind was made up, no power on earth was able to change it. The press reports of the Wright Brothers' first powered flights at Kitty Hawk in 1903 must have caused him considerable consternation, for Whitehead still believed that anything printed in a newspaper must be true. But no doubt he reconciled his opposing convictions by deciding that, while the press reports were accurate, a catapulted flight of only 852 feet was hardly *flying* in the sense *he* understood it.

Whitehead was already a dying man when on 5 October 1905 Orville Wright made a powered flight of 24.2 miles at Dayton, Ohio, to prove, beyond doubt, that a heavier-than-air machine *could* rise off the ground and fly, and his illness saved him from discovering that he had been wrong. For once his prophetic vision had failed him. But his weapon, when it got into the air, did *not*. And by the time of Taranto

199

and Pearl Harbor in World War Two the Whitehead torpedo, launched from the skies, demonstrated a sensational capacity to change the entire course of strategy by a single attack.

Despite the primitive nature of the pioneer aircraft as they stuttered and wobbled across the sky in those early days of flying it did not take long for the enthusiasts to visualize these new aerial machines as weapons of war. And it is to the eternal credit of the Royal Navy that the first glimmerings of the idea came from the ranks of the "Silent Service."

As early as 1911 two naval aviators, Commander Murray Sueter and Lieutenant Douglas Hyde-Thomson, submitted a paper to the Admiralty "stressing the potentialities of the combination of aircraft and the torpedo."[2] The idea was taken up immediately and T. 0. M. Sopwith, one of Britain's first aircraft manufacturers, was instructed to build a torpedo-carrying seaplane for which Sueter and Hyde-Thomson designed a special dropping-gear.

Sopwith's seaplane, powered by a 200-horsepower Salmson engine, won the honor of taking the first torpedo off the ground when, late in 1913, Lieutenant Arthur Longmore successfully flew the aircraft with a 14-inch torpedo slung precariously beneath its fuselage.[3] Unfortunately in the interests of economy he was not allowed to drop it.

Other pioneer aircraft manufacturers also showed an interest in the Royal Navy's experiments, and in 1914, Short Brothers produced their "folder" seaplane with a 160-horsepower Gnome engine, which within a few hours of its arrival at the RNAS (Royal Naval Air Service) base, was also fitted with the Sueter and Hyde-Thomson dropping-gear. And on 28 July, just six days before the war broke out, Longmore took the Short up from Calshot to make the first recorded live torpedo drop in history, using, for the purpose, a 14-inch Whitehead weapon weighing around 810 pounds.[4] But Britain was not alone in her efforts to translate torpedo warfare into the air, for the Italian flyer Alessandro Guidoni, experimenting at much the same time, launched an 825-pound dummy torpedo from a Farman twin-engined monoplane during a series of private trials designed to demonstrate the aircraft's carrying capacity.[5]

Britain, however, was in business for real and Shorts were quickly instructed to build a larger aircraft, to be powered by a 220-horsepower Sunbeam engine, for the specific purpose of launching torpedoes from the air and three of these projected machines were allocated to the seaplane carrier *Ben-My-Chree* for service in the Dardanelles. The Type-184 Short, as the Sunbeam-engined model was designated, proved capable of lifting a 14-inch Whitehead off the water when conditions were favorable, although it has been noted that it "would only take off with this load when feeling in the mood."[6] But despite an inclination to temperament the Short 184 was to earn its own particular niche in naval aviation history. The torpedo allocated for use, incidentally, was the old 1897 RGF Mk X, an obsolete weapon, which suggested that the Admiralty did not have a great deal of faith in this new method of attack and did not intend to risk its newer torpedoes to the air. Even so, Shorts were asked to design another machine, with a 310-horsepower engine, to carry the latest RNTF 18-inch Mk IX weighing 1,077 pounds, which was still, at that time, under development.

Ben-My-Chree, a converted cross-Channel packet steamer, left England on 21 May 1915 with her three (some authorities say two) Short 184 seaplanes, embarked en route for the Dardanelles. She arrived at Mudros the following month and for a few weeks the pilots spent their time practicing with the torpedo-dropping gear while the mechanics sweated to persuade the temperamental engines to keep running in the dusty heat of Asia Minor.

The credit for launching the first successful aerial torpedo attack is difficult to apportion. Flight-Commander C. H. K. Edmonds, DSO, flying one of the Type-184 Short seaplanes took off from the Gulf of Xeros on 12 August 1915 and headed his machine towards the Sea of Marmora in search of likely prey. It was a bumpy and precarious flight, for the rarefied air gave little lift to the already well-loaded seaplane and the engine kept stuttering as the heat affected the carburetor and fuel feed system. Passing over the Dardanelles, Edmonds suddenly spotted a 5,900-ton steamer close inshore off Injeh Burnu. Gliding down from a height of 800 feet the pilot leveled off at 15 feet and, when only 300 yards away from the target, dropped his 14-inch torpedo. The weapon behaved impeccably, arrowed straight at the enemy ship, and struck her abreast the mainmast, causing a violent explosion.

When the elated flight commander returned to base, however, he learned that the ship he had attacked had already been abandoned and beached by the Turks after being shot up by the British sub-

marines *E-11* and *E-14*. It was a cruel disappointment, but fortunately, there was not long to wait for another chance. Five days later,
on the 17th, both Short seaplanes took off again and this time Edmonds was supported by Flight-Lieutenant G. B. Dacre. Edmonds
struck first. Finding the Turkish supply ship off Ak Bash Liman he
swooped down between the towering cliffs of the Dardanelles and
scored a direct hit, which set the enemy ship on fire. She did not,
however, sink and a few days later the Turks towed her safely back to
Constantinople and salvaged her.[7]

Dacre, meanwhile, was having his own problems. The arid heat
of Gallipoli proved too much for his ailing Sunbeam engine and the
seaplane was forced to make an emergency landing in the middle of
the narrow strip of water some 5 miles southwest of Galata. The
weight of the torpedo slung beneath the fuselage made it impossible to
take off again, but rather than abandon his expensive charge to its
fate, Dacre banged open the throttle and taxied down the Strait in
search of a likely target. He found one—a small 300-ton tugboat—in
False Bay on the Asiatic side, and deliberately taxied towards it.
Then, having closed the range to the required distance, he dropped
the torpedo, which, running true, struck the tug amidships and sank
her. Relieved of the torpedo's weight the seaplane was now able to
claw its way back into the air and Dacre managed to coax it back to
Ben-My-Chree.

Three attacks and three strikes. Yet who *really* made the first
successful torpedo attack from the air? Was it Edmonds when he hit
the stationary ship already abandoned by her crew or was it his
second attack when he torpedoed the steamer that was subsequently
salvaged? Or perhaps it was the resourceful Dacre who succeeded in
hitting and sinking a moving vessel—even though his seaplane was
not airborne at the time. Honors seem equal and the credit is somewhat academic. The important point was that the torpedo had proved
itself as an air-dropped weapon and, in so doing, the tiny seeds sown
by Edmonds and Dacre took root.

Despite its lack of modern aircraft the Royal Navy persevered
with the air-dropped torpedo throughout the interwar years until, by
1939, her Fleet Air Arm pilots were probably the elite of Britain's
aviators—a claim more than substantiated by their brilliant achievements in combat with aircraft that were little better than museum
pieces. The Fairey Swordfish, the standard torpedo aircraft of the

Navy in 1939, had a top speed of barely 130 miles per hour with a duration of just over seven hours.

Gradually the technique of torpedo dropping from the air was evolved and it is to the Royal Navy that credit must be given for devising the multi-plane method of attack in which the torpedo aircraft come in on their target from all points of the compass, swamping the antiaircraft defences, and making it virtually impossible for their victim to dodge *every* torpedo. It was a technique that was also taken up by the navy pilots of the United States and Japan.

But aside from aircraft and tactics there were also a number of technical problems. One was the natural tendency of the torpedo to drop too steeply and to enter the water tailfirst after its release by the torpedo carrier. Apart from spoiling the accuracy of the pilot's aim such acrobatic evolutions also caused serious damage to the delicate rudder and propeller mechanism. It was, as Bethell commented, "a mode of entry that it resented most bitterly."[8] Bearing in mind the fuss that Robert Whitehead had made when the Royal Navy began firing torpedoes from deck tubes it is not difficult to imagine his complaints had he lived to see his weapons being dropped from a great height into the sea.

To overcome the tailfirst difficulty a wooden drogue was fitted behind the propellers, which brought the center of pressure further aft towards the center of gravity and thus ensured a more level descent. The drogue had an automatic release mechanism which allowed it to fall free as the weapon entered the water. It was, however, only a stopgap device and more sophisticated designs followed, until finally, large aerofoil vanes were fitted to the rudders of the steering mechanism, which "acted in such a way as to keep the axis of the torpedo tangential to the path of fall."[9] The vanes, of very light construction, snapped off as the weapon struck the water and a small flap opened the air supply operating the normal servomotor control valve. An even more advanced modification included a gyroscopically controlled steering mechanism which steered the torpedo throughout its entire aerial descent into the sea.

Little by little performance improved. Drops that in 1915 were limited to 15–20 feet were steadily increased until, during the war, Japanese torpedo bombers frequently made their drops from an altitude of 200 feet and, when they attacked the *Prince of Wales* and *Repulse*, an astonishing 350 to 500 feet. There were, however, other problems, for it was found that temperature falls at the rate of 3 degrees Fahrenheit for every 1,000 feet of altitude and the early experimenters soon discovered that the delicate mechanisms of the torpedoes were freezing up. The original Sopwith Cuckoo overcame this particular problem in a novel, if brutal, manner. The exhaust pipes were deflected downwards so that the hot gases from the engine played directly on to the torpedo's body "keeping it warm," as one RNAS pilot observed, "so that it could be served piping hot for the Kaiser's dinner."[10] But once again time brought a degree of sophistication and by 1939 internal heaters connected to the aircraft's own electrical system kept the torpedo's vitals comfortably warm and free from ice until it was time for the drop.

Before leaving the technical aspects of the aircraft torpedo mention must be made of one more manifestation of Robert Whitehead's genius. It will be recalled that when the Royal Navy began manufacture of its own torpedoes at Woolwich in 1872 the British pattern placed the propellers abaft the depth and steering control surfaces— a complete reversal of the Fiume layout. Although Britain remained faithful to this design for her ship and submarine torpedoes, experiments demonstrated that the Fiume arrangement was more suitable for the airborne weapon. In fact one British expert was forced to "grudgingly admit that the Fiume tail furnishes a more powerful control and therefore may be preferable."[11] And so, even though he refused to believe that heavier-than-air machines could ever be made to fly, Robert Whitehead had, quite inadvertently, produced the design most suited for launching from the air.

Of the three major navies concerned with sea flying only Japan developed their air-strike arm along the right lines. They, too, had level bombers but their tactical emphasis was on a balanced attack by dive-bombers and torpedo planes working in close conjunction from a formidable task force of fast-moving aircraft carriers. The Japanese admirals, with the sure touch one finds in men of purpose, visualized future naval warfare correctly. They realized that the aircraft, whether bomber or torpedo dropper, had extended the range of attack far beyond that of the heavy gun and that sea battles would be fought with anything up to 300 miles separating the opposing fleets. And they made their plans accordingly.

Yet, by a strange quirk of fate, it was the Royal Navy that made the Japanese attack on Pearl Harbor a practical possibility—and that is leaving aside the semi-official British Naval Mission, under Lord Semphill, which had helped the Japanese to organize and build up their naval air arm in 1921. The Fleet Air Arm attack on the Italian fleet at Taranto in November 1940 proved that a torpedo strike could be made against enemy ships lying at anchor in a heavily defended harbor, and up to that time, the Japanese had visualized their projected attack on the U.S. Pacific Fleet in terms of high-altitude bombing, dive-bombing, and torpedo attacks by midget submarines. Taranto, however, changed all that. When Yamamoto learned of the British success he called for urgent reports from the Japanese naval attachés in Rome and London.

> The reports revealed one vital fact. The depth of water in Taranto harbour was 42 feet or less. This had always been considered too shallow for aerial torpedoes. Now the British attacks on the Italian fleet had disproved this. If the British could sink ships at such a depth, why not repeat this attack on a much bigger scale? The depth of water at Pearl Harbor was 45 feet.[12]

Admiral Isoroku Yamamoto was not the only man to realize the significance of the Fleet Air Arm's achievement. The U.S. secretary of the navy, Frank Knox, observed in a top secret memorandum: "The success of the British aerial torpedo attack . . . suggests precautionary measures be taken immediately to protect Pearl Harbor . . . [author's italics] *the greatest danger will come from the aerial torpedo.*"[13]

The Fleet Air Arm's first attack against defensively screened capital ships in June 1940 had, however, proved disappointing when six Swordfish aircraft equipped with torpedoes had carried out a strike against the German battleship *Scharnhorst* at the tail end of the Norwegian Campaign. They flew 240 miles to locate their prey, but spotted by lookouts as they came down to 15 feet for their long run-in, the two subflights were met with an intense barrage from the enemy ships. Two Swordfish smashed into the sea after being shot to pieces by a hail of shell while the remainder, baffled by the almost impenetrable screen of flak, launched their torpedoes wildly—and missed.

During the following month torpedo aircraft from the *Ark Royal* made the first successful attack on a capital ship when twelve veteran Swordfish, flying in three waves, struck and immobilized the French battlecruiser *Dunkerque* at Oran during that unhappy period when Britain was forced to wage war against her former ally to ensure that the French fleet would not fall into Hitler's hands.

Taranto was the Fleet Air Arm's next trial of strength, and the overwhelming success of the attack not only confirmed the torpedo as a primary air weapon but also set the stage for Pearl Harbor and the Pacific war.[14] The Royal Navy had first considered an aerial attack on the Italian naval base as early as 1938, but as Yamamoto also discovered, the air-dropped torpedo needed a minimum depth of water in which to operate due to its tendency to "porpoise" on entering the sea. And until a suitable antidote was devised air torpedo attacks on harbors were unlikely to be successful. In the end, as always, the Royal Navy's scientists came up with the answer and now all depended on the skill and courage of the Swordfish pilots and crews.

The attack took place on 11 November. The first wave of twelve aircraft, only six of which carried torpedoes, took off from the deck of the *Illustrious* at 8:57 P.M. and set out on the hazardous 170-mile flight to the target. The flare droppers arrived over the harbor at 10:56 P.M. and a dive-bombing attack to set fire to the oil tanks for extra illumination followed immediately. The mind boggles at the idea of lumbering old Swordfish being used as a dive-bombers but they were and they succeeded.

Led by Lieutenant-Commander Kenneth Williamson, the torpedo planes came down to 30 feet and streaked for the anchored Italian battleships. There was an intensive flak barrage, and just to make things more difficult a balloon barrage.

This first wave scored a direct hit on a *Cavour*-class battleship and further hits were claimed on the other capital ships apart from the bombs from the Swordfish that were not carrying torpedoes. Yet despite the fierce ground opposition from the Italian flak batteries only one aircraft, Williamson's, failed to return to the carrier. A second strike wave of nine Swordfish cleared the carrier's deck at 9:23 P.M., although two came to grief almost immediately with the result that one had to be struck below for emergency repairs. Once again, even though the defenses were now on their mettle, the men of the Fleet Air Arm scored more successes, and this single shoestring raid, made with obsolete aircraft, put the Italian fleet out of action for several crucial months. Most of the damaged ships were repaired and recommissioned in due course, but time was of the essence and a few month's inactivity by a force of enemy capital ships can make all the difference. That victory, in the end, rested with the Allies was due in no small part to the bravery of the Royal Navy's aircrews, the sturdy reliability of the old Fairey Swordfish, and the power of Whitehead's torpedo, that night over Taranto in November 1940.

An example of the torpedo's use in slowing an enemy unit so that a surface force could close and destroy came in the famous hunt for the German battleship *Bismarck*. Weather conditions were as bad as anything the Atlantic can produce and many of the aircraft had to operate under almost impossible handicaps—the *Ark Royal*'s aircraft actually taking off while the carrier was pitching 60 feet or more into a head sea. There was a narrow escape when the *Sheffield*, mistaken for the *Bismarck* in the bad visibility, was abortively attacked by a group of torpedo planes. But success finally came to the Swordfish from the carrier *Ark Royal*, gallantly led by Lieutenant-Commander Eugene Esmonde, who flew in at point-blank range and struck the Nazi battleship with at least one torpedo that disabled her steering gear and reduced her speed. From then onwards it was only a question of time. Apart from a few anxious hours when contact was lost and literally half the Royal Navy was milling around in mid-Atlantic looking for her, the end of the *Bismarck* was as certain as the coming of dawn. And it was the torpedo that had sealed her fate.

It is sad to record that Esmonde met his end in an equally gallant attack some months later during a sortie against the *Scharnhorst*, *Gneisenau*, and *Prinz Eugen* when they made their daring Channel escape from Brest to Germany in February 1942. Esmonde's 825 Squadron, still flying obsolete Swordfish but this time operating from a shore base, were part of the huge air and surface force which the British threw against the Nazis. Ashore, the high command were in a turmoil of panic and indecision as attack after attack failed to halt the German warships. For Esmonde the responsibility weighed heavily on his shoulders. Both the RAF and Royal Navy top brass considered that, without fighter support, an attack by antiquated biplane torpedo droppers was nothing short of suicide. Even with an adequate fighter escort, opinion veered towards the view that the Swordfish could not survive the full force of the Luftwaffe and the German Navy's flak barrage. And so, instead of directly ordering Esmonde to his death, the top brass passed the buck by giving him the facts and telling him: "It's *your* decision."[15]

Esmonde had the traditions of the Royal Navy ingrained in him—not to hang back in the face of the enemy. Given the choice, and aware of the consequences, he did not hesitate.

Esmonde's 825 Squadron took off from Manston at 12:25 P.M. and headed for the Kent coast to rendezvous with its escort of fighters. But, like nearly everything else that chaotic day, something went wrong and only one of the promised Spitfire squadrons arrived. There was no time to wait, and after circling around for a few minutes, Esmonde led his group of six biplanes and ten attendant Spitfires out to sea in search of the German squadron as it stormed at top speed for the Straits of Dover. It was raining hard and visibility was closing in, but disregarding the dangers the Fleet Air Arm pilots took their planes down to wave-top height in an effort to slip beneath the enemy radar screen. Ten miles east of Ramsgate they were spotted by six Me 109s but the covering Spitfires drove them off while Esmonde, ignoring the threat from above, held his course towards the enemy warships.

Suddenly they were sighted. And with the range down to 2,000 yards every single German flak gun opened up while waves of enemy fighters screamed down to break up the attack. Gaping holes appeared in the fabric of the fuselages as cannon shells ripped the flimsy covering. The tail section of Esmonde's Swordfish caught fire as a line of tracer bullets thudded into the rudder. His rear gunner, Leading Airman W. J. Clinton, clambered out of the open cockpit and, straddling the fuselage, began beating out the flames with his bare hands as the plane jerked and shuddered from further direct hits. The other aircraft were in similar straits. But still they came on. The *Gneisenau* and *Scharnhorst* opened up with their main 11-inch guns, laying down a barrage that raised a solid wall of water in front of the Swordfish but not even this deterred them. Esmonde's lower wing broke away as a shell burst just below the biplane, and he was bleeding from wounds in his head and back. Behind him Clinton, the rear gunner, and Lieutenant W. H. Williams, his observer, were now both dead but Esmonde's determination never wavered and he forced his crippled aircraft into the dropping position. His hand moved the lever and the torpedo fell away with a clumsy splash. Seconds later the *Prinz Eugen*'s guns scored a direct hit and the Swordfish was blown to pieces.

Esmonde's aim had been true and his mission had been accomplished. The torpedo was rushing straight at the cruiser. But his skill

and courage brought no reward. *Prinz Eugen* swung 15 degrees to
port and the torpedo passed harmlessly down the side of its intended
victim. Undeterred by the fate of their leader the remaining Swordfish
kept coming in, holding a dead straight course and giving the German
gunners an easy target. All who managed to survive the murderous
barrage launched their torpedoes, but no one scored a hit and every
plane in the squadron was shot down. Of the eighteen men who had
left Manston an hour earlier only five were still alive and only two of
these were unwounded. True, they had failed, but it had been a
glorious failure. As Admiral Bertram Ramsay reported to the Admiralty: "In my opinion the gallant sortie of these six Swordfish
constitutes one of the finest exhibitions of self-sacrifice and devotion
that the war has yet witnessed."[16]

Although the circumstances were entirely different, the words
of Admiral Ito to his torpedo-boat captains before the attack on
Weihaiwei seem appropriate: "I am asking you to sacrifice your lives
for your country and to earn undying fame for yourselves." In the case
of 825 Squadron, fame was not the spur. The enemy were at the
Channel gates. In the words of the Naval Discipline Act of 1866, it was
"the Navy, whereon, under the good Providence of God, the Wealth,
Safety, and Strength of the Kingdom chiefly depend." And it was in
that knowledge that Lieutenant-Commander Eugene Esmonde made
his decision to attack with inadequate fighter cover. It was a decision
that was to lead to the posthumous award of the Victoria Cross to a
very gallant officer.

The Fleet Air Arm had pointed the way to the use of the aerial
torpedo. It was to fall to the Japanese Navy, a few months later, to
demonstrate the full power of the airborne torpedo to a shocked world
in a series of attacks that spelled the doom of the battleship once and
for all.

Yamamoto's plan for a surprise attack on the U.S. Pacific Fleet
at Pearl Harbor first began to take shape in the spring of 1940. The
annual fleet exercises made a special feature of aerial torpedo attack,
and when the results were analyzed, it was found that the successes of
the carrier-borne aircraft exceeded the most sanguine expectations.
It had been recorded that his chief of staff, Rear Admiral Shigeru
Fukudome, told Yamamoto at the end of the maneuvers, "It is beginning to look as if there is no way a surface fleet can elude aerial
torpedoes. Is the time ripe for a decisive fleet engagement using aerial

torpedo attacks as the main striking power?'' Yamamoto paused
reflectively. Then he replied quietly: "An even more crushing blow
could be struck against an *unsuspecting* enemy force by a mass
torpedo attack."[17] And thus was born the germ of the idea that was to
lead, eighteen months later, to the tactics used on the Day of
Infamy—7 December 1941.

No more was said until the British raid on Taranto when Yamamoto realized that a successful attack could be made in shallow water
and, from that time onwards, the fate of the U.S. Pacific Fleet was
sealed. Work went ahead modifying the torpedoes on lines closely
based on the British model used at Taranto and gradually the great
plan unfolded itself. A total of six aircraft carriers, supported by two
battleships and attendant small craft, made up the main striking force
under Vice Admiral Chuichi Nagumo, and for the first time in history
the main attack weapon was to be, not the big guns of the battleships,
but the bombs and torpedoes of the airplane.

Nagumo's force carried 423 aircraft. 30 were for defensive patrol
duties over the fleet and 40 were held back in reserve. Of the remaining 353, 100 were loaded with converted 16-inch shells for high-level
bombing, 131 were Val dive-bombers, 79 were Zero fighters for
combat escort duties, and 40 were Kates armed with torpedoes. The
odds were weighted in favor of the bomb. The results were to demonstrate the power of the torpedo.

The first task of the Japanese aircraft was to take out the American airfields and this operation was left to the dive-bombers under
Lieutenant Commander Kakwichi Takahashi and Lieutenant Toshio
Sakamoto. They succeeded only too well. Then Lieutenant-
Commander Shigeharu Murata's torpedo bombers, having masked
their approach by flying through cloud cover, swooped down to sea
level and roared in on the unsuspecting battleships neatly anchored
in pairs while, at the same time, Fuchida's remaining dive-bombers
fell upon the other airfields. The torpedo planes split into two parallel
lines—one headed by Lieutenant Commander Murata, the other by
Lieutenant Inichi Goto. The battleships swung squarely into view and
all was going according to plan. Or was it?

Misunderstanding a signal from the attack leader, a section of
dive-bombers chose this precise moment to swoop in on the battleships. Suddenly all hell was let loose. Despite their utter lack of

preparation the American crews managed to get some of their antiaircraft guns into action and the unplanned dive-bombing attack robbed the torpedo planes of their anticipated element of surprise. But despite an intensive screen of fire the Kates came in straight and level and as skillfully controlled as Esmonde's Swordfish had been when 825 Squadron had made the supreme sacrifice against the German warships in the Channel. One by one the torpedoes dropped away, splashed into shallow water and sped towards their targets. A series of heavy explosions split the air, the tremendous concussion dominating all the other noises of battle as the torpedoes detonated.

The *Arizona* was a total loss. Hit first by torpedoes and then struck by bombs her magazines ignited. The *Oklahoma* took the full force of three torpedoes in the first few minutes of the attack and capsized, while the *West Virginia*, also a victim of the torpedo, was only saved from a similar fate by prompt counter flooding which kept her on an even keel as she settled on the harbor bottom. The *Maryland* escaped the torpedoes but was damaged by bombs while the *California*, struck by two torpedoes and a bomb, sank into the water until her keel grounded. The *Nevada*, too, was hit by one torpedo, which, though not fatal in itself, led to her being beached after further damage by armor-piercing bombs. The torpedoes wreaked similar destruction on the cruisers and smaller craft as well, and aided by the heavy bombs raining down from Fuchida's high-level group, the carnage and confusion were almost indescribable.

The American losses were overwhelming, with 2,403 sailors, soldiers, marines, and civilians killed; 188 aircraft destroyed; and a further 159 damaged. The Japanese losses were a mere 29 aircraft, 1 fleet and 5 midget submarines. Once again the terrible torpedo had demonstrated its power to change the course of war. And once again the torpedo crews suffered most. Of the 29 Japanese aircraft lost 5 were Kate torpedo bombers—one-eighth of the torpedo attack force of 40 planes and the highest casualty rate in relation to numbers employed of all the various aircraft used in the raid.

Throughout the rest of the Pacific war the carrier and the airplane dominated virtually every battle. The torpedo, however, was not always the prime means of success. For example at the Battle of Midway the torpedo aircraft on both sides failed badly, and it was left to Rear Admiral Frank Fletcher's dive-bombers to achieve the victory which, six months earlier, would have seemed impossible. But, yet again, the torpedo demanded the lives of the men who launched it even although it rewarded them with no success.

The *Hornet*'s Torpedo Squadron Eight, commanded by Lieutenant Commander John C. Waldron, was ordered to make an attack on the Japanese carriers "regardless of consequence." His fifteen aircraft were cut to pieces by the fighter screen, yet despite everything, they held on to their attack course until nothing would keep their battered aircraft in the air a moment longer. In his final command to the squadron Waldron had said: "If there is only one plane left to make the final run in, I want that man to go in and get a hit."[18] Ensign George Gay was the last man left. And he went in with a crippled aircraft and a dead man riding shot-gun in the rear gunner's seat behind his back. But despite his heroism the torpedo missed, and it was only by virtue of a special fortune that was denied the rest of the squadron that he managed to ditch his bomber and survive. The other twenty-nine aviators of Torpedo Squadron Eight all died in action doing their duty.

Such, in terms of human life, was the price the torpedo demanded from the men who served it.

Secret Memorandum No. 83-a-42

I t was not until after the end of the First World War that torpedo scientists began to stray beyond the well-defined technical frontiers set by Robert Whitehead's original conception. In fact, before 1918 only the turbine-powered weapons of the U.S. Navy achieved any marked degree of success by deviating from the established, almost sacred, Fiume pattern.

The interwar years, however, saw a dramatic surge of activity that soon produced a bewildering array of torpedo variants. They were mostly so diverse and technically complicated that they fall outside the scope of this more personal history of the weapon. But to round off the torpedo story and to demonstrate, if further demonstration be needed, the depth of Whitehead's genius—that after some 125 years all torpedoes are based on his original concepts—it is interesting to follow, if only in broad terms, some of the modifications and designs that flowed from the original 1866 prototype.

Size had always been an important factor in the calculations of torpedo designers, for a greater size meant a larger warhead, more powerful engines, and an improvement in both range and perfor-

213

mance. Whitehead's first experimental weapon had been of 14-inch diameter, but even by 1867, it had grown to 16 inches when the constrictions of space made "plumbing" more difficult and a greater circumference desirable. The famous Fiume Mk 1 on which Whitehead's fame and fortune rested admittedly reverted to the old 14-inch size, but the diminution was due, in the main, to more precise engineering tolerances and growing experience that enabled Robert to compress the same amount of machinery into a smaller space. Even so, he himself had been reported as working on a 445-millimeter model (approximately 17.5 inches) with an overall length of just over 16 feet as early as 1875, and he obviously considered that a larger-sized weapon was desirable. For various reasons, however, the 445-millimeter model was dropped and size progressed slowly through the natural process of evolution until, by 1914, production stabilized on the 21-inch pattern weapon for surface vessels with the 18-inch version for submarines and aircraft where space and weight were at a premium. In fact, dimensions became so standardized that the 21-inch torpedo remained the primary underwater weapon throughout the Second World War and is still the regular service diameter today—even in navies where measurements are based on the metric system.[1]

Engines, too, followed the same cautious program of development. And, apart from the introduction of the "dry" and then the "wet" heater power units, no serious efforts were made to discard the tried and tested radial engines first adopted, under Robert's benevolent eye, by the Fiume factory. Two major divergencies from the old systems of motive power emerged, however, after 1918—the enriched air engine and electric propulsion. And both were to have profound effects when the naval war was resumed in 1939, for they ultimately figured as the main torpedo weapons of the Axis powers, Japan relying on the fantastic Type 93 "Long Lance" torpedo (the *Shiki Sanso Gyorai Type-93*), while Germany concentrated her production on the deadly Type G 7e electrically powered weapon.[2] Having followed the torpedo story so far it will come as no surprise to learn that both had their origins far back in the early days of development despite their apparently revolutionary design.

As noted earlier, Whitehead had first experimented with a relatively large torpedo in 1875, and his interest in big-diameter weapons was revived in 1898 when the company produced a 24-inch torpedo for the Japanese government. Despite contemporary claims that this was a shipboard weapon, such was not the case, and all available evidence confirms that it was intended for launching from shore-mounted tubes in defense of harbor entrances and narrow channels—a tactical employment similar to that of Brennan's torpedo, which, by coincidence, was also of 24-inch diameter. Unverified performance figures bandied about by naval journalists of the period suggest that the new torpedo was capable of 25 knots for 3,000 yards. It was also said to have an overall length of 16 feet and a 250-pound warhead.

There are indications that Japan ordered an even larger torpedo in 1908. But lacking Robert Whitehead's master touch this giant 27.5-inch model proved a complete fiasco and never left the Fiume works.[3] The background and technical details of these underwater monsters remain obscure and sadly little information exists outside the realm of rumor and garbled press reports. It is, however, quite certain that Japan possessed a number of 24-inch shore-defense torpedoes, designed and built by Whiteheads, at the time of the Russo-Japanese War of 1904–5.

The idea of a "big" torpedo continued to hold a magnetic attraction for designers and, in time, it became inextricably linked with thoughts of more powerful forms of propulsion. Like most other torpedo modifications such a weapon was a natural progression. Luppis had tried clockwork. Whitehead had at first used a pure compressed-air motor of his own design and then moved on to a form of combustion-ignition engine utilizing compressed air and crude oil. Finally, after Whitehead's death, came the heater units that, in simple terms, made use of steam in the process of combustion. What, then, was the next logical step to be?

It was the British who took the plunge. Realizing that the bronze four-cylinder engines in standard use at the end of the 1914–18 war had almost reached their limit of development—the main weakness being their high rate of air consumption—thoughts turned to enriched air systems, which had the advantage of enabling a greater weight of oxygen to be carried with a resultant increase in engine-running time and, thus, greater range. Trials were carried out in 1923 with hydrogen peroxide replacing air as a low-pressure oxidant, but although work continued until at least 1936 the problems involved proved too great and it was left to the German scientist Professor

Helmuth Walter to perfect the hydrogen-peroxide engine for use in Hitler's U-boats towards the end of the Second World War.[4]

Enriched air was also tried and by 1928 a Mk VII 21-inch weapon had been produced, which was capable of 33 knots at a range of 16,000 yards.[5] Unfortunately enriched oxygen proved to be a dangerously unstable substance and the Mk VII's length of 25 feet 6 inches did not endear it to the sweating torpedo crews who had to handle it in confined spaces. The oxygen, too, had a high corrosion factor which rapidly weakened the air chambers to a dangerous degree.[6] But despite the undeniable advantage that the enriched oxygen torpedo left no exhaust bubbles on the surface to warn the victim of its approach, the Royal Navy showed an understandable reluctance to proceed. Strangely, and the torpedo story is full of such coincidences, it was the Brotherhood Company's new Burner Cycle engine that killed off the enriched oxygen venture—in the same way that Peter Brotherhood's first radial engine had spelled the death of Robert Whitehead's original power unit.

The Burner Cycle engine made its first appearance some ten years before the outbreak of the war in 1939 and remains in service today in modified form—testimony indeed to a superlative engineering concept that, despite space-age technology, has never been bettered in terms of either power-weight ratio or fuel consumption per brake horsepower per hour (see Table 2).[7]

In its original form the burner cycle engine—a four-cylinder radial—was supplied with air at 840 pounds per square inch that was mixed with atomized paraffin or shale oil. The resultant gas, heated to 1,000 degrees Centigrade, was then fed into the engine through four valves where fuel injection created spontaneous ignition. The exhaust gases were expelled via a duct which formed the center of the propeller shaft. By 1945 the unit was producing some 465 brake horsepower with speeds of up to 50 knots—a far cry, indeed, from the performance obtained from Brotherhood's first three-cylinder radial of 1876.[8]

In their search for improved performance British scientists experimented at various times with ammonium nitrate, tetranitromethane, and mixtures of nitric acid propellants, but none proved satisfactory.[9] After 1945, however, and thanks to Germany's wartime research, hydrogen peroxide—the oxidant which had been discarded in 1936—regained favor. But as with all enriched air propellants hydro-

Table 2
Comparative Power-weight Ratios

Model	Total rate of fluid consumption lb/bhp/hour	Power-weight ratio
British 21-in Mk VIII	8.3	.65
British 18-in (? Mk 12)	8.9	.54
USN 21-in Mk 10	21.6	1.00
Swedish turbine	24.4	1.32
French Model W	17.5	.92

gen peroxide was still a dangerous substance and on 16 June 1955 the British submarine *Sidon* was sunk with the loss of thirteen lives when a leakage of hydrogen peroxide from a faulty torpedo resulted in a disastrous explosion.[10] Technological progress can, on occasion, exact a high price.

Britain, however, was not the only country to experiment with enriched oxygen, and although the Royal Navy hurriedly dropped development in favor of the more conventional Burner Cycle engine, Japan continued to persevere with the idea. Work had first begun in 1924 but numerous accidents led to experiments being shelved, and they were not revived again until 1927, when the Japanese discovered that Britain was working on similar lines. The main difficulty lay in the inherently confined space of the torpedo's 21-inch-diameter body, which necessitated sharp angles in the fuel pipes. These acute angles caused the oxygen to mass, heat up under compression, and then explode violently.[11] But in 1928, Rear Admiral Kaneji Kishimoto and Captain Toshihide Asakuma began a new series of experiments at the Kure Torpedo Institute, and by the mid-1930s, the technical problems had been overcome and Japan could claim to possess the world's largest, fastest, and most long-ranging torpedo—the Type 93.

But instead of proclaiming their technological triumph to the world the Tokyo admirals wisely kept it a secret and the Allies only became aware of the existence of the "Long Lance," as the Type 93 was known, when it began sinking warships by the dozen during the great sea battles for control of Southeast Asia in 1941–42.

The Japanese Navy took tremendous pains to guard the secrets of the ship-launched Type 93 when it was first introduced into service in 1933.

> Every officer was told to recover the torpedo even though in practice they were fired without warheads. We [obeyed] this order because a single torpedo then cost 5,000 yen. Moreover, we knew that we must not take any chance that this torpedo might fall into alien hands and its secret be discovered. Sometimes an entire fleet would comb a wide area of the ocean for many hours to recover one errant torpedo [and] on stormy days we even cancelled manoeuvres for fear that a torpedo might be lost.[12]

Japan's precautions would have brought a smile to Whitehead's face for he had shown a similar desire for security in the early days of development when *The Secret* of his invention was at a premium.

The Type 93 was a formidable weapon. It was almost 30 feet in length and its massive girth of 24 inches carried a 1,100-pound explosive charge. Not only was it wakeless—a characteristic that led the Allies to believe that their ships had been mined and not torpedoed in the initial stages of the Pacific war—it had an effective range of nearly 18 nautical miles and was capable of speeds up to 49 knots for 22,000 meters or 36 knots for 40,000 meters.[13] A comparison with the performance of the Royal Navy's standard RNTF 21-inch Mk VIII of the same period will emphasize the tremendous superiority of the Japanese weapon—a superiority which the Allies soon discovered to their cost in the months following Pearl Harbor.

Many writers imply that the Type 93 was also a submarine weapon but this is incorrect and, indeed, no Japanese submarines were built with 24-inch tubes—not even the mighty *I-400*-class monsters. With typical ingenuity, however, the Japanese managed to solve the plumbing problems that had bedeviled the Royal Navy; and in the late 1930s they perfected an enriched-oxygen slim-line torpedo of 21-inch diameter for submarine use, and this became the main weapon of Japan's underwater flotillas throughout the war although both the old heater model Type 91 and the Type 92 electric torpedo were brought into service when occasion demanded. Although the first boats—the *Type K-6* class—to be equipped with tubes specifically designed for the Type 95 torpedo did not become operational until 1943, it seems apparent that the weapon could be fired equally successfully from a standard 21-inch tube. There is, however, a certain amount of confusion on the point. Later in the war Japanese scientists miniaturized the design even further and produced an 18-inch version of the Type 95 known as the Type 98.

There is no evidence that any of these oxygen-powered weapons were ever air dropped and the brunt of Japan's air strikes in the first year of the war in the Pacific was borne by the well-established Type 91. This 17.7-inch weapon was a conventional heater-engined model with a contact detonator but was fitted with special tail fins to cushion the shock of entering the water.[14] Unlike air-launched torpedoes of other navies the Type 91 could be dropped from a maximum altitude of 1,000 feet—although 200 feet was regarded as optimum—and a maximum launching speed of 260 knots. The Royal Navy, in particular, was caught on the wrong foot by this level of performance, for its gunners had only exercised against Swordfish biplanes, which normally dropped their weapons from a height of 25 to 50 feet above the surface and had an approach speed in the region of 100 knots.[15]

The original Type 91 had a tendency to roll on entering the water and this frequently caused it to veer violently off course. The defect was solved by a new tail configuration and, at the same time, the warhead was increased from 330 to 450 pounds.[16] It was this larger Model 2 that destroyed the *Prince of Wales* and *Repulse* in the Gulf of Siam in December 1941.[17] In its final form, designated Model 4, the Type 91 was fitted with an awesome 925-pound warhead, but by the time it became operational the Japanese Navy had virtually no aircraft or carriers left.

The other main line of prewar development concerned the electric torpedo, so named because it was propelled by a battery-powered motor instead of a thermal engine. Once again its origin goes far back into torpedo history, although for once, it sprang not from the fertile brain of Robert Whitehead, but from an inventor of similar genius, John Ericsson, whose wire-controlled weapon of 1873 was powered by an electric current passing down an umbilical cable linking it to its mother ship.[18] Thorsten Nordenfelt took the idea a stage further in 1888 when his giant 29-inch torpedo—the largest ever built—was driven by an 18-shaft-horsepower electric motor fed by 108 storage cells carried inside the body of the weapon.[19] And it was on this storage battery system that later development was based.

Why the electric torpedo was adopted is not hard to discover.

Torpedo manufacture is a highly skilled art requiring not only considerable expertise but also a vast amount of sophisticated machinery. Even as early as 1871 the United States found to her chagrin that her engineers had insufficient skill and technical know-how to produce steel air vessels capable of containing the enormous air pressures necessary to power the conventional torpedo engine. And attempts to overcome the disadvantage by using a bronze air vessel in the 1874 experimental model met with a similar lack of success. "Prominent steel firms of this country [United States] one and all declined even attempting the construction of an air reservoir of the requisite shape and dimensions which would endure the necessary strain."[20] It is a compliment to Whitehead's practical engineering skill that, even with the limited resources of his Fiume factory, air chamber pressures never caused him any great problems. But this is by way of digression. The point was that by 1914 the construction of a single torpedo used up a tremendous number of vital man-hours. And such a prodigious consumption of highly skilled labor was not altogether conducive to mass production. In fact from September 1939 to June 1944, with all the drive and energies of a great industrial nation at war, Britain produced a total of only 17,677 torpedoes.[21]

Much of this labor cost was tied up in the production of air vessels and engines and, by its very nature, work had to be restricted to highly specialized workshops, backed by years of experience and know-how. The electric torpedo, by contrast, was a far simpler piece of machinery and it was possible to subcontract much of the power-unit manufacturing work to nonspecialized firms employing only semi-skilled labor.

The first experiments date back to 1917, but although a few weapons are said to have been issued for operational use by the kaiser's U-boats, very little is known about these early models.[22] To circumvent the restrictions imposed on torpedo manufacture by the Treaty of Versailles the first electric weapons were built and tested by German scientists in Sweden. The work began in 1923—ten years before Hitler came to power—and was concluded in 1929, when the final trials proved so successful that the designs were "frozen" and carefully stored away ready for full-scale production at the appropriate time. "It is remarkable," Kirby noted in his series of articles for the *Journal of the Royal Naval Scientific Society*, "that the British

Admiralty had no knowledge of this development work until the weapons were used in 1939."[23]

The old pre-1914 Type G—a direct ancestor of Schwartzkopff's original pirated copy of the Whitehead torpedo—was adopted as a basis for the experiments and from this stemmed first, the Type G 7a thermal-engined weapon and then, the Type G 7e electric torpedo—the latter having a battery compartment 11 feet long containing 52 lead-acid cells in ebonite cases connected in series. The batteries weighed 1,500 pounds and the electric motor had an initial rating of 950 amps at 91 volts.[24] The full specification of the remarkable Type G 7e torpedo is outside the scope of this book, but it must be admitted that its performance was somewhat inferior to that of the conventional thermal-engined weapon. Nevertheless it was widely used by the U-boat service.

The output of electric torpedoes achieved the astonishing figure of almost 1,000 units per month, and just over 75 percent of all the torpedoes fired by Hitler's U-boats were battery powered.[25] By comparison British torpedo production never exceeded 500 weapons a month, having started in 1939 at a rate of 80 a month.[26] (In the period from 1875 to 1917 Whitehead's Fiume factory only turned out a total of 12,000, i.e., less than one per working day.) The reason was not hard to discover. The German G 7e required only 1,255 man-hours for completion using semiskilled labor. The equivalent thermal-engined weapon needed 1,707 man-hours with a highly skilled work force. In the context of modern warfare the mathematics of production schedules can be as important as the tactical skill of admirals and sea commanders.

Schwartzkopffs, by then known as the Berliner Maschinenbau aG, also returned to the torpedo scene again in 1935 after discontinuing production in 1918. And by one of those strange coincidences that seem to abound in torpedo history their first task was to copy the thermal-engined Norwegian Horten aerial torpedo for use by the Luftwaffe. Unlike their initial copy of Whitehead's Fiume design, however, the Horten was a disaster and Germany was forced to go cap in hand to Italy to buy suitable weapons from Whitehead's old factory, which was now under Italian control.[27]

To return to the electric torpedo, the G 7e, like its more conventional sister, the G 7a, still owed much to Whitehead's various inventions. It was almost identical in shape and, apart from the power unit, the internal layout was similar, while the depth-keeping and steering mechanisms still adhered to the principles of *The Secret*, the gyroscope, and the servomotor. It differed in only one respect—the Woolwich system of placing the propellers abaft the rudders was adopted, a strange decision by Germany's expert designers when Whitehead's original configuration had proved to more hydrodynamically efficient.

There were other detailed changes, for by the time the Second World War started the German Navy had come down in favor of the magnetic proximity exploder in preference to the pistol contact detonator with which all torpedoes had been fitted for the previous seventy years. A refined version of the magnetic fuse formed an integral part of all Type G 7 warheads when war broke out in 1939, but the results it achieved were, to begin with, extremely disappointing due to the device malfunctioning. Otto Kretschmer, one of Germany's top U-boat aces, saw his complete outfit of torpedoes pass beneath their target without exploding on his first combat patrol, while Gunther Prien, the "Bull of Scapa Flow," estimated that at least 50 percent of his torpedoes failed to detonate when he attacked and sank the battleship HMS *Royal Oak* on 14 October 1939.[28]

The reports of weapon failures increased daily as other U-boat captains returned home with similar tales of woe and as Konteradmiral (Rear Admiral) Karl Dönitz grimly observed in his memoirs: "Faith in the torpedo had been completely lost."[29] In his capacity as *Befehlshaber der Unterseeboots* (Commander in Chief, U-boats) the admiral promptly carried out his own internal inquiry into the problem, which revealed that not only were the magnetic exploders of the G 7a and G 7e weapons totally unreliable but that the contact pistols were also faulty, and as if this was not enough, the torpedoes inexplicably suffered from erratic depth keeping. And indeed at one point, soon after the end of the Norwegian campaign, it was touch and go whether the U-boats would be committed to battle until the torpedo defects had been rectified—a view strongly supported by Kommodore Eberhard Godt, the chief of the operations branch.

While Dönitz visited combat flotillas and training bases to boost flagging morale, Konteradmiral Oskar Kummetz, the inspector of torpedoes, tackled the technical aspects of the failures, and on 20 April 1940 the commander-in-chief, Erich Raeder, intervened by setting up a Torpedo Commission to investigate the problems. The preliminary findings of the commission led to the issue of an immediate blanket ban on the use of the magnetic exploder, which the Kriegsmarine had pioneered during the interwar years. This initial setback was counterbalanced, however, by the efforts of Germany's torpedo scientists, who, working day and night, produced an improved and reliable contact pistol within a matter of weeks. And by the end of May the first of these modified impact detonators were already being fitted to G 7 warheads.

It took much longer to trace the cause of the depth-keeping difficulties, and it was January 1942 before the experts discovered that the balance chambers of the G 7a and G 7e torpedoes were not airtight. Further technical investigation revealed that the gland of the rudder shaft—which somewhat incredibly passed *through* the offending compartment—leaked compressed air into the chamber. This raised the critical internal pressure of the chamber above atmospheric, which, in turn, caused the torpedo to run deep. And accurate depth keeping was, of course, imperative for the successful operation of a magnetic exploder. Following the investigation Konteradmiral Kummetz put the failure rate of all G 7 weapons, whether triggered by magnetic influence or by impact, at 34.2 percent. Dönitz, however, considered it to be much higher.

On 11 June 1940 Raeder issued a secret memorandum in which he threatened "to call to account" the persons responsible for the failures if the Torpedo Commission found evidence of "culpable negligence."[30] And in a further secret Command Document, *No. 83-a-42*, dated 9 February 1942, he reported ominously that "this has been done."[31] Four officers and officials were court-martialed as a result of the Torpedo Commission's report and, having been adjudged guilty of culpable negligence, were punished accordingly. The trial, which lasted for six weeks, revealed that the depth-keeping fault had been first noted during running tests at the Torpedo Experimental Establishment at Eckernförde as long ago as 1936, when both the G 7a and the G 7e were found to have a tendency to run from six to nine feet below their set depth. However, "no proper and energetic attempts were made to erradicate" the fault.[32]

In view of the U.S. Navy's subsequent problems with its own Mark VI magnetic exploder Raeder's comments are not without interest. "Although sound in its basic design," he wrote, "the magnetic pistol possessed one fault, which did not come to light until it had been used in action, namely, the danger of spontaneous detonation caused by mechanical oscillations during the torpedo's run." And, even more relevant to the scandal of America's torpedo failures in 1942, he continued: "No steps had been taken, by means of firing-tests . . . to ascertain the degree of vulnerability of the magnetic pistol to disturbance of this nature . . . [and] the Torpedo Experimental Establishment neglected to subject firing parts of the [magnetic] pistol to any thorough or systematic scrutiny."[33]

The German Navy's rigorous pursuit of the faults exposed in its torpedoes during the Norwegian campaign brought its rewards. The problems with the contact pistols were identified and corrected within a matter of weeks and by the end of 1942 depth keeping was, once again, reliable. In December of the same year the first of the new pattern magnetic exploders—which could also detonate by contact—were being issued to all operational submarines. Thanks to Raeder's ruthless methods, and unfortunately for the Allies, there were few instances of a German torpedo failing to detonate when the Battle of the Atlantic raged to its savage climax the following year.

In addition to its simplicity of production and its wakeless track, the electric torpedo had a further important advantage over its thermal-engined cousin—that of silent running. And it was this characteristic that led to the acoustic homing torpedo and the multitudinous variants that followed. Germany, first in the field as usual, began experiments with a homing torpedo several years before the war started. And the results of these early sonic tests revealed a remarkable fact. It was not the power unit that provided the weapon's individual aurora of sound, but its speed; and as the electric torpedo was considerably slower than the thermal-engined weapon, it emitted less noise.[34] Further investigation showed that if both types were run at the same speed, there was an almost identical volume of background noise; and the sound source was traced back to the propellers rather than, as had been generally supposed, to the engines themselves. As a result of these tests scientists were able to demonstrate that the optimum speed of an acoustic torpedo, that is, a weapon that could lock on to its target by means of the sound waves its victim emitted, was 25 knots. Speed, it seemed, was no longer the *sine qua non* for hitting the target.

Although the first experiments had begun in 1936 a viable weapon was not produced until 1942 and the initial batch of Type T 4 homing torpedoes reached the U-boat flotillas in January 1943. Once in production modifications quickly followed, and in a very short space of time, the Type T 5 GNAT (German Naval Acoustic Torpedo) replaced the original model. They were not, however, quite so successful as the Nazi propaganda machine claimed. A total of 640 were fired operationally with a strike rate of only 6 percent[35]—a disastrously poor result when compared with Whitehead's pioneer runs in the late 1860s. And even these dismal results were only obtained after the expenditure of a further 2,500 GNATs on testing and experimental runs.

The Type T 5 was closely based on the G 7e and was a 21-inch weapon weighing 3,300 pounds with a range of just over 6,000 yards at 25 knots. It was only effective against ships traveling at between 12 and 19 knots due to the critical level of noise necessary to activate the acoustic receiver unit.

There were many variations on the homing theme, and in one instance, when the Allies began to use decoy noise floats to draw the acoustic torpedo away from its intended victim, German scientists retaliated by producing a selective weapon containing a receiver unit that would only respond to low frequency sound radiations. This new variation, code named TAUBE, was not a great success as its own noise level rendered its sensitive receiver almost totally inactive with the result that it not only avoided the decoy—it missed the target as well!

Another version, the LERCHE, used a wire-control system by which the operator could pick up sound waves received via a passive hydrophone in the nose of the torpedo, distinguish the decoy noises from those emitted by the target vessel, and then steer the weapon by means of the same wire. It was, however, produced too late in the war to become operational, which may have been a lucky escape for the U-boat crews, for the dual-purpose control wire conjures up visions of the infamous Lay torpedo and its often suicidal antics.

Ideas, each more incredible than its predecessor, were rife as scientists on both sides strove to produce better and more effective torpedoes as the war progressed. The majority, not unexpectedly, were doomed to failure and in practice very few ever got beyond the drawing board. One that failed to reach the testing stage was a British brainstorm in which the torpedo was propelled through the water by a pair of folding vanes which oscillated backwards and forwards along the axis of the torpedo rather in the fashion of a fish's gills.[36] Germany, too, had thoughts along similar lines and a G 7e was fitted with a flapping wing that to everyone's surprise actually worked! Encouraged by their unexpected success Nazi scientists went a stage further and produced a flapping-wing design that in appearance resembled the Lockheed Lightning twin-boom fighter aircraft. It proved to be a technically viable project and measured up well to the demands of the specification. There was only one snag. No one had stopped to consider how a U-boat could either accommodate or launch a twin-boom torpedo.[37]

Experiments were also carried out with hydrogen-peroxide engines, and thanks to the work of Professor Helmuth Walter, the weapon that finally emerged, the STEINWAL, actually went into production and saw operational service before the war ended. Other interesting developments included the IBIS, a wake-following torpedo that homed on its target by means of acoustic echoes from the ship's wake; circling weapons that followed a continuous course through 360 degrees until something chanced to cross their path—an ideal system for attacks on large convoys; and the LUT, a pattern-running torpedo. This latter weapon was built around a special gyroscope that, fitted to a long-range turbine-powered STEINWAL, enabled the torpedo to follow a complicated prepatterned course designed to make avoidance difficult for the target vessel.[38] It was, in many respects, the prototype of today's computerized torpedo. And—with the earlier Type T-5—it spearheaded underwater weaponry into the era of the guided missile.

Incomprehensibly Stubborn and Stupid

Although the Kriegsmarine had taken urgent steps to iden-
tify and cure the cause of the torpedo failures that bedeviled Germany's U-boats in the opening months of the Second World War, the
U.S. Navy's response to an almost identical crisis in the months
immediately following Pearl Harbor—when American submarine
commanders experienced a similar series of weapon malfunctions—
was hampered by official complacency and a determined refusal to
face facts. And the unhappy saga of the Mark 14 torpedo and its Mark
VI magnetic exploder is, perhaps, a perfect example of the mayhem
that can be created when experts bury their heads in the sand and
steadfastly refuse to face facts. The "mother knows best" syndrome
is, sadly, often little more than a cloak for ignorance and bureaucratic
lethargy.

The United States has always tended to march to a different
drummer when it comes to torpedo development, spurning Whitehead's weapon in 1869 and on two subsequent occasions on the
grounds of cost, and alone amongst the world's major maritime nations, choosing to ignore the provenly successful compressed-air

power units produced by Fiume, Woolwich, and Berlin in favor of the Howell flywheel system. Even when in 1892 the Bliss Williams Company negotiated to build the Whitehead torpedo under licence at their Brooklyn factory, it was not long before its proprietor, Frank Leavitt, discarded the Brotherhood radial engine and adopted instead the home-grown Curtis turbine. America was thus very much on her own when it came to torpedo technology, although, admittedly, the Bliss-built weapons depended on Whitehead patents for their depth-keeping mechanisms, steering controls, pistol detonators, and a host of other vital features.

In 1907 the U.S. Navy built its own torpedo production unit close to the Torpedo Station at Newport—America's only other underwater weapons factory at that time being the privately owned Bliss Company in Brooklyn. It is not generally realized that the Torpedo Station at Newport, Rhode Island, is the world's oldest official torpedo establishment, having been originally set up by the U.S. Navy in 1869 for experiments with the spar torpedo. The Royal Navy's HMS *Vernon*, although older, did not start life as an exclusive torpedo trials depot, and much of its early work was concerned with static mines and underwater explosives in addition to experiments with spar and towed torpedoes.

The wartime demand for torpedoes led to the construction of another navy factory at Alexandria, Virginia, which finally opened in 1919 but was mothballed soon afterwards as the result of pressure from Rhode Island politicians representing the vested interests of the Newport establishment. The major product of the Brooklyn and Newport plants in the First World War was the turbine-powered Mark 10 weapon—a torpedo based on the Royal Navy's latest 21-inch model, which packed a 500-pound punch of TNT in its warhead and had a maximum range of about 13,000 yards with a top speed close to 40 knots.

Torpedo research at the U.S. Navy's Newport establishment was carried out under the direction of a young lieutenant from the U.S. Naval Academy's class of 1915—Ralph Waldo Christie. In 1922 he was given the task of developing an influence, as opposed to an impact, exploder—a top secret experimental program identified merely as *Project G 53*. Germany had already invented a form of magnetic trigger for its sea mines in the latter stages of the First World War, but the "trigger" was really little more than a compass needle that deviated under the influence of a ship's magnetic field as the vessel passed overhead and detonated the explosive. While such a device was clearly impractical for use in a fast-moving torpedo, it signposted a promising direction for research into influence detonators and concentrated attention on the production of a magnetic exploder.

A working prototype had been built by the beginning of 1924, but despite repeated requests from Christie and his superior officers at Newport, the Bureau of Ordnance refused to provide a suitable target on which to test the experimental warhead. One excuse offered was based upon fears for the safety of the vessel that was to fire the torpedo. The bureaucrats clearly had little confidence in the ability of the officers on the staff of the Newport Torpedo Station.

Finally, the Navy yielded to the demands of Captain Thomas Hart—Newport's commanding officer—and on 8 May 1926 the prototype magnetic exploder was test fired at the obsolete submarine *L-8* although the torpedo was not launched from a submarine, as Christie had wanted, but from a tube on the test range. The first shot missed but the second detonated underneath the target vessel and the *L-8* went to the bottom in double-quick time. The magnetic exploder was clearly a viable proposition.

Christie was also engaged in the design of an improved torpedo for use with the latest fleet submarines, and in a process of natural evolution, it was decided that this new weapon should carry the revolutionary Mark VI magnetic influence exploder—a refined version of the experimental prototype initially tested in 1926. The new torpedo was designated the Mark 14. Powered by a heater turbine, it had a maximum speed of 46 knots, and its maximum range at reduced speed was 9,000 yards. It carried a 500-pound warhead. But incredibly, thanks to the intransigent attitude of the chief of naval operations, tests of the Mark 14 with its magnetic exploder were restricted to models equipped with dummy warheads that were fitted with a photoelectric cell in lieu of explosives, and at *no time* was a live warhead fired to test the efficacy of the magnetic exploder as the means of detonating the torpedo's charge. Even more surprisingly, the Mark VI was put into production without being subjected to a single live test.[1]

Tight security meant that the majority of submarine commanders were unaware of the Mark VI magnetic exploder, and when the first

Mark 14 torpedoes were issued to the navy's underwater flotillas, they were fitted with a dummy contact pistol, the Mark V. Thus the very men who would be called upon to operate the new torpedoes in combat were denied any practical knowledge or experience of the weapon's revolutionary Mark VI exploder. Indeed, security went to such farcical lengths that is was decided not to produce a printed edition of the exploder's Operating Manual for fear of compromising its secrets. And, having been written, it was locked away in a safe in manuscript form. The Imperial Japanese Navy suffered a similar blind spot over its *Type-A* midget submarines and enforced such stringent security that, although the two-man crews had been trained to operate them, the commanders of the *I*-class submarines from which they were to be launched off Pearl Harbor had never seen or handled one before they were hoisted aboard the mother ships in readiness for their first operational mission. It was something of a minor miracle that any of the *Type-A* midgets ever took to the water on that historic December night in 1941.

Christie had become head of the Bureau of Ordnance's Torpedo Section by 1938 and as the war clouds gathered in both east and west he expanded the Newport establishment and persuaded Congress to approve the reopening of the mothballed Alexandria factory. A short while later he also obtained an appropriation to open a third production facility at Keyport, Washington, D.C., although, even with this additional capacity, output remained insufficient to meet the navy's requirements—a problem faced by nearly all major maritime nations until the complicated thermal-engined torpedoes were replaced by the less technically demanding electric models. To add to Christie's production problems the old Bliss factory had long since abandoned building torpedoes although, happily, it returned to weapon manufacture soon after the outbreak of war.

Although the Mark VI exploders began to enter regular service in October 1941, submarine captains were given little guidance on routine adjustments or operational usage beyond a general admonition to fire deep. And although intelligence sources must have by now learned of the German Navy's difficulties with both contact and influence exploders there was still no attempt by the Bureau of Ordnance to carry out live tests.

One important advantage of the magnetic exploder was that of economy. By detonating *under* the keel of the target ship, only one torpedo was necessary to sink the average vessel as against the two or three weapons necessary to destroy a ship using torpedoes fitted with conventional impact pistols. This meant that the magnetic exploder was an important factor in maintaining an adequate reserve of torpedoes—especially with the shortfall in contemporary production schedules. The bureau therefore suffered a rude awakening when war overtook the Pacific and exposed the deficiencies of its new wonder weapon. Far from being economic, the Mark 14 was profligate in its expenditure, and submarine commanders found themselves being forced to fire an excessive number of torpedoes in order to get just one to explode under the target. Between Christmas Eve and Boxing Day, 26 December 1941, for example, the USS *Sargo* fired thirteen torpedoes in six separate attacks and not a single weapon exploded! Her skipper, Commander Tyrrell D. Jacobs, concluded that the torpedoes were running deeper than their preset depth because their combat warheads were heavier than the dummies fitted for practice runs—a fault which had caused the Royal Navy its fair share of woe in the early days of the 1914 conflict when the experts failed to allow for the variation in weight when issuing their operating instructions.

But even when the torpedoes were adjusted to run at a shallower depth *and* the magnetic exploder was deactivated there was no improvement, and breaking radio silence, Jacobs angrily reported the failures to Captain John Wilkes, the officer responsible for the Asiatic Fleet's submarine force. By coincidence, and only a few weeks earlier, Wilkes had been advised by the Bureau of Ordnance that the veteran Mark 10, which was still in service despite its First World War origins, had been found to run some four feet deeper than designed. No mention, however, was made of the Mark 14 in this context, and Wilkes did not consider it necessary to conduct tests on the new torpedo to find out if it suffered from a similar problem. Neither, so far as can be ascertained, did any other senior commander.

Although Wilkes reprimanded Jacobs for deactivating the magnetic exploder, he was wise enough to listen to the latter's complaints about the Mark 14's depth keeping and he passed word to his other skippers to employ a shallower setting. But an Ordnance Bureau expert, having investigated the problem *in situ*, blamed the failures on the *Sargo's* crewmen and reaffirmed that the Mark 14 was running at the correct depth. It should be added that this unseemly wrangle took place while the U.S. Asiatic Fleet's submarines were being withdrawn from Manila to Surabaya in Dutch-controlled Sumatra to escape destruction by Japanese bombers. Ultimately, the East Indies, too, had to be evacuated and in May 1942 a new permenant base for the submarine force was set up at Fremantle on Australia's western coast.

The excessive number of torpedoes being expended soon dented the reserve stocks, and by the time the Pacific Fleet's submarines had returned from their first patrols in December and January and replenished their empty tubes, Pearl Harbor's arsenal was down to just 101 weapons—barely enough to kit-out four *Sargo*-class boats. Even more worrying, the stocks were only being replaced at the rate of twenty-four weapons per month—the torpedo complement of a single modern fleet-type submarine.

Now that he was finally ensconced at Fremantle, Captain Wilkes, backed by his chief of staff, James Fife, sent a Report of Operations to Admiral Ernest King, commander in chief of the United States Fleet and chief of naval operations, in which he boldly asserted that the Mark 14 ran too deep and that the Mark VI magnetic exploder was unreliable. But despite this damning indictment by a senior officer little seems to have been done. And it was not only the Asiatic Fleet commanders who were complaining about defective torpedoes. The Pearl Harbor skippers were suffering similar problems—their frustrations being exacerbated by the Commander, Submarine Force Pacific Fleet, Rear Admiral Thomas Withers, who refused to authorize deactivation of the exploders and insisted that they operate by the book. As a result many submarine captains submitted misleading reports to conceal the fact that they had disobeyed orders by making unauthorized adjustments to their torpedoes—a state of affairs that was to boomerang on all concerned in due course for the doctored facts led to a distortion of the true scale of torpedo and exploder failures.

A command shake-up in March 1942 gave Commander George C. Crawford charge of Division 42, and aware that both the Kriegsmarine and the Royal Navy had quietly jettisoned their original magnetic exploders, he told his skippers to deactivate their Mark VIs—an instruction that brought Crawford a roasting from Withers, who told him: "I *know* it works. I was at Newport when it was tested."[2] And to compound the confusion a number of submarine captains were quite satisfied with the new technology. Lieutenant Commander Frank Fenno of the *Trout*, for example, had fired a total of twenty-one torpedoes fitted with magnetic exploders in the course of his March patrol and had claimed five ships sunk plus a sixth damaged.[3] His tally was confirmed by Naval Intelligence,[4] and his success gave Withers and the other supporters of the Mark VI fresh ammunition to use against their opponents.

By the end of March, however, virtually every combat captain was convinced that the Mark 14 and the Mark VI were defective. But the shore-based experts would not accept the eyewitness accounts and firsthand experiences of the submarine commanders and refused to carry out live tests of the offending weapon. In the words of submarine historian Clay Blair, their refusal to listen was "in retrospect, incomprehensibly stubborn and stupid."[5] Even worse, many of the staffers considered that the captains were at fault. And with typical lack of tact they did not hesitate to say so.

Fortunately for America's war effort the impasse ended when Rear Admiral Charles Lockwood was appointed to succeed John Wilkes at Fremantle. Lockwood listened patiently to the complaints of his captains and raised the matter with the Bureau of Ordnance only to receive the usual, almost disdainful, brush-off that the failures lay with the poor marksmanship of the submarine commanders and not with the weapons they were using. Lockwood, having failed to obtain results through orthodox channels, decided to take matters into his own hands, and during tests in Frenchman's Bay on 20 June 1942, he was able to demonstrate that the Mark 14 was running an average of *eleven* feet below its set depth. Two days later he sent details of the tests to the bureau, but as was only to be expected, his results were dismissed as inconclusive and insufficiently scientific.

The rear admiral, however, was not easily defeated, and on 18 July he staged further tests under the supervision of Jimmy Fife, now his chief of staff, which proved, yet again, that the Mark 14 was running some eleven feet below its recommended depth. This time Admiral King received a copy of the report, and as an exsubmariner himself, took up the cudgels and asked the bureau to recheck its data.

The Newport establishment's own tests were carried out by the submarine *Herring*, which fired a series of Mark 14 weapons while submerged, and at the beginning of August the experts conceded that the torpedo was running ten feet below its set depth. And in a detailed follow-up report some six weeks later it was admitted that the depth-control mechanism—the section of the torpedo known as *The Secret* in Whitehead's day—was improperly designed and inadequately tested. Within days modification instructions were issued to all submarine commands, which, the bureau claimed, would reduce the depth-keeping error to three feet or less.

Strangely enough neither Lockwood nor Rear Admiral Bob English, who had succeeded Withers as the Pacific Fleet Submarine Force commander at Pearl Harbor, considered that the magnetic exploder was suspect even though they both knew that Britain and Germany had discarded their influence detonators. And firmly of the opinion that the failure of the exploders was due solely to the excessive depth at which the torpedoes had been running, they refused to authorize deactivation of the Mark VI. Lockwood also ruled out a live test of the exploder, which, after two years of operational service and despite its questionable reputation, had still never been properly tested by *anyone.*

This situation continued for a further eight months despite increasing evidence that the exploder was faulty, and by April 1943 captains were reporting that large targets, such as aircraft carriers and battleships, were causing the warheads to detonate prematurely due to the exploder reaching activating flux density while still some 50 yards from the target. By now, and not surprisingly, even Lockwood was beginning to have second thoughts about the Mark VI.

In January 1943 Bob English had been killed in an air crash, and in the ensuing command changes Lockwood found himself transferred to Pearl Harbor, where he took over English's old job, while Ralph Christie, promoted to rear admiral, was given command of the Fremantle submarines. But although he now found himself at the sharp end of the war and in control of operational submarines, Christie retained his confidence in the Mark VI exploder despite the increasingly biting comments he was receiving from Lockwood. And in a letter to his opposite number in Hawaii he took the unusual step of assuming full responsibility: "The shortcomings of the submarine torpedo can be laid to me very properly for, for 2½ years, I had charge of the design of the Mark 14 and for three tours [of duty] at the Newport Torpedo Station was concerned with the magnetic exploder."[6] Although Christie's confidence was misplaced it was good to see a senior officer standing by his responsibilities instead of ducking and diving to escape the blame.

But more failures—including a missed opportunity to sink the carriers *Hiyo* and *Junyo*[7]—proved to be the straw that broke the camel's back and Lockwood, acting with Admiral Chester W. Nimitz's authority, ordered all Pearl Harbor submarines to deactivate their magnetic exploders. Christie at Fremantle—responsible to Admiral William F. Halsey rather than Nimitz—stuck to his guns (or more accurately his torpedoes) and refused to follow suit. As a result, for the next few months the Pearl Harbor boats were operating with deactivated exploders while those in Fremantle continued to rely on the Mark VI influence detonator.

Matters finally reached crisis point in July when the *Tinosa* fired no fewer than fifteen deactivated Mark 14 torpedoes at the 19,000-ton whale factory ship *Tonan Maru* under almost perfect conditions. Thirteen of the weapons hit the enemy vessel but only two actually exploded. Such an abortive attack by an experienced captain could only mean one thing—the contact pistol was also faulty.

Lockwood, by now almost at the end of his tether, ordered further exhaustive tests to be carried out and, at considerable risk to life and limb, was able to prove that the mechanism was defective because of poor design work. Experimental firings showed that, when the torpedo struck the target at an angle of 90 degrees—the criteria of a good shot—the exploder was crushed before it reached the fulminate caps of the detonator. Conversely, there was an improved chance of detonation with a glancing blow. Thus a captain with only mediocre skill could often claim a victim while the good marksman consistently failed to obtain results.

Once the fault had been identified it did not take long for Newport's experts to modify the trigger design, and following a series of rigorous tests on the Rhode Island range, the new contact pistol proved to be completely satisfactory under combat conditions. By September 1943 the ill-starred Mark 14 was finally fit for service—twenty-one months too late.

As Clay Blair has written in his definitive *Silent Victory:* "The torpedo scandal of the U.S. submarine force in World War Two was one of the worst in the history of any kind of warfare."[8]

The United States Navy, like Germany's Kriegsmarine, took an early interest in the electric torpedo. The Bureau of Ordnance first came up with the idea in 1915, and the Sperry Gyroscope Company was given a contract to produce a prototype. The result was a battery-powered weapon with a diameter of only 7.25-inches, weighing just 60 pounds, and measuring 6 feet from nose to tail. Its performance on paper promised a speed of 25 knots and a range of 3,800 yards; but it failed to achieve these figures in practice, and when the war ended in 1918 the project was quietly shelved although residual experimental work on a one-man basis continued spasmodically at Newport. A Mark 1 version was finally built during the twenties but was lost during trials—by coincidence the same fate as that suffered by Whitehead's original prototype in 1866—and nothing more was heard of the project until 1941 when Exide (The Electric Storage Battery Company) and the General Electric Company began work on a Mark 2 under the direct supervision of Newport's experts.

However, when the Newport establishment failed to meet the production requirements of the Ordnance Bureau—mainly because the factory was already working all hours of the day and night building turbine torpedoes for the navy and General Electric had no spare capacity for expansion—a contract was offered to the Westinghouse Electric and Manufacturing Corporation, who, after discussions and an examination of the data so far obtained by Newport, wisely decided to build an exact copy of the successful German G 7e, several examples of which had been found stranded on the beaches of the Atlantic seaboard in 1942. This new electric torpedo was designated the Mark 18.

Westinghouse surpassed all expectations by producing a completed design within six weeks of being approached by the bureau and on 2 May 1942 an order was placed for two thousand of the new weapons. Just fifteen weeks later the initial batch to come off the production line arrived in Newport for testing and evaluation. Not for the first time—nor, for that matter, the last—private enterprise had proved to be speedier and more efficient than government manufacturing sources. But unfortunately the golden promise of the Mark 18 quickly lost its glitter.

The batteries gave trouble and circuits misbehaved. In addition, the more conventional mechanical parts of the weapon proved defective because the unskilled labor force recruited to build the torpedoes was unable to work within the tolerances required. To make matters worse, Newport's experts showed little interest in what they regarded as an upstart competitor. In the words of the Inspector General who intervened at the behest of Admiral King: "The delays encountered were largely the result of the manner in which the project was prosecuted and carried out. . . . The Torpedo Station personnel competed with rather than co-operated with [Westinghouse] over the development of the Mark 18. . . ."[9] It was certainly a situation that stood in sharp contrast to the happy relationship that had existed between Whitehead and the Royal Laboratory at Woolwich in the early days of torpedo development when ideas and refinements were exchanged with eager and appreciative gratitude.

Part of the problem was due to Newport's continued involvement in the carefully engineered Mark 2, which, typically, was absorbing more time, money, and resources than expected. It was, indeed, a perfect example of official bureaucracy pursuing the "gnat of perfection"—that mythical creature of Fisher's much-quoted aphorism.

But thanks to Westinghouse's perseverence and to encouragement from the right sources, the first Mark 18 torpedoes finally began coming into service in early 1944, although their original speed was a disappointing 15 knots slower than the turbine-powered Mark 14. Six months later, however, the electric weapon was running at 40 knots and the initial trickle became a flood as production got under way. Indeed, by 1945 the torpedo complement of most U.S. submarines was made up of 75 percent Mark 18s and 25 percent Mark 14s—mainly due to the easy availability of the former. But as Clay Blair has pointed out, the increased supply of torpedoes encouraged captains to fire a full salvo at promising targets when a smaller number would have probably sufficed.[10] And for this reason, statistically, it took an average expenditure of ten torpedoes for every ship sunk. Bearing in mind the low level of output at the beginning of 1942 the vitally important part played by the Mark 18 electric torpedo in America's underwater victory over Japan is readily apparent from this summary of torpedoes fired in combat by U.S. submarines during the Pacific conflict:

1942 and 1943:	5,379
1944:	6,092
1945:	3,277

The unique characteristics of the electrically propelled torpedo led both Britain and the United States to follow Germany's example and explore the potential of the acoustic weapon. The Royal Navy

The U.S. Navy's highly successful Mark 48 torpedo. (Photograph courtesy of the U.S. Navy.)

Recovering torpedoes after testing off Puerto Rico in 1972. (Photograph courtesy of the U.S. Navy.)

tried several different designs, each being discarded in favor of the next before the previous model had been perfected.[11] As a result although each succeeding pattern was more promising than its predecessor, the final modification—code named TRUMPER and based on the RNTF 21-inch Mark VIII and Mark IX torpedoes—was still undergoing trials when the war ended and Britain had to fight to victory beneath the waves without it. Yet another example of striving for ''the gnat of perfection'' and ending up with the ''camel of unreadiness.''

America's interest initially centered on the development of the acoustic torpedo as an antisubmarine weapon, and the 21-inch Mark 24, just seven feet in overall length and the first of the modern generation of lightweight torpedoes, was put into service just under three years from its conception—no mean feat by comparison with the long drawn-out trials and tribulations of the British and German models. Its speed was, admittedly, only a pedestrian 12 knots, but this was more than adequate to catch and kill a slow-moving submerged U-boat of World War Two vintage.

Today's acoustic torpedo—unlike its American and German predecessors—is a provenly successful antiship weapon. And it emerged triumphantly from its baptism of fire on 9 December 1971, when the Pakistan Navy's *Daphne*-class submarine *Hangor* sank the Indian frigate *Khukri* and damaged the *Kirpan* during a submerged torpedo attack in the Gulf of Khambhat using French-built 550-millimeter (21.7-inch) Type E 14 or Type E 15 acoustic torpedoes equipped with passive homing devices.

The latest developments in torpedo design are, of course, shrouded under the cloak of national security and many of the details bandied about in the press are of doubtful validity. For this reason it is perhaps wiser to give only a brief outline of today's state-of-the-art technology and for the reader to bear in mind the absence of official confirmation.

The modern sonar homing torpedo relies, basically, on directional sound impulses. The more common passive sonar homing head does not transmit sonic pulses—it merely detects external sounds on a very sensitive hydrophone. Active sonar, by contrast, measures acoustic pulses which it transmits on an audio frequency band of approximately 20 to 35 kilohertz using pulse rates varying from 12.5 to 700 milliseconds. In some designs the homing device is

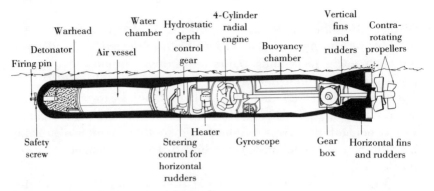

RNTF Mark VIII 21-inch TORPEDO

An exploded view of the Royal Navy's Mark VIII 21-inch torpedo. Two of these vintage weapons sank the Argentine *General Belgrano* in May 1982. (Diagram by Dominic Thomas.)

self-contained and guides the torpedo to the target without outside assistance. In other models the sonar information is passed back to the submarine, where computers feed directional instructions back to the weapon.

Although wire-guided torpedoes seem to be increasingly favored by the world's navies, they apparently have yet to achieve 100 percent reliability, particularly under combat conditions, and there have been several reports that the command wire of the German-built SST-4 weapons used by the Argentine submarine *San Luis* broke on each of three occasions the torpedo was fired at a British target during the Falklands conflict.[12] During one attack on the frigates *Alacrity* and *Arrow* off Cape Dolphin the submarine's fire-control computer broke down and Capitan de Fregata (Commander) Azcueta decided to launch a single SST-4 under manual control using the data supplied by the *San Luis*'s sonar equipment. The guidance wire broke after two and a half minutes running time, however, but the weapon apparently succeeded in reaching the target, for a small explosion was heard. When the *Arrow* retrieved her towed torpedo decoy some time later it was found to be badly damaged—conclusive evidence that British electronic countermeasures had outwitted the SST-4's homing device. The guidance-wire problem is yet another demonstration of history's inclination to repeat itself, for some 160 years earlier Robert Fulton had been complaining bitterly about the difficulties he

A Mark 48 is loaded aboard the USS *Pargo* (SSN-650)—a picture that
links Robert Whitehead to the nuclear age. (Photograph courtesy of the
U.S. Navy.)

had encountered when he tried "to preserve long wires from being torn or broken" while he was experimenting with the electrical detonation of mines.[13]

The Soviet Navy may possibly be following a different path, for its latest torpedo, the Type 65, is alleged to rely on "wake detection"— minute changes in the sea's magnetic field that take place following the passage of a ship through the water and that, it is said, can be measured by inboard computers. In order to provide sufficient space for the necessary advanced electronic technology the Type 65 rivals the Brennan for size, being, according to unofficial sources, some 30 feet in length with a diameter of 650 millimeters (25.6 inches)—a rare departure from Whitehead's standard 21-inch caliber. According to the same sources this new Soviet weapon uses an oxygen propellant supplemented by recycled exhaust gases and has an estimated range of 100 kilometers at 30 knots or 50 kilometers at 50 knots.[14]

The United States now tends, in common with other Western powers, to produce two distinct types of underwater weapons—the heavyweight 21-inch antiship torpedo, which in its latest form, utilizes OTTO (liquid monopropellant) fuel and a smaller, 12.75-inch, antisubmarine lightweight torpedo that "swims" out of a standard 21-inch tube. These lightweight models are usually powered by electricity, but the latest known weapon uses a solid propellant, which, it is said, was first devised by British scientists but never followed up.

The development program for America's Mark 48 heavyweight weapon dates back to November 1956 and series production of the torpedo, which is built by the Gould Corporation, began in 1976. Equipped with wire guidance and a digital guidance system the Mark 48 is propelled by an axial flow pump-jet propulsor driven by an OTTO monopropellant gas piston engine that gives a reputed 55-knot speed and a range of 21 miles. Its maximum operating depth of 3,000 feet is, however, only barely adequate to catch the modern nuclear submarine and work is now proceeding on DEXTOR—a deep experimental torpedo specifically designed for use against nukes operating below 3,000 feet. No other information about this new weapon is available.

Also of interest to students and practitioners of underwater warfare is the now obsolete Mark 45 ASTOR, which was built to carry an antisubmarine *nuclear* warhead—perhaps the only example of a torpedo's design being inhibited by political considerations, for U.S.

policy demanded "full control" of nuclear weapons and the government insisted that the Mark 45 should be wire guided all the way to the target. This particular requirement caused some dismay in the navy for it necessitated the use of active sonar and thus exposed the launch vehicle to electronic detection at all stages of the attack.

Britain has, perhaps, the sorriest postwar record of torpedo development of any country in the world—a sad reversal of her pioneering lead in the nineteenth century. And the disastrous saga of the Mark 24 TIGERFISH provides a salutary example of exactly what *can* go wrong with a new weapon system. Although the TIGERFISH emerged from the drawing board as a long-bodied torpedo it was, in fact, intended as a replacement for the short Mark 20 and Mark 23 models and as such should have entered service in the mid-sixties. It presented so many problems, however, that the redesigned Model 1 did not become fully operational until 1981—and then only at prodigious cost.

Wire guided on launching, but homing on the target during the latter stages of the attack with the aid of its own 3-D sonar and an inboard computer, the TIGERFISH has a diameter of 21-inches, a length of 21 feet 2 inches, and an all-up weight of 1,650 pounds. Powered by a two-speed electric motor, its contrarotating propellers give it an unofficial maximum speed of 40 knots and a range of 12,000 yards. But despite such an advanced specification, its misdeeds rate it alongside such "old favorites" as the notorious Lay dirigible torpedo.

During development runs in 1970 an unarmed TIGERFISH ran ashore on a golf course alongside the Clyde. Another struck the Rothesay ferry—fortunately without ill-effects to the vessel.[15] Following a series of disastrous trials, the Marconi Company was brought in to iron out the bugs in a two-year modification program costing an unconfirmed £40 million. But although a modified Model O TIGERFISH finally entered service in 1974, it clearly inspired little confidence, and when Commander Christopher Wreford-Brown was ordered to sink the Argentine cruiser *General Belgrano* on 2 May 1982, he chose to ignore the *Conqueror*'s wire-guided TIGERFISH and used, instead, three tried and trusted RNTF Mark VIII** thermal torpedoes that were designed nearly fifty years earlier in 1935.[16] But

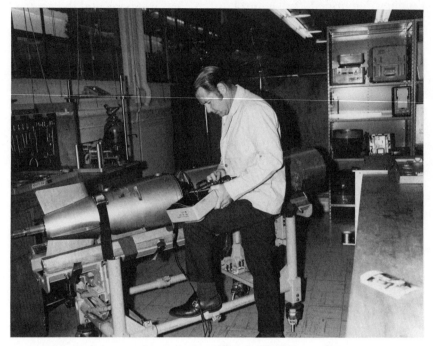

A Mark 46 under test at the U.S. Naval Torpedo Station at Keyport, Washington, D.C. (Photograph courtesy of the U.S. Navy.)

even these were not 100 percent successful, for only two weapons actually detonated while the third, which missed the cruiser and is thought to have hit the destroyer *Boucha*, failed to explode.

Wreford-Brown's caution proved to be justified, for during cleaning-up operations after the war had ended, two TIGERFISH failed to sink the burned-out hulk of the *Sir Galahad* because of battery faults while a third, working in its wire-guidance mode, made three separate passes at the wrecked *Bahia Buen Suceso* and missed on each occasion.[17] It is said that early versions of the Mark 24 suffered a 75 percent failure rate—a record of misfortune that puts it in the same class as America's wartime Mark 14—and that the Marconi modifications have resulted in a dramatic improvement in both performance and reliability. But although an improved TIGER-FISH Model 1 succeeded in sinking the old frigate *Lowestoft* during live firing trials on 8 June 1986,[18] the weapon is now being phased out in favour of the SPEARFISH.

This latter torpedo, another product of the Marconi Company, is wire guided on launching, but at an undisclosed distance from the target, directional control is taken over by an inboard computer that is fed with acoustic data supplied by an active sonar homing device—a system similar in concept to that already adopted in the TIGER-FISH. Although developed from the technology of the earlier light-weight air-launched STING RAY—a smaller weapon powered by electricity—the SPEARFISH torpedo relies on a Sundstrand gas turbine reputedly capable of producing a speed of 70 knots.[19] But here again there have been problems, for the intended fuel mixture of HAP (hydroxyl amine perchlorate) and OTTO proved dangerously lethal and after three accidental explosions, government ordnance inspectors enforced temporary restrictions on its use. According to Marconi,

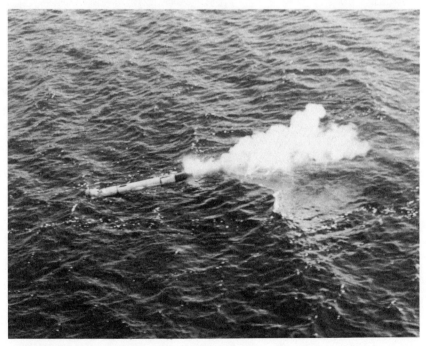

A Mark 45 Model 2 Freedom torpedo running in Dabob Bay, Washington, in 1972. (Photograph courtesy of the U.S. Navy.)

The torpedo tubes of the destroyer USS *Newman K. Perry*. (Photograph courtesy of the U.S. Navy.)

however, this particular problem has been satisfactorily resolved and the weapon is now in production.

Torpedo development costs have become astronomical since the end of the Second World War. The first Fiume weapon had a catalog price of £300, and Whitehead's total financial investment between 1865 and 1875 was estimated at around £40,000 in contemporary money terms.[20] The price had risen to £900 by 1914 and in 1939 the Royal Navy valued its RNTF 21-inch Mark VIII at £2,500. As a measure of comparison the U.S. Navy's current Mark 48 is said to cost $1 million—the new ADCAP (advanced capability) modifications adding a further $3 million to the bill. It is gratifying to learn that by 1986 the all-in cost of each Mark 48 ADCAP had been *reduced* to $3.4 million.

Britain's financial burden is, if anything, even more frightening; for whereas the United States at least has a viable weapon for its money in the shape of the Mark 48, the same cannot be said of the Royal Navy's disappointing TIGERFISH. The saga of financial disaster began in 1968, when the Mark 31's estimated development costs of £14 million so frightened Harold Wilson's Labor government that the project was abandoned after £5 million of taxpayers' money had been spent. Yet, just a year later, the modification program which Marconi undertook to overcome the design problems of the TIGER-

"Torpedoes Away!" (Photograph courtesy of the U.S. Navy.)

FISH cost the nation some £40 million, and according to the Report of the House of Commons' Public Accounts Committee issued in September 1985, the *total* development budget of this particular weapon was, by that date, in excess of £1 *billion!*[21]

The latest details to be made public reflect continually escalating costs. Press reports in 1987 revealed that Marconi Underwater Systems Ltd had won a £500 million contract for "the design, development, and production" of the new SPEARFISH torpedo—a figure intended to also include the main production run of the lightweight antisubmarine STINGRAY[22]—while an earlier report in *The Observer* alleged an overall cost of £991.1 million for 770 SPEARFISH weapons.[23] A Marconi spokesman put an estimated price of £500,000 on each SPEARFISH torpedo delivered to the Royal Navy, but if *The Observer* report is accurate, the true unit figure seems nearer to £1.25 million.

Even the prodigious expenditure on Paddockhurst, which so seriously eroded Whitehead's personal fortune, pales into insignificance alongside such fantastic amounts. Truly, as Commander Hamilton-Currey observed in 1910: "No one man has ever cost the world so much by an invention as did the late Mr Whitehead of Fiume."[24]

It seems only appropriate to conclude this account of the torpedo with a brief reference to the United States Navy's futuristic antisubmarine weapon SUBROC (submarine-launched rocket)—a marriage of torpedo and rocket missile that has translated the Devil's Device into the Space Age. SUBROC is a technological marvel of stupendous power that can be fired from a standard submarine torpedo tube while the vessel is submerged. The solid-fuel rocket motor boosts it to supersonic speed, and steered by an inboard lightweight guidance system, it follows a ballistic trajectory to the target after initially shedding the rocket motor and housing. Reentry into the water is cushioned by a shock mitigating device, and once back beneath the surface, the warhead sinks to a preset depth and then explodes. An earlier system, ASROC (antisubmarine rocket system) built by Honeywell, released an acoustic homing torpedo on reentry.

Developed by the Goodyear Aerospace Corporation the SUBROC has a range in excess of 26 nautical miles *and* it can, if required, be fitted with a nuclear warhead. Other weapons, more akin to the ASROC technology than to SUBROC, include Australia's IKARA and the French MALAFON Mark 2. Both of these weapon systems incorporate an acoustic torpedo. The sophisticated technology of SUBROC is far removed from even the most modern torpedo and it would be stretching credibility too far to classify it as such. Indeed, its relationship to the torpedo is about as close as Whitehead's 1866 prototype was to *Der Küstenbrander*. But although it is not a torpedo in the strict sense of the word it relies on another of Robert Whitehead's inventions for its initial launching—the submerged torpedo tube. Enough, surely, to recognize his contribution to the development of a space-age missile.

A cynical friend once gave this piece of advice to Hiram Maxim: "If you can devise a method by which men can kill each other quickly and efficiently you will make your fortune." Maxim took the words to heart and invented the machine gun.

In Whitehead's case it was not a matter of killing men but of sinking ships quickly and efficiently. He built the torpedo, and like Maxim, made his fortune. And yet throughout his life Whitehead never saw his weapon as an instrument of death and human tragedy. In his naivety he thought he had produced a device so terrible in its powers of destruction that no nation would ever dare to go to war again. Unfortunately and inevitably he was wrong. But the error does not detract one iota from his achievement.

AUTHORS' NOTE TO APPENDIXES

Specifications and, in particular, performance details of torpedoes must, of necessity, be treated with caution. Minor variations in established patterns and even individual weapons yield anomalies that are difficult to verify while the ever-present security considerations relating to more recent models frequently lead to the release of inaccurate data and, on occasions, deliberately misleading information. It is, indeed, rare to find two sources or two experts in total agreement and in preparing these appendixes I have found it necessary to rely on my own judgment when selecting figures.

Even impeccable sources such as official torpedo manuals contain conflicting details, although they, at least, indicate the complexity of minor variations—the Colony of Victoria manual issued in the 1890s, for example, lists three versions of the comparatively rare 15-inch torpedo: two being manufactured at Woolwich by the Royal Navy and one at Fiume by the Whitehead Company. It is clearly impossible to include *every* variant in the ensuing tables. Neither would it serve any useful purpose. And I have therefore endeavored to provide a simplified and reliable analysis of the earlier patterns.

A different and more comprehensive layout of the specification and performance tables has been adopted in this new edition and torpedoes are now listed under the Whitehead Company and individual countries. In the early days, of course, the majority of the world's navies used either Whitehead or Schwartzkopff weapons—production, in the main, not being taken over by national arsenals until the turn of the century. The Howell flywheel torpedo, which has its own table (Appendix Three) is, perhaps, the only exception to this rule.

Finally, the speed and ranges shown are *maximum* figures and it must be borne in mind that the maximum speed would result in a shorter range while the maximum range was only achieved at a lower speed.

Date	Note	Model	Diameter (inches)	Length	Engine*	Weight (pounds)	Max Speed (knots)	Max Range (yards)	Charge (pounds)
1866	a	Prototype	14	—	CO	265	6	220	18
1867	b	Austrian trials	14	11'7"	CO	346	5.7	200	14
1867	b	Austrian trials	16	14'1"	CO	650	6.7	300	67
1868	c	Austrian trials	14	11'7"	VT	346	7	600	40
1868	c	Austrian trials	16	14'1"	VT	650	7	600	67
1870	—	Sheerness Trials	14	13'10½"	VT	—	7.5	600	18
1870	—	Sheerness Trials	16	14'0"	VT	—	7+	1,000	67
1871	—	Fiume Small	14	14'0"	VT	—	16.5 (?)	800	26.5
1871	—	Fiume Standard	16	—	VT	—	7	1,000	—
1876	d	Fiume 14" Mk 1	14	14'6"	B3	529	17.5	600	26.5
1876	—	Fiume 14" Mk 2	14	14'6"	B3	594	20	600	30
1876	—	Fiume 14" Mk 3	14	13'3"	B3	554	21	600	58
1882	e	Fiume 15"	15	18'9½"	B3	904.5	23.5	—	74
1882	f	Fiume Short	14	11'0"	B3	435	21 (?)	600 (?)	—
1883	g	Fiume Baby	12	—	B3	272	21	200	33
1885	—	Fiume 14" Mk 4	14	14'9"	B3	660	23.5	600	58
1890	—	Fiume 14" Short	14	12'3¾"	B3	856	28.5	800	88
1890	h	Fiume 18" Mk 1	18	16'7"	B3	1,136	30	800	198
1891	—	Fiume 18" Mk 2	18	16'7"	B3	1,136	29.5	800	187
1905	i	Fiume 18" Mk 3	18	—	B3	1,609	29	2,190	220
1907	j	Fiume 18" Mk 3H	18	—	B3H	1,620	34	4,370	253
1909	—	Weymouth 21" Mk 1	21	—	—	1,654	—	—	—
1908	—	Fiume 18" Dry heater	18	—	H	—	42	6,560	253
1913	k	Fiume 18" Wet heater	18	—	H	1,742	44	6,560	220
1914	—	Weymouth 21" Mk 2	21	—	H	2,794	29	10,000	225

Note: Obry gyro was fitted to all torpedoes manufactured in 1895 and in subsequent years.

* For key to engine code see appendix 11.

a Made from iron boiler plates. Single screw. No balance chamber. Finned.
b As prototype but with air chamber made from solid piece of iron.
c First models to incorporate a balance chamber—*The Secret*.
d Longitudinal fins omitted for first time. Brotherhood engine with twin propellers. Servo control.
e Built in steel or bronze. Cost £350–£380.
f Built for Russia. Cost £280–£300.
g For small boat use with dropping gear.
h First Fiume 18" model.
i For small boat use.
j First "heater" model.
k First "wet heater" model. New 2-cylinder engine.

Appendix Two
Specification and Performance of Non-Whitehead Based Torpedoes 1870–1900

Date	Name	Diameter (inches)	Length	Weight (pounds)	Max speed (knots)	Max Range (yards)	Charge (pounds)	Propulsion and characteristics
1870	Quick	24	—	—	135 (?)	2,000	700	Built by George Quick of Portsmouth. Unsuccessful.
1871	USN Automobile	—	—	—	7	300	70–90	Compressed air. Built by Torpedo Test Station at Rhode Island. Unable to maintain a straight course. Bronze air chamber.
1872	Ramus	—	—	—	35	—	—	Rocket-propelled surface float with polyspheric hull.
1873	Ericsson	—	—	—	—	—	—	Powered by electricity via cable linked to weapon. Torpedo suspended beneath float. Developed into Sims-Edison (see page 257).
1873	Barber	12	7'0"	287	—	—	48	Underwater rocket. Made of cast-iron tube, wrapped in asbestos and sheathed in oak. Barber worked at the Torpedo Test Station, R.I.
?	Peck	—	—	—	—	—	—	Steam powered. Peck worked for Yarrow, the British ship builders. A Whitehead with a 60-hp steam engine.

Date	Name							Remarks
?	Cunningham	—	—	—	—	—	—	Rocket propelled. No details but was actually built.
1880 ca.	Hall	—	—	—	—	—	—	American steam-powered weapon with "wing" roll control system. Never reached production stage. Twin two-bladed propellers.
1880	Brennan	24	24'0"	7,840	30	2,825	200	Wires winding over drums inside weapon and powered from steam winch ashore. Steered by twin contra-rotating propellers. Pendulum compensator.
1880	Lay Dirigible	18	23'0"	2,500	16	4,000	200	Compressed CO_2 motor. Surface-running weapon. Steering and detonation controlled by cable linked to operator.
1880	Ericsson	16	25'0"	1,500	61	100	300	Rocket propelled. Fired from smooth-bore underwater gun using compressed air as propellant.
1880 ca.	Paulson	—	—	—	—	—	—	Propelled by super-heated water. Steered by compass and electricity.

Continued on next page

Appendix Two—_Continued_

Date	Name	Diameter (inches)	Length	Weight (pounds)	Max speed (knots)	Max Range (yards)	Charge (pounds)	Propulsion and characteristics
1880s	Borden	—	—	—	—	2,000	—	Gas-powered turbine—gas derived from gunpowder cartridges. Tiller-rope guidance system by remote operator.
1880s	Berdan	—	—	—	—	—	200	Often said to be an alternative spelling of Borden, but in view of specification this seems unlikely and it appears to be a separate and distinct weapon. Rocket propelled. The rockets fed a turbine that rotated the torpedo's six propellers.
1880 (?)	Lay-Haight	—	—	—	—	—	—	A development of the Lay dirigible, powered by gas generated by the action of sulfuric acid. Propeller near forward end and recessed. Unsuccessful.
1883	Woolwich Rocket	—	—	—	—	50	—	Experimental weapon built by Royal Laboratory.

Year	Name							Description
1884	Weeks	—	—	—	40	100	—	Surface running and rocket propelled. Directionally unreliable.
1885	Wood-Haight	—	—	—	—	—	—	Powered by 3-cylinder Brotherhood engine fueled by carbonic acid. Weapon suspended from floats.
1885	Maxim (Hudson)	—	—	—	—	—	—	Dirigible torpedo. Wire powered. Unsuccessful.
1886	Patrick	22	42'0"	6,000	21	2,000	200	Powered by 3-cylinder Brotherhood engine fueled by carbonic acid. Fired from underwater smooth-bore gun by compressed air. Suspended from floats.
1888	Nordenfelt	29	—	5,000	16	4,000	300	18 SHP battery-powered electric motor fed by 108 storage batteries. Controlled by electrical wire and suspended from floats. Unsuccessful.
1889	Sims-Edison	—	—	—	12	3,500	400	Siemens motor fed by electricity via external cable. Suspended from floats.

Note: See appendix 11 for details of the Howell flywheel torpedo.

Appendix Three
Specification and Performance of Howell Flywheel Torpedoes

Date	Diameter (inches)	Length	Weight (pounds)	Max Speed (knots)	Max Range (yards)	Charge (pounds)	Weight of Flywheel	RPM of Flywheel
1870	14	8'0"	—	8.5	400	70	—	9,000
1884	14	—	300	15.6	200	—	112 lbs	10,000
1890	14	—	—	24	400	—	—	—
1894	14	8'11"	520	26	500	70	128 lbs	10,000
1895	18	14'5"	700	30	800	180	330 lbs	12,000

Note: Special features of Howell torpedoes:
(a) Transverse azimuth pendulum control.
(b) Side-by-side propellers.
(c) Brass body casing.
(d) Later models manufactured by Hotchkiss Ordnance Company.
(e) Flywheel rotated on launching by Dow steam winch.

Appendix Four

Specification and Performance of British-built Torpedoes

Date	Note	Model	Diameter (inches)	Length	Engine*	Weight (pounds)	Max Speed (knots)	Max Range (yards)	Charge (pounds)
1872	a	RL 16" Mk I*	16	—	—	530	12	600	26
1876		RL 14" Mk I*	14	14'6"	B3	525	18	600	32
1876		RL 14" Mk II	14	14'7"	B3	575	19	600	34
1882		RL 14" Mk III	14	14'7"	B3	578	20	600	34
1883	b	RL 14" Mk IV	14	14'6"	B3	630	23	600	60
1885		RL 14" Mk V	14	14'6"	B3	654	25	600	60
1886		RL 14" Mk VI	14	14'6"	B3	648	25	600	60
1887		RL 14" Mk VII	14	15'0"	B3	707	27	600	60
1888	c	RL 14" Mk VIII	14	15'0"	B3	708	26	600	70
1890		RGF 18" Mk I	18	16'7"	B3	1,213	30	800	65
1890	d	RGF Short 14"	14	12'5"	B3	861	28	800	188
1892		RGF 14" Mk VIII	14	15'0"	B3	708	26.5	600	85
1892		RGF 18" Mk II	18	16'7"	B3	1,227	30.5	800	65
1893	e	RGF 14" Mk IX	14	15'0"	B3	726	27.5	600	188
1894		RGF 18" Mk III	18	16'7"	B3	1,213	30.5	800	77
1895	f	RGF 18" Mk IV	18	16'7"	B3	1,218	30.6	800	171
	g	RGF 18" Mk V	—	—	—	—	—	—	171
1897	h	RGF 14" Mk X	14	17'1"	B3	762	30	800	77
1905	i	RGF 18" Mk VI	18	17'10½"	B3	1,490	29	6,000	200
1908		RGF 21" Mk I	21	17'1"	—	2,100	30	7,500	225
1909	j	RGF 18" Mk VI (H)	18	—	B3H	1,490	45	6,000	200
1909	k	RGF 18" Mk VII	18	23'1¼"	B4H	1,553	41	7,000	200
	l	RGF 18" Mk IV	—	—	B4H	—	—	—	280
1909		RGF 21" Long	21	—	—	2,863	50	12,000	—
1910		RGF 21" Mk II	21	—	B4H	—	—	—	77
1917	m	RNTF 21" Mk IV	21	—	B4H	3,190	40	13,500	515
1917	n	RNTF 18" (Mk IX)	18	—	—	1,077	29	2,000	250
1924	o	RNTF 24.5" Mk I	24.5	—	EA	5,287	35	20,000	742

Continued on next page

259

Appendix Four—*Continued*

Date	Note	Model	Diameter (inches)	Length	Engine*	Weight (pounds)	Max Speed (knots)	Max Range (yards)	Charge (pounds)
1928		RNTF 21" Mk VII	21	25'6"	EA	4,106	33	16,000	740
1928		RNTF 21" Mk VIII	21	—	BC	2,253	40	15,000	750
		RNTF 21" Mk IX	21	—	BC	3,731	40	14,000	750
1939 ca.	p	RNTF 18" Mk 12	18	—	—	1,548	40	1,500	388
1943	q	RNTF 21" Mk XI	21	13'6"	Elect	—	—	—	—
1960 ca.	r	Mk 20 (S)	21	—	Elect	1,808	20	12,000	200
1970 ca.	s	Mk 23	21	—	Elect	—	—	—	—
1974	t	Mk 24 TIGERFISH	21	21'2"	Elect	1,650	40 +	12,000	—
1985	v	STINGRAY	13	7'11"	Elect	—	—	—	—
1987	u	SPEARFISH	21	27'10"	GT	4,400	70 +	70,000	—

Note: In addition to the government torpedo establishments shown in the notes below, weapons were also manufactured, at various times, by Greenwood & Batley, Leeds; The Caton Engineering Co; Morris Motor Co; and Bliss (U.S.A.). Prior to 1914 the Royal Navy also purchased torpedoes from both Whitehead & Co, Fiume, and Schwartzkopff, Berlin. The War Office purchased a number of Brennan weapons (see appendix 2) in the 1880s. There was no consistent pattern of nomenclature in the official records, and a torpedo could be identified variously as a RL 14-inch Mk VI, 14-inch RL Mk VI, or 14-inch Mk VI RL. To assist in identification the patterns listed in this appendix have been standardized with the code letters at the beginning. Models quoted in the text reflect the pattern adopted in the relevant original source.

260

* Key to engine code in appendix 11.

a First to be fitted with twin contrarotating propellers. Discontinued in 1877.

b Also known as Leeds Mk 4—some models built by Greenwood & Batley. First to use safety fan pistol and rounded nose.

c Triple-bladed propellers adopted.

d For small boat use.

e Quadruple propeller blades adopted in 1898.

f Gyroscope introduced 1895.

g Nickel air chamber of 2,200 psi.

h Adapted for aircraft use in 1910.

i New slide-valve engine with cam rollers. Cost £400.

j First British-built weapon with heater engine.

k Warhead increased to 320 lbs in 1917.

l Known as RGF 21" Long. Cost in 1914 £1,086. Warhead later increased to 433 lbs.

m Cost £1,193.

n First torpedo designed for aircraft use. 15 different Marks produced.

o Designed for use by the battleships *Nelson* and *Rodney*.

p Aircraft torpedo.

q First British electric torpedo—based on German G-7e. Development by British Thompson Houston at Rugby. First trials May 1943.

r Short antisubmarine weapon. Passive acoustic homing. Perchloric acid batteries. Limited antiship capability.

s Antisubmarine wire-guided homing weapon developed from Mk 20.

t Very unsuccessful model. Two-way wire guidance system and automatic 3-D active-passive homing. Impact and proximity fuse. Estimated development costs in excess of £1 billion. Superseded by *Spearfish*.

u Built by Marconi—official identification: NST/R7525. Heavyweight high-performance deep-depth weapon. Wire guided. Propelled by Sundstrand gas turbine engine fueled with a mixture of HAP and OTTO. Estimated cost of each weapon £500,000.

v Lightweight antisubmarine weapon. Passive-active homing. Still classified.

Appendix Five
Specification and Performance of French-built Torpedoes

Date	Note	Model	Diameter (inches)	Length	Engine*	Weight (pounds)	Max Speed (knots)	Max Range (yards)	Charge (pounds)
1904	a	1904 Model	17.7	19'6"	—	—	—	6,000	198
1904	—	450mm Long	17.7	16'6"	—	—	—	2,000	198
1904	—	450mm Short	17.7	13'9"	—	—	—	1,500	185
1904	—	380mm Long	15	18'9"	—	—	—	1,000	100
1904	—	380mm Short	15	16'6"	—	—	—	1,000	85
1905	—	356mm Long	14	16'6"	—	—	—	600	79
1905	—	356mm Short	14	15'0"	—	—	—	600	60
1912	—	Mod 1912 450mm	17.7	22'2"	—	—	—	11,000	551
1912	—	Mod 1912 400mm	15.7	—	—	—	—	6,000	317
1919	—	Type D 550mm	21.7	27'0"	—	—	—	11,000	551
1923	b	Type DT 550mm	21.7	—	—	4,620	40	15,300	680
1924	—	Model V 550mm	21.7	21'6"	—	3,285	44	—	683
1926	—	Model W 400mm	15.7	—	Tur	1,486	44	2,190	313
1929	—	Model D 550mm	21.7	—	—	—	35	22,000	—
1939 ca.	c	DAR 400mm	15.7	—	—	—	35	3,250	—
Post-1945	d	E 14 (550mm)	21.7	14'0"	Elect	1,985	25	8,300	441
Post-1945	e	E 15 (550mm)	21.7	19'5"	Elect	2,977	25	13,200	661

Post-1945	f	F 17 (533mm)	21	19'5"	Elect	2,866	35	20,000	—
Post-1945	g	K 2	21.7	—	—	2,425	50	—	—
Post-1945	h	L 3	21.7	14'0"	Elect	1,985	25	8,300	441
Post-1945	i	L 4	21	10'3"	Elect	1,188	30	—	—
Post-1945	j	L 5 (Mod 1 & 4)	21	—	Elect	2,205	35	7,700	—
Post-1945	k	L 5 (Mod 3)	21	—	Elect	2,866	35	7,700	—
Post-1945	l	Type Z-16	21.7	23'5"	Elect	3,748	30	11,137	661

Note: France manufactured Whitehead torpedoes under license at the government arsenal in Toulon from 1871. Whitehead & Co. opened its own factory at St. Tropez around 1900. This factory later merged with Schneider of La Londe. France relied heavily on U.S. torpedoes in the post-1945 period.

* Key to engine code in appendix 11.

a Whitehead made in Fiume and Toulon.
b For submarine use. Warhead charge—Tolite.
c For aircraft use.
d Antiship. Passive acoustic homing head. Free running.
e As E 14 but with additional compartment to increase range.
f Wire guided with passive acoustic homing. Built in antiship and antisubmarine variants.
g For surface ships.
h Free-running antisubmarine weapon. Acoustic homing head. Preprogrammed circular search pattern. Can operate to a depth of 985 feet.
i Lightweight antisubmarine weapon. Circular search pattern. Impact and acoustic proximity fuse. Active homing. Built by DTCN.
j Ship launched. Antisubmarine weapon with active and passive acoustic homing.
k Submarine-launched version of the Model 1.
l Obsolescent by 1975. France's standardization on the 550mm (21.7") diameter torpedo tube has been a considerable disadvantage and for a number of years many of her vessels have been unable to use NATO 21" torpedoes.

Appendix Six
Specification and Performance of German-built Torpedoes

Date	Note	Model	Diameter (inches)	Length	Engine*	Weight (pounds)	Max Speed (knots)	Max range (yards)	Charge (pounds)
1876	a	Schwartzkopff 14"	14	14'0"	CA	602	17	440	31
1883		Schwartzkopff 14"	14	—	—	581	21	640	44
1905 ca.		Schwartzkopff 450mm	17.7	—	CA	—	30	—	264.5
1906		Type G (500mm)	19.7	23'0"	—	—	36	6,560	440
1913		Type H 8 (600mm)	23.6	28'0"	H	4,410	35	18,590	616
1914		Type G 6 AV**	19.7	—	H	—	40	5,500	441
1914	b	Type G 7***	19.7	23'0"	H	2,491	36	11,700	441
1914 ca.		Type G 125	17.7	—	H	—	36	6,560	308
1917	c	?	17.7	—	—	1,680	35	1,640	350
1918		Prototype Electric	—	—	Elect	—	28	2,000	—
1937		Type G 7a	21	22'9"	4 cyl H	3,334	44	15,310	660
1939	d	Type LF5	18	—	—	1,626	30	2,500	440
1939	e	Type G 7e Mod T2	21	22'9"	Elect	3,540	30	5,470	660
WW2	f	Type G 7e Mod T3	21	—	Elect	3,540	30	5,470	—
WW2	g	Type G 7e Mod T3A	21	—	Elect	3,870	30	8,200	—
WW2	h	Type G 7e Mod T3B	21	—	Elect	2,970	18.5	4,390	—
WW2	i	Type G 7e Mod T3C	21	—	Elect	2,950	18.5	4,390	—
WW2		Type G 7e Mod T3D	21	36'0"	Elect	4,885	9	62,300	—
WW2	j	Type G 7e Mod T3E	21	—	Elect	2,960	20	8,200	—
WW2	k	Type G 7e Mod T4	21	—	Elect	—	20	8,200	—
WW2	l	Type G 7e Mod T5	21	—	Elect	—	25	—	—
WW2	m	Type G 7e Mod T6	21	—	Elect	3,870	—	8,200	—
WW2	n	Type G 7e Mod T10	21	—	Elect	3,570	30	3,280	—

Era		Name							
WW2	o	Type G 7e Mod T11	21	—	Elect	3,300	24	6,240	—
WW2	p	Type G 7e Geier	21	23'6"	Elect	—	—	—	—
WW2	q	Type G 7e Lerche	21	23'6"	Elect	—	—	6,000	—
WW2	r	STEINWAL	—	—	Tur	—	45	24,000	—
WW2	s	Type F-5b Pfau	—	—	Tur	1,810	24	6,600	—
Postwar	t	SEEAL	21	21'0"	Elect	—	35 +	12,250	—
Postwar	u	SEESCHLANGE	21	13'1"	Elect	—	—	6,000	—
Postwar	v	SST-4	21	20'9"	Elect	—	—	—	573
Postwar	w	SUT	21	22'0"	Elect	—	—	—	—

Note: Whitehead torpedoes were imported from 1873 but from 1880s were built at the Imperial Arsenal at Friedrichsort. Schwartzkopff began producing a pirated copy of the Fiume weapon in 1876 and also supplied the German Navy.

* Key to engine code in appendix 11.

a Pirated copy of Fiume 14" built by Louis Schwartzkopff of Berlin. Phosphor bronze casing. Cost £450.
b Standard weapon of First World War. Performance figures may relate to Mk 3. Type G-7 introduced in 1906.
c Aircraft torpedo. Model number unknown.
d Aircraft torpedo.
e Germany's first operational electric torpedo. 8-pole series DC motor. 91 volt. 950 amps at 1755 rpm. 26 battery cells.
f As T2 but with influence fuse.
g New battery design.
h Propulsive section of MARDER piloted torpedo.
i Torpedo component of MARDER piloted torpedo.
j Used by SEEHUND midget submarine (Type XXVIIB).
k First passive-homer torpedo. Code-named FALKE.
l Main WW2 homing torpedo. Code-named ZAUNKONIG 1. T5A and T5B had speed of 22 knots.
m Experimental.
n Wire-controlled shore defense weapon. Code named SPINNE.
o Code named ZAUNKONIG 2.
p Experimental. Active acoustic homer.
q Wire-guided weapon. Active-passive acoustic homer.
r Pattern-running torpedo with LUT gyro.
s Air-dropped weapon with passive homer.
t Wire-guided heavyweight antiship weapon. Postwar development—precise data not known.
u Wire-guided antisubmarine weapon based on U.S. Mk 37. 3-D sonar homer. Built by AEG.
v Export version of SEEAL. Active-passive homer. Wire-guided antiship weapon.
w Wire-guided dual purpose weapon. Active-passive homer.

Appendix Seven
Specification and Performance of Italian-built Torpedoes

Date	Note	Model	Diameter (inches)	Length	Engine*	Weight (pounds)	Max Speed (knots)	Max Range (yards)	Charge (pounds)
1877	—	A37-356 (Steel)	14	14'4"	CA	—	22	850	81.5
1879	—	B43-356 (Bronze)	14	14'5"	CA	—	22	850	95
1885	—	B57-356 (Bronze)	14	14'7"	CA	—	24	1,080	125
1889	—	B90-450 (Bronze)	17.7	16'3"	CA	—	30	1,100	198
1897	—	A60-450 (Steel)	17.7	16'3"	CA	—	32	850	132
1897	—	A62-450 (Steel)	17.7	16'6"	CA	—	31	2,150	137
1898	—	A90-450 (Steel)	17.7	15'7"	CA	—	34	2,150	198
1898	—	A110-450 (Steel)	17.7	16'6"	CA	—	34	2,150	242
1905	—	A68-450	17.7	14'7"	—	—	31	3,250	150
1905	—	A90-450	17.7	16'3"	—	—	31	3,250	198
1906	—	A95-450	17.7	16'10"	—	—	34	2,150	210
1911	—	A100-450	17.7	15'7"	—	—	34	2,150	220
1912	—	A100-450	17.7	16'10"	—	—	34	2,150	220
1912	—	A100-450	17.7	13'5"	—	—	38.5	2,200	220
1913	—	A110-450	17.7	17'0"	—	—	38	2,200	243
1914	—	A115-450	17.7	17'0"	—	—	41	3,250	254
1916	—	A180bis-533	21	20'9"	—	—	27	9,750	397
1916	—	A180bis-533	21	20'9"	—	—	25	9,750	397
1917	a	W270-533.4	21	23'3"	—	—	48	4,300	595

1934	a	W250-533.4 [Veloce]	21	24'3"	H	3,530	50	13,120	551
	a	W250-533.4	21	21'2"	—	—	43	11,000	551
	a	W260-533.4	21	22'4"	—	—	43	13,000	573
WW2	a	W115-450	17.7	17'2"	—	—	—	—	254
WW2	a	A110-450 [Silurotto]	17.7	16'6"	—	—	44	6,500	242
WW2	a	A110-450	17.7	17'2"	—	—	38	6,500	242
WW2	a	W200-450	17.7	18'7"	—	—	44	7,000+	441
WW2	b	SI 270-533.4	21	23'3"	—	—	48	—	608
WW2	b	SI 250-533.4	21	24'3"	—	—	40	13,000	551
Postwar	c	Whitehead G-6E	21	19'6"	Elect	—	—	—	661
Postwar	d	Whitehead G6-EF	21	20'2"	Elect	—	—	—	—
Postwar	e	Whitehead A-184	21	19'8"	Elect	2,860	—	17,600	1,212
Postwar	f	Whitehead A-244/S	12.75	8'10"	Elect	—	—	—	—
Postwar	g	Whitehead A-290	12.75	—	Elect	—	50	—	—

Note: Imported torpedoes from Fiume from 1873 onwards. After First World War Fiume became Italian territory. Weapons also produced at Naples by De Luca Daimler, which later became the state torpedo factory: *Silurificio Italiano*. The Whitehead factory at Fiume is now part of FIAT.

* Key to engine code in appendix 11.

a Built by Whitehead.

b Built by Silurificio Italiano, Naples.

c Antiship weapon now superceded by A-184. Wire guided with passive acoustic homer.

d Antisubmarine weapon—code name KANGEROO. Hybrid design: body of wire-guided G-6E with U.S. Mk 44 warhead. Active sonar homer. Now obsolete.

e Heavyweight antiship and antisubmarine weapon. Wire guided with advanced active-passive acoustic homer that controls both course and speed. Two-way communication with parent ship.

f Lightweight antisubmarine weapon. Active-passive homer. Able to institute countermeasures. Self-adaptive search pattern.

267

Appendix Eight
Specification and Performance of Japanese-built Torpedoes

Date	Note	Model	Diameter (inches)	Length	Engine*	Weight (pounds)	Max Speed (knots)	Max Range (yards)	Charge (pounds)
1930 ca.	—	Type 90	24	—	H	—	—	—	—
1931 ca.	a	Type 91 Mod 1	17.7	—	H	1,728	42	1,600	330
	b	Type 91 Mod 2	17.7	—	H	1,840	42	—	450
	—	Type 91 Mod 4	17.7	—	H	—	—	—	925
1932	c	Type 92	21	—	Elect	5,940	30	7,660	660
1933	d	Type 93 [Long Lance]	24	29'4"	EO	6,107	48	43,744	1,100
1934	e	Type 94	21	—	H	3,245	45	4,900	—
1935	f	Type 95 Mod 1	21	—	EO	—	50	13,000	900
1942	c	Type 96	21	—	O/P	3,660	48	4,900	891
1942	c	Type 98	18	—	O/P	2,000	41	3,500	770

Note: Schwartzkopff weapons were used until 1895 when Japan switched to Whiteheads. In 1905 there were three Fiume patterns in service: 14", 18", and 24"—the latter being a land-based weapon for shore defense. Japan has always been secretive about its torpedoes and virtually no details are available for patterns brought into service between 1905 and 1930. Pre-1945 torpedoes were built in the naval arsenal at Kure.

* Key to engine codes in appendix 11.
a Aircraft torpedo. Maximum launching speed 260 knots—launch height 50 to 1,000 feet. Minimum operating depth 40 feet. Special tail fins.
b Similar to the above but with modified tail configuration to overcome "rolling."
c Submarine weapon.
d One of the most successful torpedoes of all time. Fueled with petrol and liquid oxygen. Also formed basis of several suicide weapons including the *kaiten*. Official name: *Shiki Sanso Gyorai Type-93*.
e Aircraft torpedo.
f Submarine version of the Type 93 with enriched oxygen propellant. This was not a 24-inch weapon as some writers have claimed. for no Japanese submarines were fitted with tubes larger than 21 inches. Model 2: maximum range 8,200 yards. warhead 1,210 lbs.

Appendix Nine
Specification and Performance of Swedish-built Torpedoes

Date	Note	Model	Diameter (inches)	Length	Engine*	Weight (pounds)	Max Speed (knots)	Max Range (yards)	Charge (pounds)
Postwar	a	Type 42	15.75	8'5"	Elect	638	—	—	110
1977	b	Type 61	21	23'0"	HIP	3,883	60+	33,000	551
Postwar	c	Type 43X0	—	—	Elect	—	—	—	—
1987	d	Type 431	16	—	—	—	—	—	—
Postwar	e	Type 617	21	22'11½"	HIP	4,078	—	—	—

Note: Sweden began importing Whitehead weapons in 1875 and from 1911 they were manufactured under license at Karlskrona. Torpedoes built before 1945 have similar characteristics to other Fiume-based designs and do not merit listing. In the mid-1930s a turbine-powered weapon was produced.

* Key to engine codes in appendix 11.
a Swim-out antisubmarine weapon launched from 21" tube. Wire guided with passive acoustic homer. Superceded by Type 422 and Type 431.
b Heavyweight antiship weapon. Wire guided.
c Multirole weapon which can be air dropped. Wire guided with passive acoustic homer.
d Antisubmarine weapon.
e Export version of navy's Type 613. Two-way wire guidance system with acoustic homer. Thermal propulsion unit uses compressed air, alcohol, fresh water, and hydrogen peroxide mixture.

Appendix Ten
Specification and Performance of Torpedoes Built in the United States

Date	Note	Model	Diameter (inches)	Length	Engine*	Weight (pounds)	Max Speed (knots)	Max Range (yards)	Charge (pounds)
1892	a	Bliss-Whitehead Mk 1	17.7	16'5"	B3	1,161	27.5	1,000	220
1905	b	Bliss-Leavitt Mk 1	21	16'5"	Tur	—	26	3,500	180
1907 ca.	c	Bliss-Whitehead Mk 5	17.7	17'1"	H	1,452	40	4,000	200
1913	—	Bliss-Leavitt Mk 3	21	16'5"	Tur	1,928	28	3,500	318
1913	—	Bliss-Leavitt Mk 8	21	21'0"	Tur	3,050	28	10,000	300
	—	Bliss-Leavitt Mk 9	21	16'5"	Tur	3,050	27	7,000	200
1915	d	Sperry Battery model	7.25	6'0"	Elect	60	25	3,800	—
1917	e	Bliss-Leavitt Mk 10	21	—	Tur	3,050	36	13,500	385
1938 ca.	f	Mk 13	22.4	—	Tur	1,927	33.5	6,000	401
WW2	g	Mk 14	21	20'6"	Tur	3,925	46	9,000	507
WW2	h	Mk 15	21	23'0"	Tur	3,289	45	15,190	780
	i	Mk 16 & Mk 17	21	20'6"	HP	—	46	16,000	—
1943	j	Mk 18	21	—	Elect	—	?	—	—
WW2	k	Mk 20	21	—	Elect	—	—	—	—
1944	l	Mk 24	21	7'0"	Elect	—	—	—	—
WW2	m	Mk 28	21	—	Elect	—	20	—	—
WW2	m	Mk 29	21	—	Elect	—	25	—	—
WW2	m	Mk 31	21	—	Elect	—	28	—	—
WW2	n	Mk 32	21	—	—	1,200	12	—	—
Postwar	o	Mk 37 Mod 0	19	11'3"	Elect	1,428	30	8,000	330
Postwar	p	Mk 37 Mod 1	19	13'6"	Elect	1,428	30	8,000	330
Postwar	q	Mk 37 Mod 3	19	11'3"	Elect	1,428	30	8,000	330
Postwar	r	NT 37c	19	—	OTTO	—	42	15,000	330
Postwar	s	NT 37d	19	14'9"	—	1,650	—	—	330
Postwar	t	Westinghouse FREEDOM	19	18'6"	Elect	2,727	40	12,000	650
Postwar	u	Honeywell NT 37e	19	—	OTTO	—	—	—	—
Postwar	v	Mk 44 Mod 0	12.75	8'4"	Elect	—	—	—	422
Postwar	w	Mk 45 ASTOR Mod 1	21	19'11"	Elect	2,400	—	20,000+	—
Postwar	x	Mk 46 Mod 0	12.75	8'6"	Solid	570	—	—	—

Postwar	y	Mk 48	21	19'6"	OTTO	3,474	55	45,000	—	—
Postwar	z	ALWT	12.75	—			40		—	
Postwar	aa	DEXTOR		(No details were released.)						

Note: The first American automobile torpedo was built in 1871 (see appendix 2) and the Whitehead weapon was not acquired until 1891, when E. W. Bliss & Co. of Brooklyn was licenced to manufacture the Fiume pattern torpedo. Between these two dates the U.S. Navy relied on the Howell flywheel torpedo, details of which are given in appendix 3. During the First World War torpedo production was in the hands of Bliss and the Naval Torpedo Station at Newport, Rhode Island. An assembly plant was opened at Alexandria, Virginia, in 1919 but was closed down soon afterwards. During the interwar years the Bliss company withdrew from armament manufacture although it resumed torpedo work during the Second World War. The latter conflict also saw torpedoes being built by nonspecialist civilian firms including the Pontiac Division of General Motors.

* For Key to engine code see appendix 11.

a This model is identified as WH Mk 1 in *The Ship and Gun Drills, U.S. Navy, 1914*. There was also a "short" Mk 1 with a length of 11'8".

b Developed by Frank McDowell Leavitt, the chief engineer of E. W. Bliss & Co., who substituted a Curtis turbine for the Brotherhood radial. USN ordered 300 in November 1905. The turbine marked the first major departure from Whitehead's original design.

c First to be fitted with heater engine. Identified in *The Ship and Gun Drills, U.S. Navy, 1914* as WH Mk V.

d Experimental and never achieved performance shown. Work ceased in 1918.

e Still in combat service with U.S. submarines during World War Two.

f Aircraft weapon. Turbine produced 95 BHP.

g Main submarine weapon in 1941, but faults in the Mk VI magnetic exploder made it unreliable. In service for some 40 years after successful modifications.

h Submarine weapon.

i Developed from experimental Ordnance Laboratory G-49 project in 1920s and 1930s. Mk 16 was a submarine weapon while surface ships used Mk 17.

j Copy of German G 7e built by Westinghouse at government request. This torpedo sank over one million tons of Japanese shipping in World War Two.

k Antiship passive homer.

l Antisubmarine weapon with passive homer.

m Antiship weapon with passive homer.

n Antisubmarine weapon with active homer.

o Antisubmarine weapon with active-passive homer built by Northrop. Swims out of 21-inch submerged tube. Free running.

p As (o) but wire guided.

q Free running version of (p).

r Free running or wire guided.

s Three preset search modes—*not* wire guided.

t Private venture antiship weapon. Swims out of 21-inch submerged tube. Mod 0 is wire guided with terminal pattern. Mod 1 has long-range acoustic homer.

u Produced in kit form. OTTO fuel propulsion replaces the electric motor with a resultant 40 percent increase in power and doubled range.

v Lightweight antisubmarine weapon. Active homer. Can be launched by ships or aircraft.

w Nuclear warhead. Wire guided with active sonar. An antisubmarine weapon.

x Lightweight antisubmarine weapon. Passive-active homer. Mod 1 had OTTO propulsion.

y Antiship and antisubmarine weapon. Wire guided with active-passive homer.

z Lightweight antisubmarine weapon with active-passive homer.

aa Experimental deep-depth weapon intended for use against nuclear submarines.

Appendix Eleven
Key to Engine Types in Appendixes

CO	Compound oscillating air engine
VT	Whitehead Vee-twin air engine
B3	Brotherhood 3-cylinder radial air engine
B3H	Brotherhood 3-cylinder radial air engine with heater
H	Heater (thermal) engine
B4H	Brotherhood 4-cylinder radial air engine with heater
EA	Enriched air propellant
BC	Burner Cycle engine
Elect	Battery-powered electric motor
GT	Gas turbine
Tur	Turbine
CA	Compressed air
DH	Dry heater thermal engine
WH	Wet heater thermal engine
EO	Enriched oxygen fuel
O/P	Oxygen-paraffin fuel
HTP	Hydrogen peroxide fuel
HP	Hydrogen peroxide fuel
OTTO	Liquid monopropellant
Solid	Solid fuel propellant

Appendix 12
Summary of Torpedo Operations, Excluding Stationary Torpedoes, 1863–1895

Date.	Place.	Assailant Party.	Assailed Party.	Means Employed.	Type of Torpedo Employed.	Number of Torpedoes Fired.	Minimum Distance between Assailant and Assailed.	Name of Ship Attacked.	State of Ship when Attacked.	Time and State of Weather when Attack Made.	Result of Attack to Assailed.	Damage to Assailants.	Page.
April 9, '63	Charleston	Confeds.	Federals	Special launch	Spar		Seen before tor. could be used	*Ironsides*	?	?		No damage to either	i
Oct. 5, '63	Charleston	Confeds.	Federals	Special launch	Spar	1.	Contact	*Ironsides*	At anchor	Night	No damage; torpedo exploded against the side-armour	13 bullet holes in boat; two men captured	103
Feb. 17, '64	Charleston	Confeds.	Federals	Submarine boat	Spar	1.	Contact	*Housatonic*	At anchor	Night	Sunk	Boat sunk and all drowned	103
March 6, '64	N. Edisto River	Confeds.	Federals	Special launch	Spar	1.	Tor. could not be used	*Memphis*	Slipped her cables and in motion	Night		H'vy fire opened, but boat got away	104
April 9, '64	Hampton Roads	Confeds.	Federals	Launch	Spar	1.	Contact	*Minnesota*	At anchor		Severe damage	Escaped without injury	104
April 19, '64	Charleston	Confeds.	Federals	Special launch	Spar		Seen before tor. could be used	*Wabash*	Slipped her cables and in motion	Night	Sank the boat before she was hit	Boat sunk	102
Oct. 27, '64	Albemarle Sound	Federals	Confeds.	Launch	Spar	1.	Contact	*Albemarle*	Moored to shore, log boom round	Dark & rainy night	Sunk	Boat sunk; two drowned, 19 taken prisoners	111-3

Continued on next page

Appendix 12—Continued

Date.	Place.	Assailant Party.	Assailed Party.	Means Employed.	Type of Torpedo Employed.	Number of Torpedoes Fired.	Minimum Distance between Assailant and Assailed.	Name of Ship Attacked.	State of Ship when Attacked.	Time and State of Weather when Attack Made.	Result of Attack to Assailed.	Damage to Assailants.	Page.
May 29, '77	Ylo, Peru	English	Peruvian	*Shah's* launch carriage	Whitehead	I.		*Huascar*	In motion at sea	Day	Torpedo missed	Nil	309
May 12, '77	Batum	Russians	Turks	4 launches	Towing	I.	which did not explode	?	At anchor	Night	Torpedo fouled Turkish ship but failed to explode	Nil	298
May 26, '77	Brailov	Russians	Turks	4 launches	Spar	II.	Contact	*Seifé*	Stationary in River Danube	Night, dark and rainy	*Seifé* sunk; both torpedoes exploded under her	Nil	290-2
June 11, '77	Sulina	Russians	Turks	6 launches	Spar	II.	Contact?	*Idjitalié*	At anchor, had nets out	Night	Both torpedoes probably struck booms; no result	One launch sunk	292-4
June 23, '77	Danube, Mouth of Aluta	Russians	Turks	2 launches	Spar		None fired	?	In motion, nets out	Day	Attack easily repulsed	Nil	294
Dec. 27, '77	Batum	Russians	Turks	4 launches	Whitehead	II.		*Mahmudieh ?*	At anchor	Night	Both torpedoes missed; no harm done to T'rks	Nil	301-2
Aug. 23, '77	Sukhum Kalé	Russians	Turks	5 launches	Towing	I.		*Assar i Chevket*	At anchor boats, &c., round her	Night, moon eclipsed	One torpedo exploded without effect; a second fouled *Assar*, but did not explode	Nil	{298-300

274

Date	Place	Attacker	Defender	Attacking vessels	Torpedo	Mark	Range	Ship attacked	Position	Time & weather	Result	Casualties	Page
Jan. 25, '78	Batum	Russians	Turks	2 launches	Whitehead	II.	70–90yds.	?	At anchor	Night, foggy	Ship sunk; both torpedoes probably hit	Nil	$\overline{302}$-3
Aug. 27, '79	Antofagasta	Peruvians	Chilians	*Huascar's* dirigible torpedo	Lay			*Abtao* and *Magellanes*	At anchor	Day	Torpedo ran back on *Huascar*, and endangered ship	Nil	322
April 10, '80	Callao	Chilians	Peruvians	*Fanequeo*, *Guacolda*, torpedo boats	Spar	I.	Contact	*Union*	At anchor, behind boom	Night	Torpedo exploded against boom; no damage done	Nil	332 ; ii
Feb. 14, 85	Sheipoo	French	Chinese	2 launches	Spar	II.	Contact	*Yuyen*	At anchor	Dark night	Chinese ship sunk	Slight injuries to one launch	13-5
Aug. 23, '84	Foochow	French	Chinese	3 launches	Spar	III.	Contact	*Yango, Fosing*	At anchor	Day, duri'g Fr'n'h attack	Both Chinese ships sunk	One launch disabled, one man killed	8
Jan. 27, '91	Valparaiso	Congressionalists	Balmacedists	*Blanco's* launch	Whitehead	I.	?	*Imperial*	At anchor.		Missed		21
April 23, '91	Caldera Bay	Balmacedist	Congressionalists	*Lynch, Condell,* tor. gun boats	Whitehead	V.	100-20 yds.	*Blanco Encalada*	At anchor	Just before dawn, cl'udy	*Blanco Encalada* sank; one hit	*Lynch* hit four times; no damage	22-9
April 15, '93	Sta. Catherina	Peixotoists	Melloist	*Sampaio*, tor. gun boat, and 3 torpedo boats	Whitehead	IV.	160yds.	*Aquidaban*	At anchor	Night, very dark	*Aquidaban* sank; one hit	*Sampaio* 25 hits; no one hurt; no damage; other boats one hit	43-9
Sept. 17, '94	Off the Yalu	Chinese	Japanese	Torpedo boat	Whitehead	II.		*Hiyei*	In motion	D'y, during bat.	No hits; ship not injured	Boat not injured	93

Continued on next page

Appendix 12—Continued

Date	Place			Torpedo boat	Whitehead			Ship(s)		D'y	Result	Injury to boat	Page
Sept. 17, '94	Off the Yalu	Chinese	Japanese	Torpedo boat	Whitehead	III.		*Saikio*	In motion	D'y, during bat.	All torpedoes missed	No injury to boat	93
Feb. 2, '95	Wei-hai-wei	Japanese	Chinese	Several torpedo boats	None used			Chinese fleet	At anchor	Night	Seen and fired upon by Chinese; attack aband'		129
Feb. 5, '95	Wei-hai-wei	Japanese	Chinese	10 torpedo boats	Whitehead	VI.‡	330yds.	*Ting Yuen* *Lai Yuen.?**	At anchor	Dark night, 10 below zero	*Ting Yuen* struck and sunk	Only one boat uninjured; one sank; one ran ashore; 10 or 12 killed†	130-2
Feb. 6, '95	Wei-hai-wei	Japanese	Chinese	6 torpedo boats	Whitehead	?	?	*Lai Yuen,** *Wei Yuen,* *ChingYuen?*	At anchor	Dark night	*Lai Yuen* capsized	No lives in boat	132

(Range for Sept. 17 event: 50yds.)

* Three ships are allowed for in the summary for both attacks.
† Both boats were afterwards re-floated.
‡ Doubtful.

276

Summary.

Type of Torpedo.	Total Number of Attempts.	Against Ships in motion.		Against Ships at rest.				Loss to Assailant Boat.
		Number of Attacks.	Successful.	Number of Attacks.	Some success in.	Ships sunk.	Ships damaged.	
Spar	13	3	0	10	6	6	1	4
Towing	2	0	0	2	0	0	0	0
Whitehead	11	3	0	8	5	6	0	2
Lay	1	0	0	1	0	0	0	0
	27	6	0	21	11	12	1	6

Source: Reprinted from *Ironclads in Action* (1896). Table XXV, pp. 313–14. The table contains several minor errors. Where a discrepancy of fact occurs, the details given in the text are to be regarded as more accurate.

NOTES

Unless already identified in the notes full details of publishers and publication dates of all books referred to below will be found in the bibliography.

Some of the original notes and documents used in the preparation of the first edition were lost while moving residence in 1975. As a result it has not always been possible to indicate a precise date or page number in respect of certain sources.

Chapter One. As Secret as Possible

1. Although slightly dramatized the incidents in this chapter are factually based.

2. The presence of Count Georg Hoyos at the Sheerness trials is confirmed by a report in the *Illustrated London News*, 15 October 1870.

3. Admiralty letter 3/5688/6101. Quoted in *Report of the Committee on the Whitehead Torpedo*, 28 October 1870.

4. With a displacement of 649 tons and launched in 1847.

5. The Paris incident is referred to by Bradford in his *Life of Admiral of the Fleet Sir Arthur Knyvet Wilson*, 29 (hereafter cited as Bradford).

6. *Report of the Committee on the Whitehead Torpedo*.

7. Ibid.

8. Ibid.

9. Ibid.

10. Ibid.

11. Ibid.
12. Ibid.
13. Ibid.
14. The *Aigle* was a former 5th rate warship of 990 tons launched in 1801.
15. *Report of the Committee on the Whitehead Torpedo.*
16. Fisher, *Records*, 177.
17. *Report of the Committee on the Whitehead Torpedo.*

Chapter Two. Genesis of a Genius

1. Thomas Whitehead (1716–1788) was a son of David Whitehead. Educated at Glasgow University he was successively curate of Bolton (1746), Ringley, and Peel, near Westhoughton. He was appointed perpetual curate of this latter parish on 29 July 1782. Robert Whitehead, Sr. (1752–1841) was the only son of Thomas and Rachel (1724–1788). Source: Letter to the author from Denis O'Connor of the Bolton Industrial History Society.
2. Alice, daughter of Alexander Lever, owner of the Cock Inn at Bolton.
3. James Whitehead (1788–1870), the inventor's father. Source: Thomas Whitehead, interview with the author, 1972.
4. Lady John Bowman, conversations with the author, 1973.
5. *The Times*, 15 November 1905.
6. *Dictionary of National Biography*, 2nd sup., vol. 3 (hereafter cited as DNB).
7. *The Times*, 15 November 1905.
8. *Handbook of Manchester* (1842).
9. Conversation between the author and the late Count Balthazar Hoyos in 1972 (hereafter cited as Count Hoyos Interview).

Chapter Three. Der Küstenbrander

1. *The Times*, 15 November 1905.
2. Count Hoyos Interview.
3. *DNB.*
4. Ibid.
5. Ibid.
6. *Centenary Book of the Cantiere Riuniti Dell Adriatico*, 16.
7. Ibid.
8. Ibid., "Under the technical direction of the Englishman Robert Whitehead . . . [Strudthoffs] built . . . in 1856, the first cylindrical boiler."
9. Parkes, *British Battleships*, 279, 210, 220.
10. *The Engineer*, 17 November 1905.
11. Count Hoyos Interview.
12. Sleeman, *Torpedoes and Torpedo Warfare* (hereafter cited as Sleeman).
13. There are many alternative spellings of the name in torpedo literature including: Luppis, Lupins, Lupius, Lupuis, and de Lupis. The spelling adopted was supplied by Baron Geoffredo de Banfield of Trieste in a letter to the author 22 May 1972.
14. Capt. Edwin P. Gallwey, Lecture at RUSI on 6 March 1885.
15. Count Hoyos Interview.

Chapter Four. Thanks to Your First-class Engines

1. Hale, *Famous Sea Fights*, 233.
2. Ibid., 235.
3. Ibid., 236.
4. Rawson, *Twenty Famous Naval Battles*, 555 (hereafter cited as Rawson).
5. Clowes, *Four Modern Naval Campaigns*, 49.
6. Rawson, 565.
7. Text as recalled by Count Balthazar Hoyos.
8. *DNB.*
9. Rawson, 565.
10. Sleeman, 173.
11. Lt. Seaton Schroeder, U.S.N., as quoted by Sleeman, 173.
12. Major Sarrepoint, as quoted by Sleeman, 174.
13. Engine details and information relating to the Austrian trials were supplied by the late Arthur Manns, the former curator of the RNAD Museum at Gosport, and came from uncataloged and often unidentified documents held in the museum. Subsequent entries will be cited as Arthur Manns RNAD Museum.
14. ADM. 116/135, London, Public Records Office (source hereafter cited as PRO).
15. Ibid.
16. *DNB.*
17. *The Times*, 27 May 1867.
18. I am indebted to Count Hoyos for this account of how his grandfather met Alice Whitehead.
19. *DNB* and Count Hoyos.
20. Sleeman, 175.
21. Ibid.
22. Sueter, *The Evolution of the Submarine Boat, Mine, and Torpedo*, 295 (hereafter cited as Sueter).
23. Sleeman, 175.
24. Princess Flugger, *The Glory of the Hapsburgs*, 237.
25. Sueter, 303.
26. Sleeman, 176.
27. Ibid.

Chapter Five. A Barbarous Method of Warfare

1. ADM. 1. 6049/N 219. PRO.
2. Quoted material from *The Times*, 15 November 1905; Lt. F. M. Barber lecture in 1874 on the Whitehead torpedo, quoted by Sleeman, 177: "In 1869 Mr Whitehead offered his invention to our [United States] Government for £20,000. . . . "
3. Count Hoyos Interview.
4. Alex Roland, *Underwater Warfare in the Age of Sail* (hereafter cited as Roland).
5. Gray, *Few Survived*, 18.
6. Roland.
7. Autobiography 1631, as quoted by Roland.
8. As quoted by Roland.

9. Ibid.

10. Ibid.

11. Gray, *Captains of War*, 4.

12. Cowie, *Mines, Minelayers and Minelaying*, 11; and Todd, *Life and Letters of Joel Barlow*, 177.

13. Hutcheon, *Robert Fulton—Pioneer of Undersea Warfare*, 40 (hereafter cited as Hutcheon).

14. Ibid., 44.

15. Ibid., 48.

16. Fulton, *Torpedo War and Submarine Explosions*, 7n.

17. Hutcheon, 97.

18. Fulton, 22.

19. Fulton, 44.

20. *Engineering*, 17 November 1905.

21. Quoted in Hutcheon, 124–25.

22. *Royal Navy Torpedo Manual 1929*, par. 15.

23. Ibid., par. 17.

24. Peter Bethell, "The Development of the Torpedo," pt. 1, *Engineering* 159 (May 1945): 443. This article was the first in a series of seven that appeared in volumes 159–161. Subsequent references will hereafter be cited as Bethell.

25. ADM. 116/135, PRO.

26. ADM. 1. 6049/N219, PRO.

27. ADM. 116/135, PRO.

28. Mackay, *Fisher of Kilverstone*, 53 (hereafter cited as Mackay).

29. ADM. 1/6046, PRO.

30. Reference to *Engineering* and final quote from Bethell, pt. 2, 159:40; John Fisher later became Admiral of the Fleet Lord Fisher of Kilverstone, the creator of the *Dreadnaught* and first sea lord from 1904–1910 and from December 1914 to May 1915.

31. Mackay, 44; ADM. 1/6045; ADM. 1/6073.

32. Marder, *Fear God and Dread Naught*, 63.

33. Hough, *First Sea Lord*, 52–53.

34. ADM. 1/6088; details of this report appear later in the text.

35. Quoted in Mackay, 110.

36. Bacon, *Lord Fisher* 1:37 (hereafter cited as Bacon).

37. Bacon, 1:51.

38. Details extracted from Gardiner, ed., *Conway's All the World's Fighting Ships 1860–1905* (hereafter referred to as *Conway's*).

39. Parkes, *British Battleships*, 271, 413.

40. Mackay, 61.

41. ADM. 1/6088, PRO.

42. ADM. 116/135, PRO.

43. Ibid.

44. Ibid.

45. The figure of £40,000 was mentioned by Lt. F. M. Barber, U.S.N., in his 1874 lecture and is quoted on p. 177 by Sleeman.

46. Count Hoyos Interview.

47. See chapter 1 for a detailed account.

48. Jane, *The Torpedo in Peace and War*.

49. Armstrong, *Torpedoes and Torpedo Vessels*, 11.

50. *Cornhill Magazine* 1–6 (January–June 1904).
51. Quoted in Marder, *Fear God and Dread Nought,* 1:73.
52. *The Times,* 11 November 1870.
53. Arthur Manns RNAD Museum.
54. Letter from Robert Whitehead to James Whitehead, 19 July 1891.
55. G. J. Kirby, "A History of the Torpedo," part 1 of 4, *Journal of the Royal Naval Scientific Society* 27, no. 1 (n.d.): 32. Subsequent references will be cited as Kirby.
56. Kirby, pt. 1, no. 1:34.
57. *The Times,* 15 November 1905.

Chapter Six. The Offer Was of Course Declined

1. ADM. 1. 6049/N219, PRO.
2. Bradford, 29.
3. Tirpitz, *My Memoirs* 1:35 (hereafter cited as Tirpitz).
4. Bennett, *Charlie B,* 52.
5. Ibid. 62–63.
6. Armstrong, *Torpedoes and Torpedo Vessels.*
7. The account of the burglary was supplied to the author by Count Balthazar Hoyos in 1972.
8. Gallwey, Lecture at RUSI.
9. Sleeman, 172.
10. Ibid., n. 1.
11. Sueter, 313.
12. Tirpitz, 1:37.
13. Sleeman, 172.
14. Ibid., 177.
15. Arthur Manns RNAD Museum and Sueter, 304.
16. Count Hoyos Interview.
17. Alice Hoyos letter to her brother James Whitehead, 27 January 1877. Future references to this correspondence will be cited as Alice Hoyos letter(s).
18. Alice Hoyos letter, 5 October 1877.
19. Ibid., 31 October 1876.
20. *The Times,* 15 November 1905.
21. Conversation with Lady John Bowman, 1973.
22. Alice Hoyos letter, 6 December 1876.
23. *Torpedo Manual 1929,* par. 9.
24. Quotes concerning "stolen torpedo" from Alice Hoyos letter, 19 January 1877.
25. Count Hoyos Interview.
26. *Biographischen Lexicon des Kaiserrhuras Osterrich* (1887). This assessment has been confirmed in the course of recent research (1989) by Dr. Marina Cattaruzza of Trieste.
27. Alice Hoyos letter, 2 March 1877.
28. *Torpedo Manual 1929,* par. 43.
29. Marder, *Fear God and Dread Nought,* 1:84.
30. Arthur Manns RNAD Museum.

31. Quoted in Mackay, 29.
32. Bacon, 1:44.
33. Alice Hoyos letter, 7 November 1876.
34. *Torpedo Manual 1929*, par. 40.

Chapter Seven. Too Much Rough Engine Work

1. Some accounts say that the crew were persuaded to espouse the rebel cause.
2. Bethell, pt. 2, 159:41.
3. From original logbook held by the RNAD Museum.
4. Tirpitz, 1:35n.
5. Alice Hoyos letter, 28 March 1878.
6. Tirpitz, 1:25n.
7. Alice Hoyos letter, 3 May 1878.
8. Ibid., 17 May 1878.
9. Kirby, pt. 1, no. 1:35.
10. Woodward, *The Russians at Sea*, 116.
11. Tirpitz, 1:37.
12. Ibid., 35.
13. Alice Hoyos letter, 18 May 1877.
14. Ibid., 26 April 1878.
15. Tirpitz, 1:37.
16. The HMS *Vernon* Reports, RNAD Museum.
17. Bethell, pt. 2, 159:42.
18. Tirpitz, 1:37.
19. Ibid.
20. Details of the Villa Whitehead supplied by Count Balthazar Hoyos.
21. Quote from Alice Hoyos letter, 12 April 1878.
22. Conversations with Lady John Bowman, 1972.
23. Quote from *The Times*, 15 November 1905.
24. Bradford, 61.
25. Letter from Capt. Arthur Wilson dated 9 July 1881, quoted by Bradford, 61.
26. Bethell, pt. 1, 159:442.
27. Ibid., pt. 3, 160:301n.
28. In *Four Modern Naval Campaigns*, p. 79 Clowes gives some interesting, if contradictory, details of the Lay torpedo: "Patented in 1873 . . . it was a cigar-shaped automobile torpedo, driven by compressed carbonic acid gas but steered by electricity through a cable. . . . Its speed was about 12½ knots. The cable, which contained several wires, was also used for transmission of the force to stop the torpedo, to vary its immersion, and to explode its charge of 90 lbs of dynamite . . . the United States and . . . Russia accepted (it) as a weapon suitable for the purposes of coast-defence." It is difficult to know whether these details are more accurate than those of Bethell (pt. 7, 161:243) that have been given in the text.
29. Details of the action are based on the account in *Four Modern Naval Campaigns*, 89–91.
30. Bethell, pt. 7, 161:244.
31. Arthur Mann RNAD Museum.
32. Kirby, pt. 1, no. 1:35.
33. Based on official indices £436,800 was roughly the equivalent of £3,500,000

in terms of 1972 sterling values according to the Bank of England. However, this does not reflect the true purchasing power and a more sensible equivalent would be £20,000,000. Although figures are not available it is reasonable to suppose that Whitehead's profit would have been not less than 30 percent to 50 percent on turnover—and possibly considerably more.

Chapter Eight. *It Takes a Good Man to Make a Stern*

1. *The Engineer,* 17 November 1905.
2. Alice Hoyos letter, 7 November 1876.
3. Ibid., 20 July 1877.
4. Count Hoyos Interview.
5. Ibid.
6. *The Country Gentleman Magazine,* 5 October 1901.
7. *The Times,* 15 November 1905.
8. *The Country Gentleman Magazine,* 5 October 1901.
9. Undated letter from Maud Scott to Mrs. Vivienne Hancock.
10. *The Engineer,* 17 November 1905.
11. Count Hoyos Interview.
12. Details of marriage provided by Lady John Bowman.
13. *Torpedo Manual 1929,* par. 44.
14. Bethell, pt. 3, 160:301.
15. Arthur Manns RNAD Museum; also Sueter, 301.
16. *Torpedo Manual 1929,* par. 63.
17. Ibid., par. 64. It is possible that by making the drawings available to a third party the Admiralty was infringing the terms of the 1871 contract although, of course, Whitehead may have given permission.
18. Lt. L. H. Chandler, U.S.N., "The Automobile Torpedo and Its Uses," *Proceedings* of the USNI, March 1900.
19. Bethell, pt. 7, 161:243.
20. *Torpedo Manual 1929,* par. 54.
21. Ibid., par. 50.
22. Kirby, pt. 1, no. 1:38–39.
23. *Berdan Torpedo,* General Information Series No. 6. U.S. Navy, Office of Naval Intelligence, June 1887.
24. The details of the Brennan torpedo and the inventor's career have been taken from Norman Tomlinson's *Louis Brennan* (hereafter cited as Tomlinson). The author has also corresponded with Mr. Tomlinson on matters relating to Brennan.
25. British Patent No.: 3359. "Improvements in machinery for propelling and guiding vessels on land and through air and water."
26. Tomlinson, 14–15.
27. C. V. Usborne, *Smoke on the Horizon,* 156.
28. Fitzgerald, *Memories of the Sea,* 298.
29. Tomlinson, 26.
30. Brennan died in Switzerland on 17 January 1932 following injury in a road accident.
31. Tirpitz, 1:47.
32. Bacon, 1:96.
33. Bradford, 110–111.

34. Ibid.
35. Ibid.
36. Alice Hoyos letter, undated but probably 1888.
37. Alice Hoyos letter, 8 December 1888.
38. Ibid.
39. Ibid.
40. Ibid.
41. Ibid.
42. Alice Hoyos letter, 12 December 1888.
43. Ibid.
44. Ibid.
45. Ibid.
46. Ibid.
47. Alice Hoyos letter, undated.
48. Ibid.
49. *Torpedo Manual 1929*, par. 64. This was superceded by the Bincleaves range at Weymouth in 1898 (Bethell, pt. 2, 159:42.)
50. Count Hoyos Interview.

Chapter Nine. I Am Asking You to Sacrifice Your Lives

1. Phelan and Brice, *Fast Attack Craft*, 30.
2. Ibid., 32.
3. *Conway's*, 88.
4. Parkes, *British Battleships*, 254.
5. Count Hoyos Interview.
6. *Torpedo Manual 1929*, par. 76.
7. This narrative is based on the account of the Chilean revolution in *Four Modern Naval Campaigns*, 133 et seq.
8. This narrative is based on the account of the Brazilian revolution in *Four Modern Naval Campaigns*, 187 et seq.
9. Sueter, 317.
10. Bethell, pt. 2, 159:43.
11. Blond, *Admiral Togo*, 115 (hereafter cited as Blond).
12. Bethell, pt. 2, 159:43.
13. Blond, 129.
14. Sueter, 318.
15. Bethell, pt. 3, 160:301.

Chapter Ten. I Answer for Our Success

1. Kirby. pt. 1, no. 1:37.
2. Bethell, pt. 3, 160:303.
3. Ibid.
4. Arthur Manns RNAD Museum.
5. Lowis, *Fabulous Admirals*, 131.
6. *Torpedo Manual 1929*, par. 77.

7. Bethell, pt. 3, 160:303.
8. *Torpedo Manual 1929*, par. 77.
9. Ibid., par. 72.
10. Kirby, pt. 2, no. 1:43 and Bethell, pt. 4, 160:343.
11. Letter from Robert Whitehead to James Whitehead 19 July 1891.
12. Kirby, pt. 2, no. 1:43 and Bethell, pt. 4, 160:343.
13. Bethell, pt. 3, 160:301.
14. *Torpedo Manual 1929*, pars. 82, 84. The nickel-steel air chamber was introduced in 1902.
15. *Torpedo Manual 1929*, par. 86. This was the effect with a sea temperature of 48°F.
16. Thomas B. Whitehead, interview with the author, 1972.
17. *The Times*, 18 June 1892.
18. *The Times*, 20 June 1892.
19. Count Hoyos Interview.
20. Alice Hoyos letter, 13 April 1893.
21. Alice Hoyos letter, 5 June 1893.
22. Alice Hoyos letter, undated but ca. 1893.
23. Alice Hoyos letter, 28 December 1893.
24. Ibid.
25. *The Times*, 15 November 1905.
26. Count Hoyos Interview.
27. Ibid.
28. Blond, *Admiral Togo*, 156.
29. The routine described is based on the Royal Navy's *Torpedo Drill Book 1912*.
30. Blond, 159.
31. Ibid.

Chapter Eleven. His Fame Was in All Nations Round About

1. Naval writers are at variance as to the facts of the attack. Indeed some experts, such as Capt. Donald MacIntyre in *Sea Power in the Pacific* (p. 138) allege that the later destroyers fired from 1,600 yards—or perhaps even more—and this extreme range caused many of them to miss the target.
2. This would tend to support MacIntyre's view that the torpedoes were *not* fired at point-blank range.
3. Quoted in Sueter, 322.
4. Bethell, pt. 4, 160:341.
5. Count Hoyos Interview.
6. A. E. Jones produced a number of important inventions, including the blast-activated gyroscope. His son, Lewis Jones, was technical manager at Weymouth until his death in 1945. (Bethell, pt. 4, 160:366n) Count Hoyos referred to A. E. Jones as "Tell" Jones in conversations with the author.
7. Quoted in Fred T. Jane, *The Imperial Japanese Navy* (1904), 346.
8. The Japanese Official History.
9. Blond, 230.
10. Armstrong, *Torpedoes and Torpedo Vessels*.
11. *The Times*, 15 November 1905.

12. Per copy of Probated Will supplied by the Principal Probate Registry, Office of HM's High Court of Justice (London).

13. Letter to the author from John Rowland-Hosbons, 4 April 1972. Mr. Rowland-Hosbons's father, the Rev. S. Rowland-Hosbons, conducted the funeral service.

14. *The Times*, 15 November 1905. Similar sentiments were expressed in *The Engineer* on 17 November 1905. "There is reason to believe that he felt acutely that, although honoured by other countries, the country of his birth did not recognise him in the same manner. . . ."

15. Smart, Geoffrey M. "Torpedoes at Worth," Worth Parish Church Magazine (n.d.).

Chapter Twelve. This Insidious and Somewhat Sneaking Weapon

1. *The Whitehead Torpedo Companies.* An internal monograph of the Vickers Company, 20 February 1935 (herafter cited as Vickers' Monograph).

2. *The Times*, 15 November 1905.

3. Statements made by Sir Trevor Dawson at the Whitehead Company's annual dinner at Weymouth on 24 February 1931 referred to in the Vickers' Monograph.

4. Vickers' Monograph.

5. British patent no. 25003 (1904).

6. The first model to incorporate the Hardcastle or RGF heater was the 1908 RGF 18-in Mark VII. (*Torpedo Manual 1929*, par. 93).

7. Correspondence between Vickers and the Electric Boat Company made available to the author by Messrs. Vickers.

8. Ibid.

9. Count Hoyos Interview.

10. Maria von Trapp, *The Trapp Family Singers*.

11. Bacon, 247.

12. Ibid.

13. Jellicoe, *The Grand Fleet*, 401.

14. Ibid., 397.

15. Ibid., Jellicoe's italics.

16. *Torpedo Manual 1929*, par. 104.

17. Details of these foreign subsidiaries and their ultimate fates are summarized in the Vickers' Monograph.

18. Count Hoyos Interview.

19. Vickers Monograph, 2.

20. Ibid., 3.

21. Ibid., 5.

22. Ibid., 5.

23. Dr. Marina Cattaruzza and FIAT (UK) Ltd.

Chapter Thirteen. Courage! Nous mourrons ensemble!

1. Quoted in Sueter, 294.

2. For details of *Hunley*'s disastrous career see Gray, *Few Survived*, 28–34.

3. See also William Scanlon Murphy, *Father of the Submarine*, 88.

4. R. W. Jones, "The Garrett-Nordenfelt Submarines," *Warship International,* no. 4 (1968).

5. Sueter, 113.

6. Bethell, pt. 5, 160:529.

7. The late Cdr. G. Frere-Cook, former Director of the Royal Navy Submarine Museum, interview with the author, Gosport, Hampshire, 25 April 1972.

8. Gray, *The Underwater War,* 218–219.

9. Details of all British submarine operations in this chapter have been taken from *The Underwater War.*

10. Vice-Adm. David Beatty letter to Rear-Adm. Roger Keyes, 10 February 1915. Quoted in Keyes, *Naval Memoirs:* 1:163.

11. Quoted in Kirby, pt. 2, no. 1:45.

12. Gray, *The Underwater War,* 134.

13. Details of the attack and quotations have been taken from *The Times History of the War,* 12:45–46.

Chapter Fourteen. Go and Get a Hit

1. Count Hoyos Interview.

2. Bethell, pt. 6, 161:121.

3. Ibid.

4. Wragg, *Wings Over the Sea,* 18.

5. Arthur Manns RNAD Museum.

6. Bethell, pt. 6, 161:121.

7. Ibid.

8. Ibid.

9. Ibid.

10. Recollections of the late H. F. Bowers, 1972.

11. Bethell, pt. 6, 161:122.

12. Potter, *Admiral of the Pacific,* 53.

13. Ibid.

14. See Newton and Hampshire, *Taranto* (London: William Kimber, 1959) for a full account of the attack on the Italian Fleet.

15. Bowyer, *Eugene Esmonde VC,* 141.

16. Dispatch dated 16 February 1942, quoted in W. S. Chalmers, *Full Cycle.*

17. Potter, *Admiral of the Pacific,* 52.

18. Tuleja, *Climax at Midway,* 135.

Chapter Fifteen. Secret Memorandum No. 83-a-42

1. The 21-in torpedo is shown as 533mm.

2. The type numerals of Japanese torpedoes are based on the last two digits of the Japanese calendar year, in this case 2593.

3. Kirby, pt. 2, no. 1:45.

4. Kirby, pt. 2, no. 1:53.

5. Kirby, pt. 2, no. 1:49.

6. Arthur Manns RNAD Museum.

7. *The Propulsive Performance of Modern Torpedoes* (RNTF Scientific and Technical Report No. 131, 1941).

8. Arthur Manns RNAD Museum.

9. Kirby, pt. 2, no. 1:53.

10. Gray, *Few Survived*, 208.

11. Arthur Manns RNAD Museum.

12. Hara, *Japanese Destroyer Captain*, 38.

13. These performance figures must be treated with caution. Although they appear to be accurate no two sources seem to agree about the optimum performance details.

14. R. Lumley, "Japanese Torpedoes," *Warship International*, no. 1 (1973).

15. Middlebrook and Mahoney, *Battleship*, 183.

16. Lumley, "Japanese Torpedoes."

17. Middlebrook and Mahoney, 183.

18. Kirby, pt. 1, no. 1:38.

19. Ibid; Murphy, *Father of the Submarine*, 101.

20. Lt. F. M. Barber, U.S.N., lecture on the Whitehead torpedo, presented at the U.S. Naval Torpedo Station, 20 November 1874.

21. *U.K. Torpedo Production*, Command Paper no.6564 (November 1944).

22. Arthur Manns RNAD Museum.

23. Kirby, pt. 3, no. 2:81.

24. Kirby, pt. 3, no. 2:83.

25. Kirby, pt. 3, no. 2:84.

26. Arthur Manns RNAD Museum.

27. Ibid.

28. Reference to Kretschmer from Robertson, *The Golden Horseshoe*, 27; reference to Prien from Roskill, *The War At Sea*, 1:73–74.

29. Dönitz, *Zehn Jahre und Zwanzig Tage* (English translation), 89.

30. *MPA 2864/40.*

31. The text of this document is reproduced in the appendixes of the Dönitz memoirs.

32. Ibid., *Secret Memorandum No. 83-a-42.*

33. Ibid.

34. Kirby, pt. 3, no. 2:84.

35. Kirby, pt. 3, no. 2:85.

36. Arthur Manns RNAD Museum.

37. Kirby, pt. 3, no. 2:93.

38. At a late stage in the war the German Navy switched from thermal engines to turbines in order to eliminate the torpedo's wake.

Chapter Sixteen. Incomprehensibly Stubborn and Stupid

1. Clay Blair's *Silent Victory* (hereafter cited as Blair) provided useful confirmation of the basic facts pertaining to the Mark 14 torpedo story and the scandal of the Mark VI magnetic exploder, the details of which were culled from a wide variety of sources.

2. Blair, 213.

3. Hoyt, *Submarines at War*, 123 (hereafter cited as Hoyt).

4. Postwar records show that Frank Fenno had, in fact, sunk only two ships.

5. Blair, 216.

6. Blair, 414–15.
7. Hoyt, 202–3.
8. Blair, 879.
9. Kirby, pt. 3, no. 2:84.
10. Blair, 818.
11. Kirby, pt. 4, no. 2:90.
12. *Daily Telegraph*, 1 March 1985; also USNI *Proceedings* (March 1984): 119.
13. Hutcheon.
14. *Sunday Times*, 18 November 1984.
15. "The Great Torpedo Battle," *The Observer*, 11 December 1983.
16. Rice and Gavshon, *The Sinking of the Belgrano*, 102.
17. *Daily Telegraph*, 10 September 1986.
18. *The Times*, 18 June 1986.
19. *Daily Telegraph*, 10 September 1987.
20. Count Hoyos Interview.
21. *28th Report of Committee of Public Accounts*, Command Paper no. 391 (1985).
22. *Daily Telegraph*, 10 September 1987.
23. "The Great Torpedo Battle." *The Observer*, 11 December 1983.
24. Cdr. E. Hamilton-Curry, *The Man of War*. London, 1910.

BIBLIOGRAPHY

PRIMARY SOURCES

Interviews

Bowers, H. F. [Ministry of Defense, London]. Interview with the author, 1972.

Bowman, Lady John [a granddaughter of Robert Whitehead]. Interview with the author. Hungerford, Wiltshire, 8 August 1972 and subsequent telephone conversations.

Clowes, Brian [former Chief Torpedo Gunner's Mate, Royal Navy]. Interviews with the author. London, 1971–1973.

Frere-Cook, Lt.-Cdr. G. H. F. [former Director of the Royal Navy Submarine Museum]. Interview with the author. Gosport, Hampshire, 25 April 1972.

Garson, Capt. R. W. [former Commanding Officer of the HMS *Dolphin*]. Interview with the author. Gosport, Hampshire, 25 April 1972.

Hoyos, Count Balthazar [a grandson of Count Georg Hoyos]. Interview with the author. London, 12 May 1972.

Manns, Arthur G. [former Curator of the RNAD Museum]. Interview with the author. Gosport, Hampshire, 25 April 1972.

Oxenham, P. [Vickers Ltd]. Interview with the author. London, 20 April 1972.

Von Trapp, Dr. Rupert. Interview with the author. Attleborough, Norfolk, 29 August 1985.
Whitehead, Thomas B. [a grandson of Robert Whitehead]. Interview with the author. Hungerford, Wiltshire, 8 August 1972.

Correspondence

Appleton, A. H. Letter to the author, 6 April 1972.
Baggley, C. D. A. [Headmaster, Bolton School]. Letter to the author, 11 May 1972.
Banfield, Baron Geoffredo de. Letters to the author, 22 May, 12 July, and 14 September 1972.
Bank of England, Economic Intelligence Unit. Letter to the author, 22 September 1972.
Bowman, Lady John. Letters to the author, 1972–1989.
Calan, Lt.-Cdr. Jack. [HMS *Vernon*] Letter to the author, 10 January 1973.
Clarke, Vivien. Letters to the author, 11 April and 18 September 1972.
Fletcher, Mrs. Mary. Letters to the author, 4 April, 10 April, and 15 September 1972.
Heeregeschichtes Museum, Vienna. Letter to the author, 1972.
Hoyos, Alice. Letters to her brother, James B. Whitehead, 1877–1888. Courtesy of Lady John Bowman.
Hoyos, Count Balthazar. Letter to the author, 28 April and 26 September 1972.
Jordis, Baron Hans. Letter to the author, 24 April 1972.
Judd, P. H. [Vickers Ltd]. Letter to the author, 4 April 1972.
Kirby, Geoffrey [Admiralty Underwater Weapons Establishment]. Letters to the author, 1972 and 1973.
Kitson, Michael. Letter to the author, 18 May 1986.
Maclennan, Graeme G. [Editorial Director, *Marine Engineer & Naval Architect Magazine*]. Letter to the author, 20 April 1972.
O'Connor, Denis [Bolton Industrial History Society]. Letters to the author, 1972 and 1973.
Patterson, A. R. [Greenwood & Battley Ltd]. Letter to the author, 1 May 1972.
Plessing, Conrad C. Letter to the author, 11 April 1972.
Rowland-Hosbons, John. Letter to the author, 4 April 1972.
Short, Christopher. Letter to the author, 6 April 1972.
Smart, Geoffrey M. Letter to the author, 18 April 1972.
Tomlinson, Norman. Letters to the author, 27 April 1972 and 2 January 1986.
Vickers Ltd. Correspondence with Electric Boat Company, 1907–1910. Courtesy of Vickers Ltd.
Trapp, Agathe von. Letter to the author, n.d. 1985.
Whitehead, A. Letters to the author, 5 April and 11 April 1972.

Whitehead, Robert. Letters to his brother James Whitehead, 1890–1892. Courtesy of Lady John Bowman.
Whitehead, Thomas. Letter to the author, 8 August 1972.

Public Documents

Armstrong, G. E. Elswick Heater. British Patent no. 25003, 1904.
Brennan, Louis. Dirigible Torpedo. British Patent no. 3359, 1878.
London. Public Records Office. Adm. 116/135, Adm. 1/6045, Adm. 1/6046, Adm. 1/6049/N 219, Adm. 1/6073, Adm. 1/6088.
Probated Will of Robert Whitehead, Dec'd. Principal Probate Registry, Office of Her Majesty's High Court of Justice. London, 31 March 1906.

Reports, Monographs, Lectures, and Official Publications

Arthur, Capt. William. *Report of Committee on the Whitehead Torpedo.* 28 October 1870. Naval Historical Research Branch, Ministry of Defence, London.
Barber, Lt. F. M. Lecture on the Whitehead torpedo. Presented at the U.S. Naval Torpedo Station, Newport, Rhode Island, 20 November 1874. N.p. Courtesy of Admiralty Library, London.
Bedford, Captain. "Report on Action between HMS *Shah* and *Huascar*" (1877). RNAD Museum, Gosport, Hampshire.
Berdon Torpedo. General Information U.S. Navy, Series no. 6, Office of Naval Intelligence, June 1887.
Chandler, Lt. L. H. "The Automobile Torpedo and Its Uses." *Proceedings*, March 1900.
Fulton, Robert. *Torpedo War and Submarine Explosions.* New York, 1810.
Gallwey, Capt. Edwin P. Lecture at the Royal United Services Institute, London, 6 March 1885. Courtesy of RUSI, London.
HMS *Vernon*, Annual Reports. RNAD Museum, Gosport.
Official Catalogue of the Paris Exhibition. 2nd ed. May 1867.
Parish Account Books of Bolton (1796–1798). Courtesy of Bolton Library.
Parliamentary Reports of the Paris Exhibition. HMSO [Her Majesty's Stationery Office]. London, 1868.
Propulsive Performance of Modern Torpedoes. RNTF Scientific and Technical Report no. 131. 1941.
Raeder, Erich. *Memorandum MPA 2864/40.* Quoted in Dönitz memoirs (qv).
———. *Secret Memorandum No. 83-a-42.* Reproduced in Dönitz memoirs (qv).
Royal Navy Torpedo Manual 1929. HMSO. London, 1929.
Summary of Aircraft Torpedo Data. RNTF Scientific and Technical Report no. 200. N.d.
Torpedo Drill Book 1912. HMSO. London, 1912.
Torpedo Manual. Colony of Victoria, Australia. Ca. 1891.

United Kingdom. Parliament. *Torpedo Programme: 28th Report from Committee of Public Accounts.* Command Paper no. 391. HMSO. London, 1985.
United Kingdom. Parliament. *United Kingdom Torpedo Production.* Command Paper no. 6564. HMSO. London, November 1944.

SECONDARY SOURCES

Unpublished

O'Connor, Denis. *A Brief Textile History of Bolton.* Ca. 1972. Bolton Library.
The Whitehead Torpedo Companies. Monograph for internal information dated 20 February 1935. Courtesy of Vickers Ltd, London.

Memoirs and Autobiographies

Dönitz, Grand Adm. Karl. *Zehn Jahre und Zwanzig Tage.* Athenäum Verlag: Bonn, 1958. (English translation: *Admiral Dönitz Memoirs.* London: Weidenfeld & Nicolson, 1959).
Fisher, Adm. Lord. *Records.* London: Hodder & Stoughton, 1919.
Fitzgerald, Adm. Penrose. *Memories of the Sea.* London: Edward Arnold, 1913.
Keyes, Adm. Lord. *Naval Memoirs.* London: Thornton & Butterworth, 1934.
Paget, Adm. Lord Clarence. *Autobiography of Admiral Lord Paget.* London: Chapman & Hall, 1896.
Tirpitz, Grand Adm. Alfred von. *My Memoirs.* 2 vols. London: Hurst & Blackett, 1919.
Trapp, Maria von. *The Trapp Family Singers.* London: Geoffrey Bles, 1953.

Books

Archer, Denis, ed. *Janes Pocket Book of Naval Armament.* London: Macdonald & Janes, 1976.
Armstrong, G. E. *Torpedoes and Torpedo Vessels.* London: Bell & Co., 1901.
Bacon, Adm. Sir Reginald. *Lord Fisher.* 2 vols. London: Hodder & Stoughton, 1929.
Bennett, Geoffrey. *Charlie B.* London: Peter Dawnay, 1968.
Blair, Clay, Jr. *Silent Victory.* New York: Bantam Books, 1975.
Blond, Georges. *Admiral Togo.* London: Jarrolds, 1961.
Bowyer, Chaz. *Eugene Esmonde V.C.* London: Kimber, 1983.
Bradford, Adm. Sir Edward. *The Life of Admiral of the Fleet Sir Arthur Knyvet Wilson.* London: John Murray, 1923.
Centenary Book of the Cantiere Runiti Dell Adriatico. Trieste, 1957.
Chalmers, Rear-Adm. W. S. *Full Cycle.* London: Hodder & Stoughton, 1959.

Clowes, Sir William Laird. *Four Modern Naval Campaigns*. London: Hutchinson, 1906.
Couhat, Jean Labayle. *French Warships of World War II*. London: Ian Allen, 1971.
Cowie, J. S., *Mines, Minelayers and Minelaying*. Oxford: Oxford University Press, 1949.
Dommett, W. E. *Submarine Vessels*. London: Whittaker, 1915.
Fleet Air Arm. London: HMSO and Ministry of Information. Ca. 1943.
Flugger, Princess. *The Glory of the Hapsburgs*. London: Harrap, 1932.
Fraccaroli, Aldo. *Italian Warships of World War I*. London: Ian Allen, 1970.
———. *Italian Warships of World War II*. London: Ian Allen, 1968.
Gardiner, Robert, ed. *Conway's All the World's Fighting Ships 1860–1905*. London: Conway Maritime Press, 1979.
Gray, Edwyn. *Captains of War*. London: Leo Cooper, 1988.
———. *A Damned Un-English Weapon*. London: Seeley Service, 1971.
———. *Few Survived*. London: Leo Cooper with Secker & Warburg, 1986.
———. *The Killing Time*. London: Seeley Service, 1972.
———. *The Underwater War*. New York: Scribner's, 1971.
Grenfell, Russell. *Main Fleet to Singapore*. London: Faber & Faber, 1951.
Grey C. G. *Sea Fliers*. London: Faber & Faber, 1942.
Hale, J. R. *Famous Sea Flights*. London: Methuen, 1911.
Hamilton-Curry, Cdr. E. *The Man of War*, London: T. C. & E. C. Jock, 1910.
Hara, Capt. Tameichi. *Japanese Destroyer Captain*. New York: Ballantine, 1961.
Hill, Rear-Adm. J. R. *Anti-submarine Warfare*. London: Ian Allen, 1984.
Hough, Richard. *First Sea Lord*. London: Allen & Unwin, 1969.
———. *The Fleet That Had to Die*. London: Hamish Hamilton, 1958.
———. *The Hunting of Force Z*. London: Collins, 1963.
Hoyt, Edwin P. *Submarines at War*. New York: Stein & Day, 1983.
Hutcheon, Wallace, Jr. *Robert Fulton—Pioneer of Undersea Warfare*. Annapolis: Naval Institute Press, 1981.
Jackson, G. Gibbard. *The Romance of the Submarine*. London: Sampson Low, 1930.
Jane, Fred T. *The British Battle Fleet*. 2 vols. London: Library Press, 1915.
———. *The Imperial Japanese Navy*. Reprint of 1904 edition. London: Conway Maritime Press, 1984.
Kemp, Lt.-Cdr. P. K., ed. *The Fisher Papers*. 2 vols. London: Naval Records Society, 1960.
———. *Fleet Air Arm*. London: Herbert Jenkins, 1954.
———. *HM Destroyers*. London: Herbert Jenkins, 1956.
Lord, John. *A Memoir of John Kay*. James Clegg, 1903.
Lord, Walter. *A Day of Infamy*. London: Longmans, 1957.
———. *Incredible Victory*. New York: Harper & Row, 1967.
Lowis, G. *Fabulous Admirals*. New York: G. P. Putnam's Sons, 1957.
Macintyre, Donald. *Sea Power in the Pacific*. London: Arthur Barker, 1972.
Mackay, Ruddock R. *Fisher of Kilverstone*. Oxford: Oxford University Press, 1973.

March, Edgar J. *British Destroyers.* London: Seeley Service, 1966.

Marder, Arthur J., ed. *Fear God and Dread Naught* [the correspondence of Admiral Lord Fisher]. Vol 1. London: Jonathan Cape, 1952.

Martin, Christopher. *The Russo-Japanese War.* New York: Abelard-Schuman, 1967.

Middlebrook, Martin, and Patrick Mahoney. *Battleship.* London: Allen Lane, 1977.

Miller, David, and John Jordan. *Modern Submarine Warfare.* London: Salamander, 1987.

Murphy, William Scanlon. *Father of the Submarine.* London: William Kimber, 1987.

Okumiya, Masatake, and Mitsuo Fuchida. *Midway.* Annapolis: Naval Institute Press, 1957.

Parkes, Oscar. *British Battleships.* London: Seeley Service, 1970.

Phelan and Brice. *Fast Attack Craft.* London: Macdonald and Janes, 1977.

Potter, John Deane. *Admiral of the Pacific.* London: Heinemann, 1965.

———. *Fiasco.* London: Heinemann, 1970.

Rawson, Edward K. *Twenty Famous Naval Battles.* New York: Crowell & Co., 1899.

Rice, Desmond and Arthur Gavshon. *The Sinking of the Belgrano.* London: Secker & Warburg, 1984.

Robertson, F. L. *Evolution of Naval Armament.* London: Constable, 1921.

Robertson, Terence. *The Golden Horseshoe.* London: Evans, 1955.

Roskill, S. W. *The War at Sea.* 4 vols. London: HMSO, 1954–1961.

Roland, Alex. *Underwater Warfare in the Age of Sail.* Bloomington: Indiana University Press, 1978.

Scholes, J. C. *History of Bolton.* 1892.

Sleeman, C. *Torpedoes and Torpedo Warfare.* Portsmouth: Griffin & Co., 1880.

Snyder, L. *The Blood and Iron Chancellor.* N.p., n.d.

Stafford, E. P. *The Far and the Deep.* London: Arthur Barker, 1968.

Sueter, Cdr. Murray. *The Evolution of the Submarine Boat, Mine, and Torpedo.* Portsmouth: Griffin & Co., 1907.

Temple-Patterson, A., ed. *The Jellicoe Papers.* 2 vols. London: Naval Records Society, 1966.

Todd, Charles Burr. *Life and Letters of Joel Barlow.* New York: G. P. Putnam's Sons, 1886.

Tomlinson, Norman. *Louis Brennan.* Chatham: John Howell Publications, 1980.

Tuleja, Thadeus V. *Climax at Midway.* London: J. M. Dent, 1960.

Usborne, C. V. *Smoke on the Horizon.* 1940. Black Jacket ed. London: Hodder & Stoughton, 1940.

Watts, Anthony. *The Imperial Japanese Navy.* London: Macdonald: 1971.

Whitehouse, Arch. *Subs and Submariners.* London: Muller, 1961.

Wilson, H. W. *Ironclads in Action.* 2 vols. London: Sampson Low, 1896.

———. *Japan's Fight for Freedom.* 2 vols. London: Amalgamated Press, 1905.

Woodward, David. *The Russians at Sea.* London: William Kimber, 1965.
Wragg, David. *Wings Over the Sea.* New York: Arco Publishing Inc., 1979.
Young, Desmond. *Rutland of Jutland.* London: Cassells, 1963.

Periodicals and Newspapers

Armstrong, Lt. G. E. N.t. *Cornhill Magazine* (January–June 1904).
Bethell, Cdr. Peter. "The Development of the Torpedo." Parts 1–7. *Engineering* 159–161 (25 May 1945 to 15 March 1946).
The Country Gentleman Magazine, 5 October 1901.
The Engineer, 17 November 1905.
"First Successful Aerial Torpedo Attack." *Warship International.* N.v. (Ca. 1969).
Fisher, Edward C. "Japanese Torpedo Cruisers." *Warship International,* no. 2 (1972).
"The Great Torpedo Battle." *The Observer,* 11 December 1983.
Hancock, Vivien F. "Worth Priory." *Sussex County Magazine* 12 (1983): 750–757.
Jones, Robert J. "The Garrett-Nordenfelt Submarines." *Warship International,* no. 4 (1968).
Kennon, John W. "U.S.S. *Vesuvius.*" *Proceedings* (February 1954): 183–190.
Kirby, G. J. "A History of the Torpedo." Parts 1–7. *Journal of the Royal Naval Scientific Society* 27, no. 1 (n.d.): 30–55; no. 2 (n.d.): 78–95.
Lumley, R. "Japanese Torpedoes." *Warship International,* no. 1 (1973).
Neve Freie Presse, 15 November 1905.
Smart, Geoffrey M. "Torpedoes at Worth." *Worth Parish Church Magazine.* N.v., n.d.
"Torpedo Boats." *Warship International,* no. 2 (June 1970).

Annual Publications

Almanac de Gotha (1904).
Biographischen Lexicon de Kaiserrhuras Osterrich (1887).
Brassey's Naval Annual (various).
Dictionary of National Biography, 2nd sup., vol. 3.
Directories of Bolton & District (1816–1834 and 1841).
Jane's Fighting Ships (various).

ABOUT THE AUTHOR

Born in England within sight and sound of the London docks at a time when ocean freighters unloaded their exotic cargoes in the heartland of the capital, Edwyn Gray has always had a deep interest in the sea and the Royal Navy. He counts among his ancestors John Philipot, who led a makeshift English fleet to victory in the fourteenth century.

Educated at the Coopers Company School in London, the Royal Grammar School in High Wycombe, and London University, he began writing for magazines in 1953 and had his first book published in 1969. His work on submarine and torpedo history has earned him an international reputation as a naval author; he has also written eight novels with underwater warfare backgrounds. His books have been published in both Britain and the United States and have been translated into Dutch, German, Italian, Danish, Swedish, and Japanese. He continues to produce features on a variety of historical subjects for leading British and American periodicals.

An accomplished jazz organist in his leisure time, Gray and his wife now live in Norfolk, England, with an ever increasing family of cats and dogs.

The **Naval Institute Press** is the book-publishing arm of the U.S. Naval Institute, a private, nonprofit professional society for members of the sea services and civilians who share an interest in naval and maritime affairs. Established in 1873 at the U.S. Naval Academy in Annapolis, Maryland, where its offices remain today, the Naval Institute has more than 100,000 members worldwide.

Members of the Naval Institute receive the influential monthly magazine *Proceedings* and discounts on fine nautical prints, ship and aircraft photos, and subscriptions to the quarterly *Naval History* magazine. They also have access to the transcripts of the Institute's Oral History Program and get discounted admission to any of the Institute-sponsored seminars regularly offered around the country.

The Naval Institute's book-publishing program, begun in 1898 with basic guides to naval practices, has broadened its scope in recent years to include books of more general interest. Now the Naval Institute Press publishes more than sixty new titles each year, ranging from how-to books on boating and navigation to battle histories, biographies, ship and aircraft guides, and novels. Institute members receive discounts on the Press's more than 375 books.

Full-time students are eligible for special half-price membership rates. Life memberships are also available.

For a free catalog describing the Naval Institute Press books currently available, and for futher information about U.S. Naval Institute membership, please write to:

Membership & Communications Department
U.S. Naval Institute
118 Maryland Avenue
Annapolis, Maryland 21402-5035

Or call, toll-free, (800) 233-USNI. In Maryland, call (301) 224-3378

THE NAVAL INSTITUTE PRESS

THE DEVIL'S DEVICE
Robert Whitehead and the History of the Torpedo

Designed by Alan Carter

Set in Bauer Bodoni
by TCSystems, Inc.
Shippensburg, Pennsylvania

Printed on 50-lb. Glatfelter Antique Cream
and bound in ICG Devon Starch
by The Maple-Vail Book Manufacturing Group
York, Pennsylvania